ONE VOTE, ONE VALUE

One Vote, One Value

Electoral re-districting in English local government

COLIN RALLINGS
University of Plymouth, UK
MICHAEL THRASHER
University of Plymouth, UK
JAMES DOWNE
University of Warwick, UK

Ashgate

Published by
Ashgate Publishing Limited
Gower House
Croft Road
Aldershot
Hampshire GU11 3HR
England

Ashgate Publishing Company
131 Main Street
Burlington, VT 05401-5600 USA

Ashgate website: http://www.ashgate.com

British Library Cataloguing in Publication Data
Rallings, Colin
One vote, one value : electoral re-districting in English local government
1. Local Government Commission for England 2. Apportionment (Election law) - England 3. Election districts - England
4. Local government - England
I. Title II. Thrasher, Michael III. Downe, James
328.3'345 '0942

Library of Congress Control Number: 2001099648

ISBN 0 7546 2152 9

Printed and bound in Great Britain by
Antony Rowe Ltd, Chippenham, Wiltshire

Contents

List of Tables

Preface

The idea for this book grew out of a project to determine the likely electoral consequences of the Fourth Periodical Review of parliamentary constituency boundaries (Rallings and Thrasher, 1995). It struck us that the ward level building blocks from which constituencies were constructed were themselves subject to boundary review and change, and that the particular way of conducting such reviews gave a pivotal role to (partisan) local authorities. We also realised that almost nothing was known about the electoral review work of the Local Government Commission for England, about the process of local electoral re-districting, or about how far political parties tried or were successful in exploiting it for their own ends.

A research proposal on this theme found favour with the Leverhulme Trust and we are grateful to the Director and Trustees for generous funding and a lightness of touch in overseeing the project through to completion. Once the research began we needed to seek the co-operation of a very large number of individuals. It was gratifying that almost everyone approached was willing to help us. Our contacts with the Commission were initially conducted through Colin Wilby, the then Director of Reviews. He was instrumental in arranging for us to attend Commission meetings and to see relevant papers, and without his enthusiastic support our progress would have been that much slower. We must also thank Barbara Stephens (Chief Executive of the LGCE), Archie Gall (Head of Policy), Bryan Davey (Review Manager) and Professor Michael Clarke (Deputy Chairman of the Commission) for exceptional levels of assistance in providing information and contacts and commenting on draft reports and manuscripts. And that is quite apart from the other Commissioners and Commission staff who talked to us about their roles and even, in some cases, acted as 'tour guides' during visits to particular local authorities. We were also fortunate in being able to interview three people who played prominent roles in the Local Government Boundary Commission (1972-92). Sir Geoffrey Ellerton (Chairman 1983-92), Professor Michael Chisholm (Commissioner 1972-8), and Stephen Garrish (Secretary to the Commission 1985-90) provided an essential link with the past and kind hospitality. Much of the documentary material on the LGBC we were able to obtain through the good offices of Rob Clements in the House of Commons Library.

Those who helped us in local authorities are literally too numerous to mention.

The councils which were the focus of our case studies bore a particularly heavy burden from our inquiries and intrusions, and in every one of them there are councillors and officers who freely gave their time. Thanks are also due to the even larger numbers who responded to the questionnaire sent to the chief executive and party group leaders of all those councils that had undergone a Periodic Electoral Review during or prior to our research.

Among academic colleagues, Professor Ron Johnston of the University of Bristol deserves special mention. Not only did he read our manuscript in full, but he is directly responsible for the analysis of electoral 'bias' in Chapter 8 and for suggesting that the book might be enhanced by a few maps! Professor David Denver of the University of Lancaster also read the entire book with his customary hawk-like eye for detail and grammatical infelicities.

The final drafts were put together whilst Thrasher was working in Plymouth, Downe in Warwick, and Rallings in Canberra, Australia. He acknowledges with gratitude the time and space to finish the book provided by the award of a Visiting Fellowship at the Australian National University. Special thanks are due to his hosts, Professor Ian McAllister, Director of the Research School of Social Sciences, and Professor Marian Sawer, Head of the Political Science Program at ANU.

Last, but certainly not least we must mention two colleagues in Plymouth. Brian Cheal often found himself called upon to check a fact or ferret out further information in addition to his other duties, and Dawn Cole turned a word-processed manuscript into an impressive camera-ready file quickly and with great skill.

One of the fascinating and yet frustrating aspects of this project has been the feeling that we have been trying to describe and analyse a constantly evolving process. The publication of the LGCE's fifth edition of Guidance in October 2001 and its imminent transfer into the Electoral Commission are both further significant developments. We have endeavoured faithfully to report and interpret what we found at the time of our research. By now, however, it is likely that the target will have moved again!

COLIN RALLINGS, MICHAEL THRASHER and JAMES DOWNE

Plymouth and Warwick

October 2001

Chapter 1

Introduction

That each vote should be of equal value is a fundamental principle of elective democracy. In Britain, primary responsibility for ensuring that this is the case rests with those charged with drawing up the boundaries of the various electoral units. Although there is a sizeable academic and professional literature on the theoretical and practical considerations of electoral re-districting in many different contexts, no work has ever been undertaken on the case of local government in England. Until 1972 the construction and review of electoral boundaries within local authorities was a haphazard process, often left to the discretion of the authorities themselves. Inertia tended to rule the day, so that over time population movement and housing developments produced considerable imbalances in the numbers of electors in each ward. The Local Government Boundary Commission (LGBC), created by the Local Government Act 1972, was given the statutory task of periodically reviewing ward boundaries to ensure the maintenance of acceptable levels of electoral equality. In 1992 these functions were handed over to its successor body, the Local Government Commission for England (LGCE). This book is a study of how the LGCE goes about the task of conducting Periodic Electoral Reviews (PER), how local authorities prepare for and contribute to the process, and what, if any, are the party political consequences of the boundary changes which follow.

There is no doubt that the work of the LGCE receives considerably less attention and prominence than that accorded to the Parliamentary Boundary Commissions. The impact that the latter can have on the careers of individual Members of Parliament and on the prospects for whole parties ensures that their deliberations are followed closely and that every opportunity is grasped to influence their decisions. That is not to say, however, that what the LGCE does is without significance. For local politicians and parties the opportunities and threats presented by an electoral review are real enough. Indeed, local authorities and other groups are invited to submit initial proposals for the Commission's consideration. This gives PERs much more of a 'bottom up' flavour and allows political parties to try to devise schemes to their own electoral advantage rather than, as is the case with parliamentary reviews, having to respond to provisional recommendations drawn up by the Boundary Commissions themselves. Nor is the significance of any success which councils or parties have in persuading the Local Government Commission to adopt their suggestions restricted to the local government arena. The Parliamentary Boundary Commissioners use local wards as the building blocks for constituency boundaries and, therefore, how those wards are constructed is of direct relevance to that process too.

Data sources

This book draws on a wide range of primary and secondary source material. Interviews have been conducted with staff and Commissioners from both the Local Government Boundary Commission and the Local Government Commission for England, and we have had the opportunity to attend meetings of LGCE Commissioners and to observe Commission staff at work. We were allowed access to Commission minutes, private papers and to the 'stakeholder' survey used to elicit reaction from each local authority after its review. The process of electoral review has also been studied from the perspective of local authorities, with detailed case studies conducted in 13 councils undergoing a PER. These were the districts of East Devon, Kennet, North Wiltshire, Salisbury, West Devon and West Wiltshire, Swindon unitary authority, Northamptonshire county council, and the London boroughs of Barnet, Croydon, Harrow, Richmond-upon-Thames, and Westminster. We attended various meetings at which the review was discussed, interviewed key participants among both councillors and officers, and surveyed coverage in the local media. In addition, we constructed a database for the total of 127 local authorities whose ward boundaries were reviewed during the period from September 1996 to September 1999. This database contains details on many variables including electoral equality at various stages of the review, type and number of wards, number of councillors, the number and success of local submissions, and a comparison of the Commission's recommendations at the draft and final stages. Questionnaires were also sent to officers and to the three largest party political groups in each of these authorities asking for their comments on the review process. Information from either or both sets of respondents was received for 89 councils – 70% of the total surveyed. Finally, we have drawn on our own records contained in the British Local Elections Database 1973-2001 to enable us to measure and assess any electoral impact stemming from redistricting.

Plan of the Book

We begin in Chapter 2 by examining the process of electoral re-districting in both an international and national context. Although the institutions and mechanisms employed for defining and adjusting boundaries vary, it seems that no system can avoid disputes between those who insist that electorate numbers in each unit should be equal and those who argue that such units should also be drawn to reflect definable communities and interests. These tensions often cross-cut those engendered by party political involvement in boundary drawing. In the United States, for example, a partisan re-districting process is constrained by the expectation of zero deviance in population between electoral units. In other countries, on the other hand, non-partisan commissions have tolerated considerable variations in size between electorates and even the weighting of representation between areas. What appears to be common to all, however, is the attempt over time to impose tighter regulations on the process. In Britain, the initial formal review of parliamentary boundaries by Commission in 1947 has been followed by five Periodical Reviews, each subtly enhancing the prominence given to achieving equally sized electorates. In local government, the LGBC was the first body charged with a national responsibility for ensuring that 'as nearly as may be' there was electoral equality between the wards in each local authority. However, the fact that it was also obliged to have regard to fixing boundaries which would be 'easily identifiable' and not break 'local ties', made it inevitable that it too was thrust into the debate about conflicting re-districting criteria.

The Local Government Commission for England took over responsibility for Periodic Electoral Reviews in 1992 and Chapter 3 outlines the rules to which it worked, together with the procedures that it adopted and the ways in which these have been adjusted over time. The Local Government Act 1992 covered much the same ground as its 1972 predecessor and the crucial role of local authorities in preparing their own proposals for future electoral arrangements was retained. However the LGCE has considerable discretion as to the detail of how it operates and it set out in published guidance how it intended to interpret various aspects of the legislation. This covered such potentially difficult and ambiguous areas as the appropriate size for councils, the problem of sparsely populated areas and the forecasting of future electorates. Such guidance has frequently been amended to reflect changing circumstances and experience, and the reaction of its stakeholders. During the period of our research the Commission also found itself caught up in uncertainty about government policy on the appropriate structure of local authority wards and the likely frequency of local elections. This caused it to change the tone of some of its guidance to authorities and sometimes left it having to pacify those which thought that the goalposts had been moved during the course of their electoral review.

Having set out the formal framework within which the LGCE conducts Periodic Electoral Reviews, we move on in Chapter 4 to try to give an impression of how the Commission actually undertakes a review. Here we begin to get an insight into the culture of the organisation and come face to face for the first time with the perennial tension between achieving electoral equality and respecting community identities and interests. Using interviews, observation and documentary evidence we examine the work that is involved at each stage of a review. It is clear that although the LGCE places a premium on a co-operative and constructive relationship with its 'client' local councils, it is also at pains to convince them that redressing electoral imbalance has to be their prime focus. Each stage allows for extensive consultation and dialogue and the Commission does have the power to hold a public meeting if it feels that this might assist it in refining its proposals. However, these are not formal public inquiries of the type which occur during parliamentary boundary reviews and neither local authorities nor any other interested parties have the right to insist on a meeting being held. In the final analysis the Commission holds all the cards. For although representations are invited concerning the Final Recommendations which it submits to the Secretary of State, government policy is to preserve the LGCE's independence by not modifying the substance of the electoral arrangements proposed.

In Chapter 5 we turn the focus on to the subjects of electoral review. For local authorities the attention of the Commission can come as an unwanted irritant, bringing it with it considerable demands on resources. How they respond varies widely. In some cases the review is seen as purely an administrative matter to be dealt with by local government officers with minimal political oversight; in others the parties are well aware of the stakes and become closely involved at every stage, often through *ad hoc* working groups. Both approaches can lead to tension between elected members and officials. Councils can find themselves in conflict with the Commission if, as often seems their natural reaction, they try to pursue minimal change. Such a policy makes it easier for them to draw up proposals and is less likely to excite adverse party political or electorate opposition. However it can mean that they are unable to meet the Commission's required standards on electoral variance. The Commission also takes an interest in the degree of consultation undertaken by local authorities and in public responses to re-warding schemes. A scheme for which there is evidence of widespread local support is likely to weigh more heavily than one on which there has been no consultation. The debate about contentious proposals can spill over into the local media, with changes affecting the integrity of long-standing boundaries a particular bone of contention.

Chapter 6 puts the process under the spotlight by presenting case studies of the Periodic Electoral Review in six local authorities. These make clear the importance of internal council dynamics in determining how re-districting proposals were drawn up and the nature of the interaction with the LGCE. For each authority we present a brief portrait of its demographic and political character, followed by an examination of how its submissions were prepared, its relationship with the

Commission, and the role played by party politics in the review process. Most councils began with the aim of achieving a cross-party consensus, but even where that was not possible, disputes tended to centre on particular wards or localities. There were few attempts at wholesale gerrymandering, not least because the Commission's requirements about the shape of and degree of equality between wards acted to limit what it was possible for authorities or political parties to propose. Not that attempts to gain electoral advantage from the review were wholly absent, with political parties and others using electorate projections, arguments about community interests and a range of other devices to persuade the Commission of the validity of their proposals.

Although the case study method provides a wealth of detail and flavour, it is vulnerable to the charge of being based on atypical examples. In Chapter 7, therefore, we present findings from our database of all 127 authorities for which the Commission completed its Final Recommendations in the period from December 1996 to September 1999. We measure the extent and magnitude of the changes proposed by the Commission, examining in turn the electoral cycle, the size and structure of wards both within and across local authorities, the size of the council, the calculation and accuracy of electorate projections, and the impact of review on both councillor/elector ratios and electoral equality. The data show how the interests of the Commission and of the local authorities both contribute to the overall outcome of PERs. Radical change to anything except ward boundaries and electorates is rarely proposed by councils or initiated by the Commission. Equally, although the Commission successfully insists on measurable reductions in electoral variance between wards, it does not always achieve an optimum solution. Changes made between the publication of its Draft and Final Recommendations suggest that it will listen to claims about community ties even at the expense of numerical equality, and the policy of basing proposed wards on projected electorates has the potential to undo the most carefully crafted scheme if those projections prove inaccurate.

For many observers, however, the key question about Periodic Electoral Reviews is whether they have any party political impact. In Chapter 8 we examine this issue from a number of perspectives. For its part, the Commission appears confident that it has become attuned to spotting and weeding out any blatantly partisan attempts to hijack the process, and believes that its rules and procedures severely limit the scope for such activity in any case. Strangely enough, the parties appear to agree. The national parties concentrate their efforts on providing procedural information and advice to their local members. Locally, most parties are active during a review, often proselytising their own favoured (and usually favourable) re-warding scheme. In both cases, however, the need to satisfy the Commission's criteria was acknowledged as an important constraint. We sought confirmation of this in our attempt to quantify the electoral advantage or disadvantage accruing to the parties through the electoral review in their local authority. Whilst it did seem possible to manoeuvre to add the occasional new ward to a party's safe seat tally, any overall disproportionality in election results was far more likely to reflect factors such as differential turnout, uneven patterns of party competition or the operation of the first past the post electoral system than a successful gerrymander.

Our final substantive chapter, Chapter 9, attempts to evaluate the PER process and its outcomes. Evidence is drawn from a range of sources including the Commission's own self-audit and analysis, its stakeholders in both local and central government, and the quinquennial Financial Management and Policy Review which happened to coincide with our own research. For both the LGCE and the local authorities electoral reviews involved a good deal of learning 'on the job'. Complaints fell and satisfaction grew in direct proportion to the number of reviews the Commission had completed. Councils whose turn was later in the cycle benefited both from the experience of others and the Commission's surer touch. Indeed, the consensus from every side – Commission, local authorities, political parties and the FMPR– was that the system of electoral review required adjustment rather than overhaul. However, it should come as no surprise that the biggest criticism of both the Commission and the system focused on the perceived significance attached to achieving electoral equality even at the expense of breaking local ties and identities. That is an issue that constantly resurfaces throughout the book and that dominates discussion of re-districting whether in an international or local community context.

Chapter 10 draws all these themes together and, additionally, attempts to place the electoral review work of the LGCE in wider context. There are two aspects to this. On the one hand, it has often appeared as if this study was trying to describe and analyse a moving target. The election of the Labour government in May 1997 and its subsequent expressions of interest and intent about constitutional and local government reform had a significant impact on the Commission's on-going work, guidance and timetable. Now, the LGCE is to be absorbed into the new Electoral Commission, where it will be joined after 2005 by the Parliamentary Boundary Commissions as well. What better time to offer a few observations on how the electoral review process might be reformed. We would also claim that the process of re-districting local government ward boundaries itself forms an excellent case study of the policy-making process in Britain. A small and rather forgotten corner of the overall political system it may be, but there are lessons to be learnt, not only about the relationships between councillors and officers, local and central government, and the political parties, but also about the way policy is devolved and implemented.

Chapter 2

Re-districting by Commission

Nations with single member electoral districts and/or plurality voting systems need mechanisms for boundary reviews. In most countries this process has become formalised over time as the move towards universal franchise brought in its wake a demand that each vote should be of equal value. However, that is a goal more easily stated than achieved. Partitioning an area so that each unit has an equally sized electorate can be done crudely or subtly, and with partisan interests to the fore or kept firmly in check. Those who argue that equal numbers are the only things that matter are countered by claims that boundaries need to make sense in terms of acknowledging local communities and – in some cases – social and ethnic divisions in the population. The trade off between these mathematical and organic approaches has dominated discussions about re-districting. Of no less importance has been the issue of who is responsible for boundary drawing. In cases where party driven legislatures have undertaken the task there has been understandable concern about a tyranny of the majority for its own advantage. Where, by contrast, a neutral body has been established, there remain questions about the appropriateness of the rules to which it works and its susceptibility to party political influence. In this chapter we wish briefly to review how re-districting is carried out in a range of different countries, and how they address the seeming contradictions we have noted. We then turn to a more detailed examination of the evolution of the process at both parliamentary and local government level in Britain.

International comparisons

The example most frequently used by commentators wishing to point to partisan gerrymandering in the drawing of electoral boundaries is the United States. In the US redistributions take place after every decennial census, with the population at the time of the census rather than the electorate used in all calculations. This can immediately give rise to controversy if it is thought that potential boundaries might be based on mis- or under-counting. Re-districting is also a devolved process, with '50 congressional re-districtings and 1000s of state and local ones, each conducted under different conditions and constraints' (Butler and Cain, 1992: 15). Although neutral electoral commissions are used either first up (e.g. Hawaii) or as back up to resolve disputes (e.g. Montana) in a few small states, in most cases state legislatures have re-districting powers. Naturally this provokes considerable political excitement and speculation about how far the majority party will be able to ensure that its will prevails. In practice, however, it seems that changes in the law have had the effect of limiting the scope for implementing partisan fixes. Butler and Cain point out that the courts now tend to insist on the 'one person, one vote' principle even down to the level of local school boards and, as a result, 'among the alternative plans that would be acceptable to a judge…the difference in most instances between the best and the worst plans would only alter the party balance by a handful of seats'(1992: 5). In particular, although US law does not set down specific tolerance limits concerning the allowable variance in population between electoral units, it is likely that any deviation away from zero might be challengeable. One probable outcome of these trends will be to dampen state variations even further.

Even if parties can still find a way to impose their will on the process, they face a difficult dilemma. In an era of political volatility it could be quite hard to predict where and whether a change in boundaries will lead to change in partisan composition. Is a party best advised to try to safeguard its safe seats, or should it adopt the very risky strategy of supporting the construction of more 'potential' seats? Such a decision is thrown into sharp relief by the requirement in the United States that, where relevant, a certain number of so-called 'majority-minority' congressional districts must be created. That is, districts in which the ethnic minority (usually Afro-American) population forms a numerical majority. During the 1991 re-districting in Georgia this had the effect of weakening the Democrat position as party supporters were drawn from surrounding areas to form 'max black' districts (Bonfili, 1998). The law also came into play. Although the initial attempt at re-districting had attracted 'solid bipartisan and biracial majorities in both houses', it was rejected by the scrutinising Department of Justice on the grounds that it could have been even better (Bonfili, 1998: 8–9). A subsequent iteration resulted in the drawing of bizarrely shaped districts in order to meet both the population equality and 'max black' criteria and this, in turn, was challenged by whites on the grounds that it amounted to a 'racial gerrymander' violating the Equal Protection Clause of the 14th Amendment. The need to consider race when drawing boundaries adds a further dimension to the trade-offs involved, and has given rise to numerous other examples of the tensions seen in Georgia between political interest groups, the Department of Justice and the courts. The principle of pursuing one vote, one value is fine, but it can disrupt the democratic process in other ways. Moving voters from area to area can break both community interests and continuity of representation. Each redistribution is not only a chance to equalise numbers, but also presents the opportunity for a new gerrymander. From the American perspective, choosing among the re-districting trade-offs and options properly falls within the political domain.

The experience of the United States differs from that of most other western liberal states in that it has retained a system of boundary determination which relies for the most part on legislative decision-making. However, it has not been immune to what we can see as an international trend towards the greater regularisation of redistributions. In the US, this has meant a greater role for the law and legal determination; elsewhere, it has involved the evolution of Commission based processes. Commissions are politically impartial and operate free from interference by the government of the day. Their legitimacy in carrying out boundary reviews rests on those qualities. The older Commonwealth countries provide a good example of variations in history and practice. In Australia, federal redistributions are provided for under the Commonwealth Electoral Act 1918 and are conducted by an independent public body, known since 1984 as the Australian Electoral Commission (AEC). Redistributions are required every seven years and can be held more frequently under certain circumstances (McAllister *et al.,* 1997). The AEC determines the number of members entitled to be elected from each state according to a quota derived from national electoral enrolment. All seats have to have an electorate within 10% (20% prior to 1970) of the state's quota at the start of the process and, since 1987, must be projected to fall within 2% of it after three and a half years (that is, at the halfway point between boundary reviews). In the Australian states responsibility for boundary reviews rests either with the state legislature or the state electoral commission. Western Australia retains a system of rural weighting so that there are fewer electors per seat in sparsely populated parts than in urban areas, and Queensland was divided into electoral zones in order to achieve the same effect until about a decade ago. Elsewhere rural weighting has been abolished. The states have a similar role in determining local government electoral boundaries, with the method and frequency of review usually laid down by statute.

A Commission charged with reviewing boundaries has existed in New Zealand since 1887, although unusually it contains one government and one opposition nominee in addition to independent members (Bush, 1995). Reviews are conducted every 5 years and no constituency is allowed to vary by more than 5% from the quotas calculated separately for the North and South Islands. The issue of whether there should be wards in local government and, if so, how they should be apportioned was for a long time left to local decision. Wards are now compulsory for Territorial Local Authorities with a population in excess of 20,000. However, because there tend to be only a very few multi-member wards in each authority and because elections are based on simple plurality, disproportionate rewards for the 'winner' are common regardless of the equity in the number of electors. In Canada, electoral redistribution was the responsibility of parliament until the 1960s when a federal Commission was set up (Small, 1991). A quota is devised for each Province, with individual seats being allowed to vary by up to 25% from this and 'exceptionally' by more. Additionally, each Province is protected against ever having to lose a seat, so that the House of Commons will inevitably grow and never shrink in response to population changes and movements. There have been three re-districtings conducted by the Delimitation Commission in India for both national and state legislatures. Despite a rule that electorates should be 'as equal as possible', wide tolerances were in practice allowed in order to respect established boundaries. In 1975 it was agreed that there should be no further redistribution until at least the end of the century and variations in electorate are now very considerable. European countries that provide good case examples of re-districting include Germany and France. In Germany, the use of the Additional Member System to compensate parties for any discrepancy between the share of the vote received and the number of seats won has meant that drawing boundaries with precisely equal electorates has been perceived as less important. A permanent Commission allows tolerances of up to 25%, with boundaries compulsorily redrawn once the variance from the average in any seat reaches 33.3%. In France, boundary reviews have tended to coincide with changes between Republics and/or electoral systems. Parliament was responsible for the last review in 1986, but was required to respect the boundaries of *departements* and ensure that each seat was within 20% of the quota for the *departement*. Butler and Cain concluded that 'the majority party did try to draw boundaries in its own favour, but was constrained by its own deputies seeking boundaries congenial to themselves' as well as by the courts (1992: 128).

These examples point up the variety of mechanisms and regulations used in the redrawing of electoral boundaries. The United States retains the most decentralised and potentially party political driven system, but in practice tough legal requirements concerning electoral equality and the representation of minority groups have limited the effective scope for malpractice. In other countries it is common to try to take boundary determination out of the political arena by appointing Commissions to undertake the task. Nonetheless, the rules to which these Commissions work will have been drawn up by politicians and there are considerable variations in the degrees to which electorates are allowed to vary in size and representation is weighted between areas. Indeed re-districting criteria appear to be inherently conflictual and trade-offs therefore a frequent requirement, regardless of whether Commission or legislative based systems are adopted. In Britain, formal boundary reviews only began in the twentieth century and were initially subject to Act of Parliament. It was not until 1944 that permanent Parliamentary Boundary

Commissions were appointed to provide assurance about the integrity and neutrality of the process. In local government, boundary changes began as the responsibility of the councils themselves, but they too gradually – and in comparative terms, rather unusually – became subject to Commission oversight. This was not least because the wards so established were then used, as we noted in Chapter 1, as the building blocks for the construction of parliamentary constituency boundaries. To provide historical context to the current work of the Local Government Commission for England it is worth examining the evolution of both the parliamentary and local government boundary review procedures in more detail.

The evolution of review procedures in Britain: parliamentary constituency boundaries

Until the second world war parliamentary boundary changes were carried out by Act of Parliament and tended to be prompted by extensions of the franchise. Each new redistribution brought with it an *ad hoc* increase in the formality of the procedures, with a Speaker's Conference in 1917 drawing up the first set of general rules for issue to the Boundary Commissioners (including a requirement that constituencies should be of roughly equal size). The period between 1918 and 1947 saw no further boundary alterations, but it was characterised by an increasing disparity in constituency electorates (by 1939, 30 constituencies had more than 100,000 electors and 13 fewer than 30,000) and a further acceptance that the periodic review of constituency boundaries should become a fixed part of the political agenda. In 1942 the Report of the Committee on Electoral Machinery recommended the establishment of permanent boundary commissions to review constituencies once in the lifetime of each Parliament, and the 1944 Speaker's Conference drew up more detailed rules for how the Commissions would calculate and apply an electoral quota and the circumstances under which discretion might be allowed. These proposals were incorporated into the House of Commons (Redistribution of Seats) Act 1944 and some very large constituencies with electorates in excess of 100,000 were sub-divided in time for the May 1945 general election.

The Initial Review 1947

Following the end of the war and the compilation of new registers, the Parliamentary Boundary Commissions set to work. There were four Commissions, one each for England, Wales, Scotland and Northern Ireland. Each was nominally chaired by the Speaker, although the effective control rested with the Deputy Chairman, a High Court judge. In addition, there were two other members, usually also lawyers, two 'expert' assessors – the Director-General of the Ordnance Survey and the Registrar General or their equivalents in each nation – and a staff of civil servants. They reported in 1947 – see Table 2.1. According to one source the 'redistribution seems to have been fairly painless', though David Butler notes that the then Labour government asked the Commissioners to create seventeen additional seats drawing protests from the Conservatives (House of Commons Library, 1992; Butler, 1954). Legislation enacting these proposals and some amendments to the rules – including a requirement for general reviews to be undertaken at intervals of not less than three and not more than seven years – was consolidated in the House of Commons (Redistribution of Seats) Act 1949. It is interesting to note that although the 1944 Act required the Commissions to respect the boundaries of local government areas in drawing up constituencies, it was 'entirely silent' (Rossiter *et al.*, 1999: 85) on which spatial units in England were to be used when such areas had to be divided into two or more constituencies. In practice however, as Rossiter *et al.* go on to point out, wards and civil parishes were the chosen building blocks and the English Commission noted with satisfaction in its report how rarely these had had to be split in forming constituencies.

Table 2.1 The work of the Boundary Commission for England

	Work commenced	*Report published*	*Act/order passed*	*Total seats (England)*
Initial report	January 1946	October 1947	July 1948	506
1st periodic review	July 1953	November 1954	Jan/Feb 1955	511
2nd periodic review	February 1965	April 1969	November 1970	516
3rd periodic review	February 1976	February 1983	March 1983	523
4th periodic review	February 1991	June 1995	June 1995	529

Source: C. Rallings and M. Thrasher, *British Electoral Facts 1832–1999,* Ashgate 2000

First Periodical Review 1954

In order to meet the requirement for a further review within 3–7 years, the Commissions set to work again in 1953. On this occasion their work caused considerable controversy, culminating in two unsuccessful attempts to persuade the Courts to prevent the Home Secretary from presenting draft Orders in Council giving effect to the Commissioners' recommendations. Many reports were considered to be too brief and without adequate explanation and the Commissioners were felt to be working without clear guidance on how far they should adhere to or depart from the 'rules'. Moreover, the redistribution came too smartly on the heels of its predecessor. As David Butler puts it in his definitive work on the British electoral system, 'There were few gross anomalies, but the rigorous pursuit of mathematical equality meant that, after only 5 years, 170 constituencies had their boundaries altered, often drastically' (Butler, 1963). Following such criticism, and although the Orders were made effective in time for the May 1955 general election, inter-party consultations led to a new House of Commons (Redistribution of Seats) Act 1958. The routine interval between reviews was changed to between 10 and 15 years; the electoral quota was to be calculated separately for each of the four parts of the United Kingdom; it would be required that a High Court judge be the deputy chair of each Commission, and that a local inquiry be held if the Commission's original proposals were objected to by a local authority or 100 or more electors.

Second Periodical Review 1969

The second periodical review of boundaries ran from 1965 to 1969. On this occasion the procedures were not in dispute, but controversy surrounded the Labour government's decision not to implement the Commissions' proposals. Ostensibly, the government wished to delay implementation pending the reorganisation of local government. More cynical observers thought it was trying to avoid the loss of Labour seats which seemed an inevitable consequence of the review. Instead the government introduced a limited Bill to alter boundaries in Greater London and in a few, very large constituencies. This measure was blocked in the House of Lords and James Callaghan, as Home Secretary, then presented to Parliament the necessary Orders to give effect to the Boundary Commission recommendations only to use the government majority to defeat them. The 1970 general election was therefore fought on unchanged boundaries, with the Conservative party promising in its manifesto rapidly to put in place the Commissions' proposals. This was done in November 1970. At both this and the First Periodical Review the English Commission adhered to its practice of avoiding crossing local ward boundaries in its construction of constituencies. However it noted that this was difficult to achieve where ward boundaries had become out-of-date and where local authorities had not conducted ward reviews to resolve the problem (Boundary Commission for England, 1969: 5). This frustration at the piecemeal way in which local boundary changes were undertaken and implemented was, as we shall see, soon to be addressed by the formation of a Local Government Boundary Commission.

Third Periodical Review 1983

The third review of boundaries began in 1976 and was obliged to take account of new local government units formed by the Local Government Acts of 1972 and 1973. Indeed two general elections, those in October 1974 and May 1979, took place with constituencies located in local government areas which no longer existed. For example, the Stockport constituencies were still deemed to be in Cheshire despite being located in the new County of Greater Manchester, and Bath and Bristol were now in a new County of Avon rather than in Somerset and Gloucestershire respectively. The instruction to the Commissions not to allow constituencies to cross county boundaries 'so far as is practicable' and their decision to use the now many fewer wards of the new district (in Scotland, regional) councils as the building blocks for parliamentary constituencies made large scale change inevitable.

The Commissions were delayed in their work first by awaiting the deliberations of the separate Local Government Boundary Commissions, and then by two pieces of litigation. In the first legal case three local authorities in the County of Tyne and Wear challenged the English Commission's recommendation to reduce the number of members of parliament in the county from 14 to 13. Their application was dismissed in December 1982. The second case involved four prominent members of the Labour party, including the leader Michael Foot and the party's general secretary Jim Mortimer, acting as individual, private electors. They challenged the English Commission's failure to use its discretion to cross county and London borough boundaries where to do so would lead to a reduction in the disparity in size between constituencies. They also disputed the time taken by the Commissions to come up with their proposals, in particular the fact that constituencies based on 1976 electorates would by that time be seriously out of date. Their application was dismissed by both the High Court and the Court of Appeal and they were refused leave to appeal to the House of Lords. The legal process having been exhausted, the Orders were placed before parliament and passed in time for the new constituencies to be adopted at the June 1983 general election.

The failure of litigation did not quell the criticisms of the third periodical review, and indeed the Court rulings had served to emphasise the considerable freedom available to the Commission in determining when and when not to use its discretion. The Court of Appeals' opinion stated,

> 'It is important to realise that Parliament did not tell the Boundary Commission to do an exercise in accountancy...It told it to engage in a more far-reaching and sophisticated undertaking, involving striking a balance between many factors which point in different directions. This calls for judgement, not scientific precision.'

In particular, as Johnston *et al.* argue, the Court seemed to indicate 'that the Commission should be more prepared to consider, and more open to challenge on, issues of disruption due to change and to the breaking of local ties than disparities around the electoral quota' (Johnston *et al.*, 1993). Despite this judgement concern was expressed not so much at the Commissions' use of their discretion as at the seeming inconsistency of their interpretations. As Waller put it, 'Quite frequently when presented with similar problems different recommendations were made in different counties' (Waller, 1983: 197). This was especially the case following public inquiries. Such inquiries, chaired by various Assistant Commissioners appointed on an *ad hoc* basis, tended to err on the side of recommending no disturbance to the status quo rather than pursuing an arithmetical equality of electorates.

Many of these issues were given further attention by the enquiry of the Home Affairs Select Committee into the redistribution of seats during the 1986/87 parliamentary session. The Committee's agenda was dominated by a concern to curtail the seeming inexorable increase in the number of constituencies (and thus members of parliament) which followed each boundary review. They argued,

> 'Since the Rules for the Redistribution were formulated in 1949 a fundamental defect has come to light. Rule 1 provides a total number of seats for Great Britain (613) which should not be substantially exceeded. Rule 8 provides that the electoral quota (i.e. the target size for the electorate of each constituency) should be determined by dividing the electorate of each region in the United Kingdom by the number of constituencies in existence there at the start of each general review. Rule 6 allows for constituencies in sparsely populated parts of the Kingdom to have smaller electorates than the quota, and Rule 5 also provides circumstances in which quota entitlements to seats may be exceeded. Whenever extra seats are awarded under these Rules the number of constituencies will exceed the previous number. Those higher numbers will in turn be used for determining the electoral quota next time. The result is a progressive and cumulative increase in the number of seats in the House of Commons. The total for Great Britain is now 633. We do not believe this to be an intended consequence of the Rules, and we regard the continuation of this tendency as being undesirable' (Home Affairs Committee, 1987: para 6).

It was also noted that the Commissions had a tendency to round an area's theoretical entitlement up rather than down where this would produce seats whose average electorate was closer to the national quota. For example. With a quota of 60,000 and an electorate of 327,600 a county would be entitled to 5.46 seats. With 5 seats, the average constituency would have 65,520 electors and deviate from the quota by 5,520. With 6 seats, the average constituency would have 54,600 electors and deviate from the quota by 5,400. In such cases it had been the Commissions' practice to award 6 rather than 5 seats. Such thinking led the Committee to recommend the adoption of a permanently fixed divisor to cap future growth of the House of Commons. The Committee was also conscious of the different levels of representation in the different parts of the United Kingdom. They noted that the electoral quotas in 1985 were 68,700 for England; 55,100 for Scotland; 56,400 for Wales; and 63,400 for Northern Ireland. However, although they demonstrated that it would be technically quite easy to achieve a uniform UK quota, they accepted that 'it would not be feasible on political grounds to change the Rules' to provide such uniformity and made no recommendation.

Fourth Periodical Review 1995

Although the Parliamentary Constituencies Act 1986 was enacted to consolidate previous legislation on the redistribution of seats, no legislative slot was found to incorporate even those aspects of the Home Affairs Select Committee report which the government had accepted in principle before the fourth periodical review was announced in February 1991. However, the English Commission did make clear from the outset that there would be a number of changes in its interpretation of the Rules. Quite the most significant was the Commission's view that 'in order to give effect to rule 1, it would be proper for them in the exercise of the discretion given to them in rules 5,6, and 7 to limit any further increase in the number of seats' (Boundary Commission for England, 1991). The Commission also noted that the discretion to cross county and London borough boundaries does exist and 'might be exercised if the interplay of the rules, including the limit on the number of seats in rule 1, so required'. Similarly, it expressed the view that ' the "special geographical considerations" justifying departure from rules 4 and 5 occur mainly in Scotland and Wales and seldom in England'. The identification of 'local ties' as specified in rule 7 has also been an area of controversy. The Commission is clear that district wards are the smallest unit in the process of 'building' a constituency and that proposals for splitting wards between constituencies would be considered a *prima facie* case of breaking local ties. However, local ties are claimed in other instances too and the Commission's evidence to the Home Affairs Select Committee gave an insight into how such claims were assessed. It commented,

> 'The Commissions must rely heavily on the advice given by assistant Commissioners following their investigations into local ties...Many of the political arguments are put to us cloaked in arguments about local ties. We must rely on the assistant Commissioners to sift through the conflicting information often presented and to guide us accordingly. It is of course inevitable that those who have not succeeded in persuading the assistant Commissioner of the validity of their arguments on local ties should thereafter loudly affirm that justice has not been done' (Boundary Commission for England, 1986).

The Commission ends its briefing paper with what might be termed a trenchant defence of inconsistency. The rules, it says, are

> 'interrelated in a complex way and obviously designed to allow the Commission a very wide discretion in their application...there is ...usually no one perfect way to distribute constituencies...In practice, in one area the Commission may feel able to allow the requirement of rule 5, for electorates to be as near the electoral quota as practicable, to be given effect whereas, in another area, other factors such as the requirement of rule 4, to respect county and London borough boundaries, or the existence of strong local ties, may prevent this. Elsewhere a compromise solution may be found. These subjective decisions are difficult, but the Commission reach

> their independent and impartial conclusions on the basis of all the information available to them' (Boundary Commission for England, 1991: 32–33).

It was against such a background of no legislative change, but a clear determination to limit any increase in the number of seats and to assert the Commissioners' discretion, that the English Boundary Commission began work. However, before any final recommendations had been made and in the wake of the Conservative general election victory in April 1992, it found itself working to a new and tighter timetable. Having been returned with a narrow majority, the Conservatives decided that a rapid boundary review would net them valuable extra parliamentary seats. The Boundary Commissions Act 1992 revised the interval between boundary reviews in general from not less than 10 or more than 15 years to not less than 8 or more than 12 years from the submission date of the last report, and required all four Commissions to submit their report to the relevant Secretary of State no later than 31st December 1994 – some three years in advance of the original deadline. Only the Scottish Commission, which was required by the 1986 Act merely to 'have regard' to local government boundaries, was able to meet this target, although its report was not submitted to Parliament until February 1995. The other Commissions were late, but the Act had allowed for that possibility by stating that 'a failure…to submit a report within the time limit…shall not be regarded as invalidating the report for the purposes of enactment' (Boundary Commissions Act, 1992: 2 (4)). Not least the explanation for this delay was that in England, Scotland and Wales the Periodical Review coincided with changes to local government structure. These impacted on the boundaries not only of council areas, which the Commissions were statutorily obliged to respect, but also of their building blocks, the wards. It was little wonder that calls grew for the better synchronisation of local and parliamentary boundary reviews.

The Fourth Periodical Review did not provoke either the political controversies or legal challenges that had characterised some of its predecessors, but it did serve to highlight a number of major issues concerning the Commission approach to boundary drawing. In particular, as Rossiter *et al.* point out in their standard work, although 'the Commissions' bona fides have only rarely been queried…Their work is not immune from the political process' (1999: 399). At national level, the timing was changed in 1992 by a Conservative government seeking early benefit from an electoral advantage it knew would be the unintendedly partisan product of any review. In individual local areas, by contrast, the Labour party proved itself better able to make representations at Local Inquiries and, through these, to sway the recommendations made to the Commissions. At the same time, however, 'there was very much less variation in the size of constituencies after the Fourth Periodical Review than had been the case heretofore' (Rossiter *et al.,* 1999:

194). Although the current legislation lays down no formal guidance concerning the allowable variation in constituency size around each country's electoral quota, this trend towards privileging the mathematical rather than organic approach to review was clearly driven as much by the desire to limit the growth in the number of seats in the House of Commons as by philosophical concerns about the equal value of each vote. Such a policy itself has the potential to provoke those who place a high premium on the representation of communities and, as we shall see, their arguments have perhaps an even greater resonance when local electoral boundaries are being drawn.

The evolution of review procedures in Britain: local government electoral boundaries

Electoral boundaries in English local government have also been the responsibility of a developing system of determination by Commission. Unlike their Parliamentary Boundary cousins, however, those reviewing local government had two sets of borders to consider. Much of their work, and certainly the majority of any public attention that it attracted, has been concerned with the structure of local government itself. That is reshaping the boundaries between principal local authorities and effecting changes in their functions. The Commissions' other role, to set the boundaries of electoral divisions and wards within local authorities, was often seen as secondary. Indeed until 1972, when the establishment of the Local Government Boundary Commission (LGBC) put electoral reviews on a statutory footing for the first time, local authorities themselves played the major role in prompting, devising and implementing such boundary changes. We have already seen how this had become a source of frustration to the Parliamentary Boundary Commission, and the attempt to address such concerns was destined to give the decisions of the LGBC significance beyond local government and to charge its review procedures and criteria with potential party political implications.

Prior to 1972

The practice of dividing local authorities into wards followed the 1835 reform of municipal corporations. Tory politicians in particular were concerned that they might not win any council seats at all if elections were conducted 'at large'. However, as the boroughs were also to have annual elections, most of the wards created were multi-member and this helped to simplify and, in some cases, avoid altogether the need for warding. Calls for piecemeal and incremental changes to be made to the boundaries, status and functions of local authorities accelerated following the formalisation of county government in 1888. Initially such change came about through local initiation or Private Bills in parliament. Between 1888 and 1927 a total of 270 Urban District councils and 118 Rural District councils were created (Pearce, 1980), but with many being 'unwarded' there was little reason to focus on electoral arrangements. The principle of systematic review was not established until the 1929 Local Government Act charged County Councils with reviewing the 'subordinate' authorities that fell within their boundaries. Once again, however, little attention was paid to the construction of electoral units at a time when party politics had made few inroads into local government outside the major cities.

The first Local Government Boundary Commission (the Trustram Eve Commission) was established to help adjust the structure of local government following the end of the second world war in 1945. It had the power to make Orders for change, but none were forthcoming as Commissioners decided that a wholesale overhaul of the functions of local authorities and of the relationship between them was required (Young and Rao, 1997). The government took the view that this was beyond the Commission's remit and competence and, following its dissolution in 1949, the earlier arrangements for taking boundary changes through a special parliamentary procedure were reactivated. Other Commissions followed. The Royal Commission on Local Government in London 1957–60 (the Herbert Commission) did lead to radical changes in the capital, including the creation of the Greater London Council. The Local Government Commission (the Hancock Commission), appointed following the 1958 Local Government Act, had wide powers to recommend the pattern of local government it felt appropriate, but got into difficulties over changing boundaries between local authorities and the long-winded public consultations these involved (Keith Lucas and Richards, 1978). When it did recommend changes, often involving the expansion of county boroughs, it risked hostility from ministers concerned about their electoral implications. In a revealing passage in his Diaries, Richard Crossman noted,

> 'I've also had to deal during the first 5 weeks with the whole question of the LGBC (*sic*)… I've talked to my colleagues about it, and I've got them to agree after a great deal of humming and hawing that I can't delay my decisions on the recommendations of the Commission any further, and that I am bound to announce these decisions in the near future…My colleagues know this, and this gives me an odd detached power in dealing with them. After all, I can make or mar George Brown at Belper, Bert Bowden in Leicester, Bill Wilson in Coventry, Ted Short in Newcastle: each of them knows that as Minister of Housing the decision I make may be life or death for them in terms of representation at Westminster' (Crossman, 1975:Vol.1, 441).

A particular example occurred in Northampton in 1965. The normal procedure was for the Home Office to draw the boundaries of any new wards required after consultation with local councils and electors. On this occasion, however, the local Labour and Conservative parties each put forward rival schemes. The Labour Home

Secretary, Sir Frank Soskice, formally ruled in favour of the Conservative scheme and then reversed his decision following party protests. The issue served to concentrate minds on 'whether a minister in such circumstances should pretend to be totally blind to party considerations, or should be a realist and recognise, what everyone knew, that drawing ward boundariess affects election results' (Keith Lucas and Richards, 1978: 21). It was not long before Crossman put the whole matter on the back-burner by appointing the Royal Commission on Local Government in England 1966–9 (the Redcliffe-Maud Commission) to review the entire structure.

In the meantime local government was left with a haphazard set of rules for reviewing electoral boundaries – see Box 2.1.

BOX 2.1 Procedures for reviewing ward boundaries prior to 1972

County councils: single member divisions could be varied by Order of the Home Secretary on representation by the county or by the council of a district within it.

Greater London Council: divisions defined by the Home Secretary and varied on representation from London local authorities.

Boroughs: may be divided into wards for electoral purposes. Number of wards fixed by borough charter, or may be fixed/altered by Order in Council on petition by the Borough.

Urban districts: may be divided into wards for electoral purposes. These determined or altered by county council after local inquiry. UDCs could apply to Home Secretary if county unwilling to initiate procedure.

Rural districts: divided into areas based on parishes/parish wards. Areas and number of councillors determined/altered by county council.

Source: W. Eric Jackson, *The Structure of Local Government* 5th edition Longman 1966

In practice, as in Northampton, electoral arrangements tended to be considered only as part of the creation of new county boroughs or at the time of other structural changes. With few of these taking place, discrepancies in the number of electors represented by each councillor grew. The trend affected both urban and rural areas. In Chester, there had been a reluctance to redraw boundaries following the incorporation of Hoole in 1954 with the result that by 1964 one ward had 3,106 electors and another 10,058. The extension of the city's boundaries and its retention of county borough status, as recommended by the Hancock Local Government Commission, was mooted as being the springboard for a rewarding (Lee in Sharpe (ed), 1967: 73). Elsewhere population movement out of the cities meant that inner city councillors had fewer and fewer electors in their wards, and suburban ones more. Leeds, for example, last had its ward boundaries reviewed in 1950. By 1964 this stasis was badly disadvantaging the Conservatives (Hill in Sharpe (ed), 1967: 161). Some 50% of all Municipal Boroughs and Urban Districts with populations under 10,000 were still unwarded in the mid 1960s, and the whole parish base of much Rural District representation made those councils particularly hard to change. Stanyer notes that, in the 1960s, one parish in Oakham RDC in the East Midlands returned one member despite having no resident electors, whereas another with 3,950 electors similarly had a single district councillor (Stanyer, 1967: 22).

The last hurrah of the unreformed local government system came, ironically, with the inaugural elections for the new authorities set up under the 1972 Local Government Act. The government was more concerned that these elections, held in 1973, should be administratively feasible than democratically fair. It was accepted that electors would be voting in temporarily constructed wards that would be bound to change. The government itself prepared draft schemes for 'informal consultation' as regards the counties and the new metropolitan authorities, and the Local Government Boundary Commission – which had not yet formally come into existence – took responsibility for the non-metropolitan districts. The result was a 'set of elections, based normally on existing wards or their amalgamation, which often were hardly fair to either candidates or voters' (Wood, 1976: 168). In many counties, for example, multi-member divisions were used despite the fact that the Act specified that all county divisions should return a single member. The LGBC would not finally manage to abolish these until the 1985 election. Equally common were gross disparities in electorates, with divisions in Cheshire varying between one councillor per 6,000 electors and one for every 16,000! Among the districts, perhaps the greatest anomaly was the number of candidates to be elected in each ward. For example, some wards in Beverley district council had twelve members, and in the Clitheroe ward of Ribble Valley there were no fewer than 31 candidates for ten vacancies. The fact that one party, on this occasion the Conservatives, was able to win eight of the ten seats despite polling little more than 40% of the total votes cast only served to emphasise the need for a rapid review of boundaries.

The Local Government Boundary Commission for England 1972–92

It was the 1972 Local Government Act that, for the first time, charged a Commission with reviewing, at intervals, the electoral arrangements for all counties, districts and London boroughs. Until then such reviews had effectively been permissive rather than statutory, except when they accompanied the relatively rare adjustments to the structure or boundaries of local authorities. The Act laid down the criteria for the Commission to follow, but its clauses were a mixture of a centralised, 'top down' approach combined with the accordance of important roles and responsibilities to the local authorities themselves. The Commission was to take into account not only 'the need to secure effective and convenient local government' (a recurring phrase in local government legislation before and since), but also 'the wishes of the people'. Nevertheless it was to ensure 'as nearly as may be' that there was electoral equality between the wards in each local authority. All county councils were to have single member divisions, each of which should be located within a discrete district council area and have regard to the boundaries of district wards. The Greater London Council also had single member divisions, based on both boroughs and parliamentary constituencies. Where a constituency lay wholly within a London borough, then that area would constitute a GLC electoral division. Where a constituency crossed boroughs, the Commission was obliged to create a new division. This must fall within a single borough and its electorate should equate not only to other divisions in the borough but, as far as possible, to the average number in each electoral division in London as a whole. The districts and London boroughs were not restricted to single member wards but individual ward electorates were, of course, to be equitable. In every case the Commission was required to take into account 'any changes in the number or distribution of the local government electors of the [local authority] likely to take place within the period of five years' immediately following an electoral review (Local Government Act 1972: Schedule 11). The same Schedule also charged it with having regard, subject to the considerations of electoral equality, to 'the desirability of fixing ward boundaries which are and will remain easily identifiable; and any local ties which would be broken by the fixing of any particular ward boundary'. The final proposals resulting from each electoral review were to be reported to the Home Secretary.

The Chairman and members of the LGBC were appointed by Ministers, but it was an independent body. Its staff consisted solely of civil servants drawn from a number of different departments. Many of these people had no experience of local government, and were moved about at regular intervals. A former Secretary to the Commission told us, 'You didn't make a career in the Boundary Commission' (interview with Stephen Garrish, 1/10/1998). However, because the Commission was working in new territory, it seems to have had a relatively free hand in developing its own methods of working and interpretations of the statutory criteria. Among its first concerns was drawing up a timetable for the programme of reviews it was required to begin immediately following the 1973 local elections. Indeed the haphazard and piecemeal nature of the wards put together for those elections only served to emphasise the urgency of this task. The Commission committed itself at the outset to consult widely on its activities, and it soon learnt from the local authority associations and political parties that most councils would need to settle down following vesting day on 1 April 1974 before being ready for an electoral review. The decision was therefore made to start the process in May 1974 and to proceed county by county. Immediately this delay put in doubt the target which the Commission had been given to review the electoral boundaries of all 332 districts and 45 counties before the local elections due in either 1976 (districts) or 1977 (counties). The Commission was, however, sensitive to the fact that 'the initial electoral arrangements have produced anomalous wards in a number of districts' (LGBC report 6, 1973: para 14). It proposed to start with those counties where the electoral anomalies seemed greatest, and to invite other authorities to 'volunteer' for an early start if they felt sufficiently prepared. In an early acknowledgement of the relationship now formally drawn between the LGBC and the Parliamentary Boundary Commission, it set itself a revised target by aiming 'to complete the review of local government electoral arrangements before the PBC complete their review, probably in 1979' (6: para 11).

Timing was also at issue when the Commission came to judge how long it would take to complete an individual review. It noted that, 'This is the first time that a body has been charged with the task of carrying out a complete electoral review of all local authorities outside London as a single operation. The statutory requirements covering the operation are also new. We are therefore without guidance from past experience as to the time that the various stages in the process can reasonably be expected to take' (LGBC report 6, 1973: para 26). Opportunities for consultation were again seen as important, but these would themselves introduce uncertainties. The Commission needed to rely on local authorities to produce draft schemes for it to consider as well as promptly meeting other requests for the supply of information. In addition it took the view that, 'there will be comparatively few cases where we can proceed to formulate final proposals without arranging a local meeting for the resolution of differences of local opinion or of points on which local opinion is at variance with our draft proposals. Assistant Commissioners will be appointed to hold such meetings' (6: para 23). The published indicative timetable for reviews tried to take these factors into account – see Box 2.2.

In practice, of course, the Commission's ability to adhere to this schedule was heavily dependent on the co-operation received from local authorities, and there were tensions between the need to make progress and achieve targets and demands for additional time for consultation. Indeed the Secretaries of State for the responsible Departments (the Home Office and the Department of the Environment) responded to the LGBC report by expressing the hope that having gained experience the Commission would 'find ways of speeding up the programme as a whole without prejudicing the quality of the review or the opportunities for public involvement in this very important matter.' (quoted in LGBC report 141, 1976). Not for the first time the government wanted to have its cake and eat it too.

BOX 2.2 LGBC Procedure and Timetable for Reviews of Electoral Arrangements

LGBC give notice of intention to conduct review and of procedure to be adopted	week 1
Council prepare scheme of representation in consultation with local interests and send it to LGBC within 20 weeks	week 20
LGBC consider council's scheme and views of local interests and formulate draft proposals	week 24
LGBC publish draft proposals and invite comments within 8 weeks	week 28
Deadline for comments	week 36
LGBC consider comments	week 40
Asst. Comm. to hold meeting and submit report to LGBC	week 48
LGBC consider report and decide final recommendations	week 52
LGBC proposals submitted to Home Secretary and published	week 56
A further 6(minimum)-8 weeks allowed for Home Secretary to reach a decision and make an Order.	

Source: LGBC report 6, 1973: Appendix

There were other matters to which the Commission needed to pay early attention. Because the Act contained no provisions concerning council size it was decided to adopt the ranges used for the 1973 elections. That is, that counties should have a membership of between 60 and 100; metropolitan districts between 50–80; and districts between 30–60. A range of 50 to 70 councillors was adopted for the London boroughs when their reviews were added to the Commission's task list in June 1974. A lower figure might be appropriate in districts with small populations, but a council should only be larger if an 'exceptional' case was made. Authorities were invited to prepare schemes accordingly, with the Commission actually suggesting to counties and metropolitan districts what their overall council size should be. 'It was made clear that any special factors the authority might wish to identify in support of a modified figure would be considered...the Commission...fully recognised that they must examine each case on its merits' (LGBC report 443, 1983: para 38). By the end of the review process six metropolitan districts together with Bristol had been allowed councils larger than the range, and 15 districts and the London Borough of Barking and Dagenham were smaller. It was indeed a dispute over council size which led to a suspension of electoral review work in February

1978 and the reference of a Commission decision to the House of Lords. The London Borough of Enfield argued that the LGBC had exceeded its powers in insisting that the borough should have 66 councillors rather than the 69 it itself had proposed. The Law Lords supported the Commission arguing, in the words of Lord Denning, that, 'there are the words at the beginning of section 47 of the 1972 Local Government Act...[namely] 'changes appearing to the Commission desirable in the interests of effective and convenient local government'. These words seem to me to be overriding words which the Commission must apply in the whole of their consideration' (quoted in LGBC report 688, 1992: para 3.3). In short, the Act gave the Commission wide discretion to do almost whatever it saw as fit. This judgement can be seen as neatly foreshadowing the similar decision, noted earlier, made in the case brought by Labour party members against the English PBC in 1982.

The Commission had earlier exercised its discretion in determining limits on the number of councillors to be elected from each ward. In the metropolitan districts it was obliged to ensure that this number should be divisible by three, but it was a Commission rather than statutory decision to make all wards three-member. It was felt that six member wards, for example, would be 'undemocratic' and could lead to 'unacceptably disproportionate' results (interview with Professor Michael Chisholm, 17/6/1998). Even so, there remained some feeling that the requirement for all wards to be multi-member deprived the Commission of the flexibility to respect local ties. The structure of non-metropolitan district council wards was to be set by Order following electoral review. Here the Commission took the view that 'only in the most exceptional circumstances' should it be necessary for wards to elect other than one, two or three members. This led to very considerable changes not simply to the temporary wards set up for the 1973 elections, but also to what were long-standing patterns of warding in many areas. By the end of the review process there were 38 districts with universal three-member wards and 5 with wholly two-member ones. The rest had a mixture which suited 'the often conflicting requirements of electoral equality and preservation of local ties' (LGBC report 413, 1981: para 11). The Commission sanctioned just four cases of five-member wards and a single four-member configuration. These usually reflected a district's unwillingness to divide a parish council area into wards, and led the Commission – doubtless emboldened by the Enfield judgement – to emphasise that it was,

> 'in the last resort empowered by the 1972 Act to divide a parish ward or an unwarded parish for district warding purposes if satisfied that it is in the interests of effective and convenient local government...If a district council refuses to make a parish warding order this could mean in a particular case that it was not 'reasonably practicable' for the Commission to comply with the relevant paragraphs of Schedule 11. If this were not so, the Commission might be obliged to make proposals for wards which they considered inappropriate in order to conform to the parish warding

> arrangements or the non-warding of a parish determined by a district council, and which were contrary to other provisions of the Act regarding effective and convenient local government or electoral equality' (413: para 15).

The requirement in the Act that attention should be paid, when defining ward boundaries, to likely changes in the electorate in the five years following review posed problems for the Commission. How were these projections to be made, by whom, and how reliable were they likely to be? The Commission felt it had no option but to accept that 'the forecasts made by councils with their local knowledge must in general be regarded as the most reliable indication available' (413: para 18). Councils were likely to adopt different methods for making their calculations and to approach the task with different levels of sophistication. However, as one LGBC member put it to us, 'the fact that the system asked local authorities to do most of the work for you meant that it was difficult to impose algorithms about how they should make their projections' (Chisholm 17/6/1998). The Commission claimed not to take everything it was told at face value,

> 'Where convincing evidence has been produced by other parties to cast doubt on council forecasts or where we ourselves have detected what seemed to us inherent improbabilities or inconsistencies in them, we have not hesitated to ask the council concerned for further comments and explanations. In some instances this has led to councils revising their forecasts; in others the issue has been pursued further at local meetings. We have then made such allowance as we thought fit for any remaining legitimate doubts in arriving at our final recommendations...' (413: para 18).

Interestingly, though, two of our interviewees who were involved with the Commission at a later stage seemed less confident that this process worked in practice. A former Chairman was clear that 'population estimates from local authorities were routinely accepted and *not* checked' (interview with Sir Geoffrey Ellerton 16/7/1998), and one of the Secretaries who worked with him recalls that 'we did not have the means to challenge the population projections, but were sceptical and could have looked more closely at them' (Garrish 1/10/1998). Overall, and taking into account the likelihood of a wide margin of error in such an exercise, there seemed to be a tendency for councils to over-state the projected growth in their electorates. The Commission did not dispute the intention behind attempting to look ahead in devising electoral arrangements, but pointed out that 'anything approaching a perfect degree of electoral equality at the end of 5 years is unlikely to be attainable, particularly where rapid population changes are occurring or are planned e.g. in new or expanding towns and in inner city areas. This may mean more frequent electoral reviews in such cases than would otherwise be desirable' (LGBC report 413, 1981: para 19).

Although the Commission was obliged by the Act to keep electoral equality at the forefront of its deliberations, this too was open to interpretation. In its March 1983 progress report, the Commission noted,

> 'We seek to ensure that as few cases as possible result in a level of representation greater or less than 10% from the average for the authority as a whole, and that representation departing more than 20% from the average is backed by very strong reasons and has public support. This does not mean that we do not take into account community ties but they cannot be allowed to override equality of representation unless there are the most cogent reasons. Where the level of representation is within 10% of the average, greater weight can be given to geographical and community factors' (LGBC report 443, 1983: para 8).

With hindsight this seems quite a lax measure of electoral equality and it is difficult to check what was achieved in practice. An examination of five LGBC reports, chosen at random across the period 1974–89, shows that they contain no information at all on individual ward electorates and very little analysis of the degree to which they vary about the mean in either the existing or proposed schemes. However, an analysis from our own records does indicate that each of these electoral reviews did improve electoral equality and that only a small minority of wards continued to have variances in excess of + or -10% – see Table 2.2.

The Commission may have been influenced by its own doubts about whether perfect equality was 'attainable' in a practicable way, as well as by a concern to make boundaries identifiable, readily definable, and reflective of the pattern of people's lives. In March 1988, for example, it commented 'we continue to regard local ties (like identifiable boundaries) as important even though they rank as secondary criteria. We seek to reflect them in our proposals as far as we can, without causing a *significant* reduction in equality' (LGBC report 550, 1988: para 83, emphasis added). Similarly, in a Commissioner's eyes, the type and range of information available meant that 'judgements not algorithms were the order of the day. You could pursue equality to within a 1% variance as in the United States, but this would override communities and still be based on 'variable' data' (Chisholm, 17/6/1998). The need to meet 'often conflicting' criteria proved particularly difficult when trying to match the boundaries of county divisions and district wards while at the same time pursuing intra-county electoral equality. Frustrated by this the Commission contrasted its position with that of the Parliamentary Boundary Commission,

> 'although the Act requires that electoral divisions...should have regard to district ward boundaries, the overriding consideration must nonetheless be the question of numerical balance between divisions. This is in contra-distinction to the thinking behind the criteria which the PBC have been given, namely, that numerical considerations are subordinate to questions of geography' (LGBC report 443, 1983: para 7).

Table 2.2 The impact of some LGBC reviews on electoral equality

	Before review	*After review*
Watford, LGBC report 11, 1974		
Max councillor/elector ratio	1850	1853
Min councillor/elector ratio	1284	1310
Max +ve variance	16.7	20.6
Max – ve variance	-19.0	-14.8
%wards with variances > +/- 10%	54.5	33.3
Trafford, LGBC report 300, 1975		
Max ward electorate	10831	9545
Min ward electorate	5402	7069
Max +ve variance	35.9	18.1
Max – ve variance	-32.2	-12.6
%wards with variances > +/- 10%	80.9	19.0
Reading, LGBC report 331, 1977		
Max councillor/elector ratio	2217	2490
Min councillor/elector ratio	1159	2028
Max +ve variance	10.9	9.5
Max – ve variance	-42.0	-10.8
%wards with variances > +/- 10%	23.1	6.7
Preston, LGBC report 567, 1988		
Max ward electorate	9325	5592
Min ward electorate	3295	4441
Max +ve variance	84.2	12.4
Max – ve variance	-34.9	-10.7
%wards with variances > +/- 10%	47.4	10.5
Colchester, LGBC report 575, 1989		
Max councillor/elector ratio	3006	2333
Min councillor/elector ratio	1335	1425
Max +ve variance	66.0	26.4
Max – ve variance	-26.3	-22.8
%wards with variances > +/- 10%	59.3	25.0

Source: Local Government Chronicle Elections Centre, University of Plymouth

However, before such evaluations could be made, the LGBC had to get on and conduct some reviews. At the outset the Commission met weekly with eight or more schemes under review at a time. Together with the necessary homework, one

Commissioner estimated that this amounted to 'a two day per week commitment' (Chisholm, 17/6/1998). By the end of 1975 130 reviews had been completed, and the Home Secretary was asked to continue making Orders well into 1976 so that the new boundaries could be used for the next local elections in as many districts as possible. After 1980 electoral reviews became 'a sideshow' (Garrish, 1/10/1998) – see Table 2.3. The Commission met no more than fortnightly and its focus switched to area reviews. These attracted more attention from both public and ministers 'who made it clear they would veto proposals' (Ellerton 16/7/1998). Arguably the tapering off of electoral reviews was not without longer term significance, for when the LGCE began its programme in 1996 it was fully 15 years since anyone, either Commissioner or staff member, had had experience of being intensively involved in the process. Even during the later life of the LGBC it seems that 'Commissioners were a little uneasy on electorals... their heart was in the geography...estate management not radical change' (Garrish, 1/10/1998). As time went on the Commission became, in tune with the times, even more aware of the need to make its decisions as transparent as possible. It acknowledged that,

> 'When we publish draft proposals or modifications we think it desirable that the reasons why we have taken this action should be clear to those who may be affected. This has not always been the case... This is not entirely satisfactory and we therefore intend as a matter of routine in the future to ensure that any relevant representations or other documents are placed on deposit for inspection at the district council offices along with our draft proposals and modifications' (LGBC report 443, 1983: para 28).

Those making representations were assured that 'draft proposals are just that, not unratified final decisions, and there have been many occasions on which we have changed course in the light of public comment' (LGBC report 688, 1992: para 5.5). Local public meetings were common, being held in two thirds of all cases and in up to 80% of London boroughs and metropolitan districts. However, there was a move away from using Assistant Commissioners towards less formal meetings run by Commissioners themselves. These were seen as 'an opportunity for testing the strength of particular aspects of arguments which have already been deployed in the material we have before us. We do not arrange a meeting simply because there is great public interest and people want to have their say' (LGBC report 443, 1983: para 33). Indeed great reliance was placed on these consultations to uncover attempts at gaining partisan electoral advantage from a review. Commissioners were 'aware of the considerable political stakes and that parties (the dominant group in the local authority in particular) might seek to obtain political mileage' (Chisholm, 17/6/1998). They therefore 'relied on objections as a way of smelling a rat' (Ellerton, 16/7/1998). The Commission also tried to improve the visibility of reviews by improving its publicity beyond formal public notices, and by making its final reports more 'user-friendly' and accessible with a summary of findings and clearer mapping.

Table 2.3 Number of Electoral Review final reports published

Years	*No. of reports*
1973–76:	166
1977–80:	224
1981–84:	23
1984–1992:	19

Source: Calculation made from LGBC report 688, 1992

The LGBC's willingness to explain and evaluate what it was doing led it to produce a long and illuminating valedictory report. This tended to concentrate on area rather than electoral reviews, but did highlight a number of perceived problems with the current re-districting rules and offered advice to any body charged with conducting the process in the future. Although the Commission was gratified to note that 'our integrity has almost always been accepted' (LGBC report 688, 1992: para 4.2), it was only too aware that many of its decisions ranged over highly contentious issues. On council size, for example, 'we have found it necessary to work within the existing parameters of size and organisation' (para 4.10), but could not help noticing the resultant 'large variations in elector/councillor ratios not only, as might be expected, between metropolitan and shire districts but between neighbouring authorities such as Brent (one for every 2561) and Westminster (one for every 1829)' (para 4.8). Whilst a former Commissioner was prepared to defend such outcomes as 'a rare example of protection from centralisation' (Chisholm, 17/6/1998), the corporate view by 1992 was that clearer [statutory] 'criteria on matters such as council size and the broad range of councillor/elector ratios might facilitate the restructuring process to be undertaken by the Local Government Commission' (para 4.8). The fact that 'the most obvious and superficially attractive remedy for electoral imbalances tends to be one requiring an increase in council size…[had] no clear justification' (para 4.9) and the Commission 'welcomed… the recent ministerial statement that some of these issues of local authority internal management merit further investigation' (para 4.11). On more immediately practical matters the LGBC recommended a tighter timetable for reviews and the establishment of a culture in which this time scale would be adhered to. This could be achieved through a 'more concerted and organised effort…to command the high ground of information, [entailing] a basic structure of key information requirements to which the participants would be asked to respond according to an agreed methodology. This approach to information gathering, together with simultaneous consultation on various proposed options...may be of particular interest to the new LGC' (para 5.14). It was also up to individual authorities to provide 'information about local ties. Unless they discuss this aspect more fully, telling us, for example, about alternative boundaries they have considered and their reasons for rejecting them, it is very difficult for us to know whether they have given any weight to local ties' (LGBC report 550,1988: para 83). In any event, 'it is important to set the ground rules for information so that responses can be assessed on a consistent basis' (LGBC report 688, 1992: para 7.5). The Commission also drew attention to its regret that the Act did not allow it to make minor (and swift) adjustments in response to structural or population changes or transfers of land, rather than have to conduct full scale second reviews.

The story of the Local Government Boundary Commission seems to be 'an episodic process of learning over time' (Chisholm, 17/6/1998). There is also a thread running through all its reports which reflects the degree to which the Commission was being pushed to and fro by changing government thinking on the structure of local government and how this might come to impinge on its work. Through it all though it upheld the idea that 'an impartial and non-political body, to consider and make recommendations on local authority boundaries, is very important. Local government in modern Britain has been acclaimed for its honesty and democracy; it has been going through a period of profound change, and an independent mechanism for considering boundary changes is an important bastion' (LGBC report 688, 1992: para 7.1). This view was supported by each of our three interviewees independently. The Commission 'takes these acutely political issues out of the political sphere' (Ellerton, 16/7/1998). This becomes even more important if it is accepted that 'boundary decisions are an art not a science' (LGBC report 688, 1992: para 4.3). The LGBC had noted, and clearly had some sympathy towards, a 'recent tendency for community identity and the wishes of the people to figure more prominently in the submissions we have received...' (para 6.3). This was often accompanied by an expressed preference for the status quo. Although 'boundaries become out-of-date, as population shifts, new housing developments are built and the pattern of industry alters' (para 7.6) and change is subsequently required to ensure equity of representation, there is a case for 'recognising that this should be seldom as people are attached to the ways things are' (LGBC report 550, 1988: para 8) and that 'there are advantages of not having more change than you have to' (Chisholm, 17/6/1998). This did not amount to a call for a return to the rigidity which had characterised local government in the 85 years prior to 1972, but should strike a warning that 'any attempt to reduce the exercise of judgement, as distinct from accumulating facts on which judgement is based, in favour of the application of numerical techniques would be dangerously illusory' (LGBC report 688, 1992: para 4.3).

Conclusions

In this chapter we have reviewed the evolution of British parliamentary and local government re-districting processes within an international context. Although the system of review by Commission is widely admired for removing decisions about electoral boundaries from the cut and thrust of party politics, standards are by no means universal. For example, different countries have different rules for matters such as the allowed variation about the mean electorate and the protection of the interests of sparsely populated areas. Moreover, because the Commissions have statutory protection, the courts have tended to give them a relatively free hand to interpret the often 'unavoidably conflictual' (Bonfili, 1998) criteria that parliaments have given them. Ironically, this has meant that legislative driven redistributions – typically the United States – can often result in tougher controls over the exercise of discretion precisely because they are subject to judicial review concerning any infringement of constitutionally protected rights. One universal trend appears to have been the attempt to tighten re-districting criteria over time. In some countries this has been reflected in a reduction in tolerance limits or in an expansion of the number of elected bodies subject to a formal review process. In England, for example, the Parliamentary Boundary Commission has used its discretion to try to hold back the growth in the number of members of parliament. At the local level, the mere establishment of the Local Government Boundary Commission as late as 1972 meant that local electoral boundaries were, for the first time, to be dealt with in a 'centralised, independent, formal and regular' manner (Chisholm, 17/6/1998). The LGBC's successor, the Local Government Commission for England, began work in 1992. In Chapter 3 we set the scene for our detailed, empirical examination of how Periodic Electoral Reviews have been conducted under its jurisdiction by considering some of the issues and constraints which it faced and to which it had to adapt.

Chapter 3

Periodic Electoral Reviews

This chapter introduces the Local Government Commission for England (LGCE) and examines its statutory role in periodic electoral reviews. It outlines the rules to which the Commission works, together with its procedures and the ways in which these have been adjusted over time. The chapter serves as a necessary information resource for later discussions about how electoral reviews are conducted and their consequences for local authorities and political parties.

The Local Government Commission for England is an independent body set up by Parliament in 1992 to carry out two main functions. The first is to undertake reviews of local authorities as directed by the Secretary of State, and to make recommendations for any structural, boundary or electoral changes. The second is to carry out a periodic electoral review (PER) of every local authority in England. In the years following its creation the LGCE was heavily involved in structural reviews. These attracted a good deal of political and academic attention, and resulted in some significant re-drawings of the local government map. In particular 46 all-purpose unitary authorities were established in place of the previous two-tier county/district structure in some parts of shire England. During the period from 1992–96 the Commission found itself the centre of considerable controversy over issues such as how widespread the system of unitary authorities should be, how far the century old county structure should be preserved, and whether different parts of the country were being treated equitably in terms of their desire for either unitary status or the preservation of the status quo. Most studies of the Commission during this period suggest that it succeeded in fully satisfying no one (see, for example, Leach, 1994; Stewart, 1997; Johnston and Pattie, 1996; Chisholm, 2000).

Since 1995 the major part of the LGCE's work has focused on its second function – a rolling programme of periodic electoral reviews. These involve looking at the boundaries of electoral units (wards) within individual local authorities and coming up with recommendations for how they might be adjusted the better to equalise the size of the electorate between them. Although, as we shall see, this task too has the potential to stir local feelings and political sensibilities, it has proved less sensitive than the earlier structural reviews. Partly that is because the

LGCE is required to work to more clearly defined rules, and partly too because the Commission has taken great care to consult with local authorities on its procedures and on how it interprets those rules. There is also much less scope for local authorities being able, or feeling the need, to compare what is happening to them with the experience of neighbouring or demographically similar councils.

The rules of the Periodic Electoral Review process

Although in shorthand a PER is concerned with ensuring that each ward in a local authority has a similar number of electors, other factors enter the equation. Box 3.1 sets out the rules as they apply to shire district councils – that is, local authorities which continue to share their functions with a county council.

BOX 3.1 The rules governing a shire district PER

Under section 13 (5) of the Local Government Act 1992, the Commission is required to make recommendations to the Secretary of State for any changes to the electoral arrangements within the areas of English principal authorities as appear desirable to it, having regard to the need:

i) "to reflect the identities and interests of local communities"; and
ii) "to secure effective and convenient local government".

In reporting to the Secretary of State, the Commission may make recommendations for such changes to electoral arrangements as are specified in section 14 (4) of the 1992 Act. In relation to principal authorities, these are:

- the total number of councillors to be elected to the council;
- the number and boundaries of electoral areas (wards or divisions);
- the number of councillors to be elected for each electoral area, and the years in which they are to be elected; and
- the name of the electoral area.

The Commission is required to comply so far as is reasonably practicable with the rules set out in Schedule 11 to the 1972 Act. In relation to shire districts:

Having regard to any changes in the number or distribution of the local government electors of the district likely to take place within the period of five years immediately following the consideration (by the Secretary of State or the Commission):

a) the ratio of the number of local government electors to the number of councillors to be elected shall be, as nearly as may be, the same in every ward in the district;
b) in a district every ward of a parish council shall lie wholly within a single ward of the district;

Contd./

Box 3.1 continued

c) in a district every parish which is not divided into parish wards shall lie wholly within a single ward of the district.

The Schedule also provides that, subject to a) - c) above, regard should be had to:

d) the desirability of fixing ward boundaries which are and will remain easily identifiable; and

f) any local ties which would be broken by the fixing of any particular ward boundary.

Different types of authority have different rules depending on their defined electoral arrangements. In the counties, for example, a single councillor is elected for each county division once every four years. In the metropolitan boroughs, on the other hand, each ward has three councillors, of whom one is elected in three out of every four years. In both these cases, therefore, the councillor/elector ratio is calculated by reference to a fixed divisor. In a similar way to their parliamentary boundary counterparts, the rules for local electoral reviews contain the seeds of ambiguity. As we shall see, the requirement that the councillor/elector ratio 'shall be, as nearly as may be, the same in every ward in the district' can come into conflict with the desire that ward boundaries should be 'easily identifiable' and that any changes do not break 'local ties'. It is also interesting to note that the phrase regarding the need 'to reflect the identities and interests of local communities' did not form part of the 1972 Act, and in that respect it can be argued that the 1992 Act provides a more stringent statutory test for the LGCE than the equivalent criteria did for the LGBC.

The Periodic Electoral Review Process

The single most important thing to understand about the PER process is that the initial plans for re-warding originate at the local authority level. Councils themselves, political parties, and even private groups and individuals are entitled to submit schemes covering either the whole or part of the area under review. The Commission then reacts to these, where necessary proposing amendments and engaging in further consultations. This process is covered by a timetable. In 1995 the Commission consulted local authorities on a proposed review timetable based around four stages identified in Section 15 of the 1992 Act – see Box 3.2. Stage One is where schemes are submitted to the Commission. Stage Two is used by the Commission to analyse these schemes and all other information received. It then produces and publishes formal Draft Recommendations for consultation at Stage Three. Finally, at Stage Four, the Commission scrutinises the representations received on the draft scheme and publish its Final Recommendations. The Commission suggested that each review should be completed within a period of nine months.

The first edition of the Commission's Guidance indicated that the length of Stage One and Stage Three was fixed, but that the other stages may be shortened if circumstances dictate. The length of a review could thereby vary between 34 and 40 weeks. In the second edition of the Commission's Guidance, the length of the stages was changed. Stage One and Stage Three were only slightly altered to read 'typically twelve weeks', but Stage Two and Stage Four were lengthened to 'typically 12 to 16 weeks'. While authorities often complain about the short timetable of the review from their perspective (Stage One and Stage Three), these times have remained largely unaltered during the course of the review. The Commission have only lengthened the stages, Two and Four, when they are 'active' reviewing submissions and producing the draft and final reports. The length of a review can now vary between 44 and 52 weeks, with the Commission expecting to complete a review in a period of about a year rather than the original 40 weeks. In addition the Commission has introduced an informal Preliminary Period before the PER gets under way. This enables it to give local authorities better notice of the forthcoming review and to provide briefing sessions and launch meetings for both members and officers.

BOX 3.2 The stages of the PER process

	March 1996 guidance	***March 1998 guidance***	
Stage One	12 weeks	typically 12 weeks	Commencement of review and submission of proposals for changes (or no changes) to electoral arrangements*.
Stage Two	8–12 weeks	typically 12–16 weeks	Commission considers proposals, determines draft recommendations and prepares public consultation report**.
Stage Three	8 weeks	typically 8 weeks	Commission publishes draft recommendations report and invites representations.
Stage Four	6–8 weeks	typically 12–16 weeks	Commission considers representations, reaches conclusions on final recommendations and submits a final report to the Secretary of State.

* This was changed in the 1998 guidance to read, 'Commencement of review and submission of proposals for *future* electoral arrangements'. The Commission are trying to make it clear that 'no change' is not an option.

** This was changed in the 1998 guidance to read, 'Commission considers proposals, determines draft recommendations and prepares *draft recommendations* report'.

It appears that the length of the various stages was altered largely to enable the Commission to cope with undertaking a greater number of reviews. Staff work in such a way that they are involved in several reviews at the same time. Review Leaders will usually be dealing with four or five reviews, each at a different stage in the process, while Review Managers oversee around eighteen reviews at the same time. The timetable has been arranged so that at any one time officers will be busy on some reviews and quiet on others, thereby providing a consistent workload. (See Chapter 4 for more detail on how the Commission and its staff actually undertake electoral reviews.) The Commission is continuing to increase the number of reviews it completes year on year – see Table 3.1. It usually proceeds county by county, and expects all local authorities to have been reviewed by 2004.

Table 3.1 The Commission's throughput of reviews

	Started new reviews	*Published Draft reports*	*Published Final PERs*
1996–7	53	30	29
1997–8	48	43	32
1998–9	57	54	39
1999–2000	58	57	57

The phasing of reviews

The Local Government Act (Section 13(3) and (4), 1992) provides that, so far as reasonably practicable, PERs should be undertaken at intervals of not less than 10 years and not more than 15 years after the initial review by the LGBC of the *county* in which the area is situated. Only six authorities in our database were last reviewed between 10 and 15 years ago: Halton (last reviewed in 1985, Draft Recommendations published in September 1996), Warrington (December 1986 and September 1996), Blyth Valley (December 1986 and October 1996), Taunton Deane (July 1985 and June 1997), Swindon (November 1984 and September 1998), and South Gloucestershire. This unitary authority was formed by combining the former Avon county districts of Kingswood and Northavon. These authorities were reviewed in 1986 and 1975 respectively. The draft report for South Gloucestershire was published in December 1997. Two further councils, South Somerset (last reviewed in 1988, Draft Recommendations published in June 1997), and Welwyn Hatfield (June 1989 and July 1997), experienced a more rapid cycle following successful requests to the LGBC for an interim review to deal with electoral anomalies. All other authorities had had to wait much longer, as first the LGBC was wound down and then the LGCE found itself pre-occupied with structural reviews.

The Commission has attempted to carry out reviews according to when the boundaries were previously changed, but has not always found this possible. All authorities in Shropshire (except The Wrekin) were last reviewed between July 1975 and June 1976 and the Final Recommendations of the new PER were published in August 1999 – a gap of up to 24 years. By contrast, although the last reviews in the Devon authorities were carried out between February 1977 and June 1979, they were reviewed at an earlier stage in the timetable with the Final Recommendations being published in January 1999. In exceptional circumstances, reviews can take place out of order. For example, the Secretary of State has the power to direct the commission to undertake reviews. This occurred with the eight proposed unitary authorities (Blackburn, Blackpool, Halton, Medway Towns, Peterborough, Thurrock, Warrington, and The Wrekin) which started their review in September 1996. These councils were brought forward in the timetable because they were due to hold inaugural elections in May 1997. They will still have to undergo a normal PER during the current round. In other cases, for example Isle of Wight and South Hams, rapid and/or unbalanced growth in the electorate has led the Commission to invite the council to submit proposals for its future electoral arrangements 'out of turn'. In South Hams this resulted in Final Recommendations being published some two months before PERs began in the other Devon districts. Purbeck was also reviewed before other Dorset councils, in its case because the recommendations previously made by the LGBC in 1992 were never implemented by the Secretary of State. Both the Commission and the Local Government Association are in favour of changing the legislation so that electoral inequalities, rather than the gap since the last review, become the key to PER timing.[1]

The timetable for review also contained a loophole that inhibited the Commission's PER programme in London and the metropolitan districts. For the London boroughs, and for two of the six metropolitan county areas (where the county councils had been abolished before the LGBC could get to work), there was no county review to use as a reference point. In London, boroughs were reviewed according to their warding structure. Those boroughs with the largest number of three-member wards were tackled first. For example Barnet, which had twenty three-member wards, was included in the first tranche, whereas Camden, with nineteen two-member wards and seven three-member wards, was part of the final tranche of boroughs reviewed. Metropolitan district reviews are scheduled to start in 2001/2.

The Commission seemed to change its policy on the timing of county council

---

[1] The Political Parties, Elections and Referendum Act 2000 has now abolished the requirement to carry out reviews on a set time-scale, so that in future the LGCE will be able to 'accord priority to the needs of authorities with the most significant levels of electoral imbalance' (Guidance, 2000: para 2).

reviews in relation to the district reviews. It stated in its 1995 Consultation Paper which discussed the work programme and timing of reviews that,

> 'Given that county division boundaries should be based on district ward boundaries, the Commission is minded to defer submitting reports on the districts until it is also in a position to submit reports on the county council's electoral arrangements' (Consultation, 1995: para 78). 'In shire county areas, the Commission will simultaneously review electoral arrangements for the county, its constituent districts and any unitary authorities that are encompassed by the boundary of the ceremonial county' (para 80).

This order of reviews changed with the publication of the Commission's first edition of Guidance. The policy now was that,

> 'In reviewing shire county areas, the Commission will first examine the electoral arrangements of the constituent district councils, and those of the local councils within their areas. Reviews of county council electoral arrangements will take place once the Secretary of State has taken decisions on any recommendations for changes to district warding arrangements' (Guidance, 1996: para 33).

The Commission published its initial three-year timetable of reviews in the same month in which the process began – March 1996. This gave those authorities whose PER was scheduled at the beginning of the programme very little, if any, advance warning. Subsequently, more notice of the Commission's programme has been given. For example, the full timetable of reviews to 2004 is already known and set out in the Commission's quarterly newsletter and on its web-site.

As well as consulting and issuing guidance on the staging and phasing of PERs, the Commission has also sought to clarify its position on other matters pertaining to the interpretation of the rules for Periodic Electoral Review.

Electoral Cycle

The Local Government Act 1972 states that London borough and English county councils will hold whole council elections on a four year cycle, while metropolitan boroughs must have elections by thirds. Shire district councils (and this now includes the recently created unitary councils) have the option of using either method of electing members. Local authorities can request the Secretary of State to change the method of election if there is a two thirds majority in favour of a change. Arrangements can also be changed through a recommendation from the Commission as part of an electoral review.

In the Commission's Consultation Paper the advantages and disadvantages of whole-council elections and elections by thirds were discussed. It concluded, 'The Commission considers that there may be some merit in having whole council elections for authorities which have a mix of one, two and three member wards' (Consultation, 1995: para 67). This would reduce confusion, as all electors within an authority would have the opportunity to vote at the same time. In the first edition of its Guidance (1996), however, the Commission is less prescriptive, acknowledging that as there are supporters of both types of electoral cycle, it will not override the preferences of an authority. In the second edition of Guidance (1998), the Commission moved again. It referred to the government's stated intention in the White Paper, *Modern Local Government – In Touch with the People*, of introducing more widespread annual elections and advised stakeholders to take account of this in formulating their proposals. We return to this issue later in the Chapter.

Council structure

The first edition of Guidance asserts that 'The Commission generally supports the conclusions of the Report of the Committee of Inquiry into the Conduct of Local Authority Business, (HMSO, 1986, Cm 9797) – the 'Widdicombe Report' – in its preference for single-member wards' (Guidance, 1996: para 26). It offers an assurance that it will have regard to local preferences, but also asserts that, '...single-member wards have considerable advantages in terms of their clarity of accountability and, where they are appropriate and enjoy local support, [the Commission] will seek to promote them' (para 27). By March 1998, however, the Commission's guidance has been changed. Having carried out a number of reviews and rounds of consultation, it drops its stated preference for single-member wards and puts more emphasis on a mixture of types,

> 'We have not been prescriptive and have generally made recommendations which provide for a combination of single and multi-member wards. Our recommendations have tended to reflect the present pattern of multi-member wards in most urban areas and single-member wards in many rural areas. ...Three-member wards may create sharper accountability in authorities where there are to be elections by thirds' (Guidance, 1998: para 49).

This more even-handed approach to the merits of single- as opposed to multi-member wards seems to be a pragmatic response to local authority proposals already received, and an invitation to those yet to be reviewed to worry less about trying to produce a common pattern of warding. The one exception to this was the London boroughs who were consistently advised, following publication of the government's Green Paper in February 1998, to plan for three-member wards in order to facilitate the introduction of annual elections. This advice was later extended to those urban unitary councils still awaiting review.

In Scotland, all wards are single-member. In Wales, however, the structure of councils is not so clear cut. The Local Government Act 1972 (Schedule 11) (as amended by the 1994 Act) requires the Welsh Local Government Boundary Commission to provide for there to be a single member for each electoral division. However, the Secretary of State for Wales may direct the Commission to consider the desirability of providing for multi-member electoral divisions for the whole or part of a principal area. So, there is a preference for single-member divisions, but multi-member divisions can be enacted if there is local support. Before the most recent (1999) electoral review in Wales there were a significant number of single communities represented by more than one councillor. In these multi-member divisions, it would only be possible to create single-member divisions if the community was split. As the Commission must have regard to any local ties which would be broken by the fixing of any particular boundary, it is unsurprising that the most recent ward boundary changes in Wales made few inroads into the number of multi-member divisions.

Council size

When conducting its own reviews the LGBC determined the appropriate size of a council by the use of a banding system. In the first edition of its Guidance, the LGCE adopted a similar approach. The ranges used for each type of authority are shown in Table 3.2.

The Commission argues that the range band approach for council size '...provides sufficient flexibility to take account of the particular circumstances and characteristics of individual local authority areas and the communities within them'. However, it also asserts that 'these ranges are not prescriptive and there will be occasions when an authority's council size will fall outside the range' (Guidance, 1998: para 34). Moreover, 'The Commission is unlikely to seek reductions in the size of those local authorities which currently exceed the Commission's indicative ranges' (Guidance, 1996: para 18). A Commissioner revealed to us that the idea behind the banding of council sizes was to encourage councils to think seriously about the issue, especially the possible reduction in council size. Unfortunately this had rather back-fired as instead councils looked at their size, saw that it fitted within the bands and did not consider any change. The size bands did successfully perform one function. They stopped either authorities or individuals proposing excessively large or small councils. On the other hand, the council size banding for London boroughs seemed inappropriate to councillors in the London Borough of Barnet we interviewed. They could not understand why the maximum size of a council could be 80, when they had the second largest electorate in London, the second largest council (of 60) in London, and the largest councillor/elector ratio of all boroughs.

Table 3.2 Council size bands

Local Government Boundary Commission to 1992	
Type of Authority	***Number of Councillors***
County council	60–100 councillors
Metropolitan district council	50–80 councillors
Non-metropolitan district council	30–60 councillors
London borough council	50–70 councillors
Local Government Commission for England since 1996	
Type of Authority	***Number of Councillors***
County council to 1998	60–100 councillors
County council from 1998*	40–80 councillors
Shire district	30–60 councillors
All unitary authorities (including shire unitaries, metropolitan districts and London boroughs)	40–80 councillors

* This change was in response to the restructuring which created the shire unitary councils.

The Local Government Boundary Commission for Scotland has a different way of proceeding to that of the LGCE. There are defined lower (18 councillors) and upper (80 councillors) limits on council size, which itself depends upon population density and distribution of the population. The Local Government Boundary Commission for Scotland write,

> 'Regarding equity as between voters, we considered that ideally each elector's vote should possess the same weight and significance in local government elections throughout the country; furthermore, ideally, there should be similar mutual accessibility between electors and councillors. However, since Scotland is a country of great diversity, both geographically and demographically, a fact reflected in the areas for which councils created by the Act of 1994 are responsible, and since we are satisfied that, in the interests of good local government, the number of councillors in any council must fall within certain limits, we concluded that these ideals are unattainable in practice. In this situation, recognising that a fair degree of homogeneity exists within certain groups of councils, which exhibit broadly similar geographic and demographic characteristics, we resolved to strive for equity in the senses mentioned within these groups, so far as that is possible within the constraints of the legislation which we operate' (Third Statutory Review of Electoral Arrangements, August 1998).

Mainland councils were therefore placed into categories according to their population density and how the population was distributed across the authority. After consultation with all Scottish councils, six categories were produced and the ratio of councillors to electors for each category was set. The ratio for the three island councils was set at 1:750. The six categories and the ratio for each are as follows,

Category 1.	Large Cities – Glasgow and Edinburgh (1:6,000).
Category 2.	Cities – Aberdeen and Dundee (1:4,000).
Category 3.	Authorities with less than 60% of the population living outwith settlements of 10,000 or more persons AND an overall population density of one person or more per hectare (1:3,500).
Category 4.	Authorities EITHER 60% or more of the population living outwith settlements of 10,000 or more persons OR an overall population density of less than one person per hectare (1:3,000).
Category 5.	Authorities with 60% or more of the population living outwith settlements of 10,000 or more persons AND an overall population density of less than one person per hectare (1:2,500).
Category 6.	Authorities with 60% of more of the population living outwith settlements of 10,000 or more persons AND an overall population density of less than 0.2 persons or more per hectare (1:2,000).

The Local Government Boundary Commission for Wales is directed to recommend council sizes to be within the range of 30 to 75 members. The Secretary of State for Wales has also issued guidance which states that, '...the aim should be to achieve electoral divisions with a member to electorate ratio no lower than 1:1,750' (Review of Electoral Arrangements Draft Proposals, County Borough of Bridgend, Local Government Boundary Commission for Wales, December 1996: 2). In reality, the Commission has not complied with this guidance. Not only are there many divisions with a councillor:member ratio of less than 1,750, but there are more than ten councils in Wales which have an average ratio for the whole authority less than the recommended figure (e.g. Gwynedd (1,223), Blaenau Gwent (1,318), and Powys (1,322)).

The Local Government Commission for England noted in its internal report on the second year of electoral reviews that,

> 'Some Commissioners have expressed unease about the non-prescriptive approach the Commission has taken to council size in England ... The key difference in England to Scotland and Wales is that the Commission is primarily dealing with established authorities, already reviewed by the LGBC. The Scotland and Welsh Commissions, on the other hand, are dealing with new authorities where temporary electoral arrangements were put in place which, it was widely understood, would be subject to review' (LGC (98) 58).

The LGCE had the opportunity to move to the Scottish system of banding but, having listened to stakeholders during its consultation in 1996, it retained the current system. A senior officer at the Commission commented that the Scottish legislation has caused a number of problems in that country. The rules regarding the number of councillors had proved to be contentious and provoked difficulties in the early stages of the review. One Commissioner suggested to us that there was envy in Scotland of the English system because it allows for the recognition of diversity in local government and takes communities into account.

In 1998, the Commission began to relate the government's modernising agenda to council size. The Commission states that,

> 'We support the concept of diversity and innovation in local government and, where appropriate, are willing to promote proposals for experimentation in different democratic styles and structures. A PER provides the opportunity for council size to be changed if that should be a desirable corollary to implementing a reform' (Guidance, 1998: para 37).

In 1999, the Commission reconsidered its council size range bands in the light of the government's proposals for executive styles of political management. It advised stakeholders that,

> 'We do not wish to inhibit the full and proper consideration by local authorities and other interested parties of what may be the most appropriate council size for their area by suggesting a range which may be suitable for their proposed political management structure, and *have therefore decided to dispense with range bands*' (Guidance, 1999: para 3.8).

In a number of reviews since the publication of the White Paper and the removal of the Commission's bands on council size, schemes have been put forward to the LGCE which proposed significant alterations to council size. However the Commission took the view that,

> 'It was far from clear from the supporting evidence how, in detail, the authorities concerned intended to take forward the Government's proposals or what new political management structures they planned to put in place. There was no implicit or explicit assumption in the Government's proposals that a greater or smaller number of councillors would be required' (April 1999 meeting).

An argument can be made for either an increase or a decrease in the number of councillors being necessary as a result of modernisation. More backbench councillors may be needed to scrutinise policy made by the executive, or fewer councillors in total may be required because there are fewer committees and more of an executive structure in place. The Commission had no government lead on its approach to council size, although it was made clear by the government that it did not expect significant changes to council size being made. The decision was taken by the Commission not to put forward radical solutions itself, but to support those schemes (within the rules) that were derived locally as these were likely to be lasting.

Electorate forecasts

Schedule 11 of the Local Government Act 1972 states that the Commission should conduct electoral reviews, 'Having regard to any changes in the number or distribution of the local government electors of the district likely to take place within the period of five years immediately following the consideration (by the Secretary of State or the Commission)'. Projections of the electorate five years ahead are a vital, yet contentious area of the review. For example, the Local Government Boundary Commission highlighted in its Report No. 413 (1981) the fact that there were problems with the forecasts of electorates. The projections provided by authorities had been challenged by opposition parties and in some instances had caused particular controversy. Although the LGBC noted that local authorities had a tendency to overestimate their projections, it made no suggestions for an improved system of forecasting.

The basis for using projections is that a scheme will not date immediately from its publication, but will take account of expected changes in population in the near future. The Commission has to judge the relative weight to be given to current and projected electorates. In September 1996 it stated that,

> 'With the exception of areas where there is a clear expectation of population growth, the current year electorate is likely to provide the most reliable basis for any changes...[the Commission]...may recommend, although it will, of course, have regard to the forecasts' (Guidance, 1996: para 23).

Yet it appears from an internal document that greater weight is given to the projections. 'Current electorates have the advantage of certainty. However, it is clearly preferable for the Commission's electoral schemes to show an improvement in electoral balance over time' (LGC (97) 154).

The Commission admits that calculating the projections is an 'inexact science', as there is no standard way of producing the figures and no check on their accuracy. It does not issue guidelines on how to calculate electorate projections, but looks to the council's Chief Executive to form a professional judgement about them. The Commission does expect the projections to be calculated according to the most up-to-date information the council has. The projections should be realistic and only take account of housing developments that have received planning permission at the time of the review and have a reasonable degree of certainty of completion within five years. Likely occupancy levels per dwelling should also be considered. In 1998, the Commission wrote that,

> 'We have found the most constructive approach in two-tier county areas has been for all district councils and the county council to agree a protocol to secure a

> consistent and rigorous approach to electorate forecasts in each district' (Guidance, 1998: para 43).

Most London boroughs use the London Research Centre to provide information on electorate forecasts. These figures are then adjusted by the boroughs themselves using their local knowledge of potential developments.

Under-registration of electors

Determining the accuracy of current electorate figures can be as difficult as making future projections. The Commission was asked by a number of local authorities if it would take evidence about the under-registration of electors into account on the grounds that they also had to provide services for people not on the electoral register. Whereas the Parliamentary Boundary Commissions are required to use the 'number of persons whose names appear on the register of parliamentary electors' as the building blocks for their own calculations, the LGCE has more flexibility on the issue. The guidance states that,

> 'We will take claims of under-registration into account for the purposes of five-year forecasts where credible evidence is provided, both of the existence of under-registration, and of steps being taken which are likely to increase registration in a particular area' (Guidance, 1998: para 46).

This issue has the potential to provoke controversy as a party may claim under-registration in an attempt to gain political advantage. In the case, for example, of a ward which the party currently holds but which is under-sized for the purposes of the review.

Councillor/elector ratio

The Commission found in its 1995 consultation exercise that local authorities were in favour of different council sizes even where there were similarly sized electorates. Such differences could stem from historical patterns of council size or reflect population densities. The Commission and authorities are happy that in Northampton, for example, one councillor serves an average of 3,003 electors, while in neighbouring South Northamptonshire a councillor represents just 1,316 electors. As long as councillors represent approximately an equal number of electors *within* an authority, differences in councillor representation *between* authorities are not thought important. Nevertheless questions about the validity of this practice remain. Do electors across the country receive equitable representation from their elected representatives, and is it right that councillors should have such different workloads in similar authorities?

Internal Commission documents indicate that the issue of the variation of the ratio of councillors to electors between authorities has had a significant airing. In one report it is noted that,

> 'Notwithstanding some unease on the part of some Commissioners – relating, for example, to the wide variation in the number of councillors serving Blackpool (44) and Blackburn (62) – the previously established inconsistencies in council size have not generally been corrected' (LGC (97) 154).

Eight months later in the second edition of its guidance, the Commission uses these two unitary authorities as an example of its support for diversity in local government,

> 'Council size is normally a reflection of an area's population or electorate. However, there can be wide variations in council size between local authorities which have similar electorates. Some local authorities with larger electorates have historically had smaller council sizes than some councils with smaller electorates. Much depends on the area concerned. Some examples are:

	Council size	***Electorate***
Blackpool	62	101,647
Blackburn	44	115,891'

> (Guidance, 1998: para 35).

The 'unease' of some Commissioners seems to have dissipated, at least in public.

Electoral equality

Schedule 11 of the Local Government Act 1972 states that, 'The ratio of the number of local government electors to the number of councillors to be elected shall be, as nearly as may be, the same in every ward of the district'. The phrase, 'as nearly as may be', allows the Commission some flexibility in drafting its recommendations. The Commission's predecessor, the LGBC, used bandings of tolerance for electoral equality which were also adopted by the Commission. According to the first edition of guidance,

> 'Proposals for change in electoral arrangements should therefore be based on variations in each ward of no more than plus or minus 10 per cent from the average councillor/elector ratio for the authority, having regard to five year forecasts of change in electorates. Imbalances in excess of plus or minus 20 per cent may be acceptable, but only in highly exceptional circumstances, and again will have to be justified in full' (Guidance, 1996: para 25).

The Commission's task is, however, not purely mathematical because it also has to take into account the 'identities and interests of local communities' and ensure that the new boundaries result in local government which is 'effective and convenient' (1992 Act, section 13(5)). The balance between these competing drivers is the most important factor in an electoral review.

At an early stage the Commission held meetings to determine its approach. It decided that the prime criterion should be electoral equality. The definition of communities and 'local ties' was, it was argued, subjective and likely to be contested, whereas electoral equality – notwithstanding the problems in arriving at accurate base figures – could be measured. It was inevitable that some local authorities or individuals would disagree with the Commission's decision. An internal paper records, 'The Commission has determined that electoral equality, having regard to local circumstances, is the prime objective of its reviews. Given the circularity of the legislation, this may have been challengeable' (LGC (97) 154). Although a few authorities such as Durham and West Wiltshire have made complaints about the review process to the Secretary of State, there has been no legal challenge to the Commission since the 1979 Enfield case – see Chapter 2.

In the second edition of guidance the LGCE came down even more firmly in support of the primacy of electoral equality, and explicitly advised authorities that they must produce evidence for any schemes that would divert from it. Whilst recognising that achieving perfect electoral equality is impossible in reality,

> '...Local authorities and other interested parties should start from the standpoint of absolute electoral equality and only then make adjustments to reflect relevant factors, such as community identity. Each such adjustment should be justified, using the approach of *proposition*, *argument* and *evidence*. The degree of argument and evidence required will largely depend on the level of electoral imbalance being proposed. For example, we will require particular justification for schemes which would result in, or retain, an imbalance of over 10 per cent in any ward. Any imbalances of 20 per cent and over should arise only in the most exceptional of circumstances, and will require the strongest justification' (Guidance, 1998: para 39).

Taking a strong and consistent line on electoral equality was often the focus of Commission meetings. At one meeting a new Commissioner argued that the starting point of the LGCE's work is electoral equality. He stated that, 'Achieving good electoral equality is what we are here for; it's what we get paid for'. Another Commissioner agreed by commenting that the Commission had so far taken a vigorous line on electoral equality. If it departed from this line, it would be setting a precedent. One factor which helps to drive the Commission is that its sponsoring government department (now, the Department of Local Government, Transport and the Regions), checks that it is achieving its stated aim of improving electoral equality figures. The Commission publishes figures on patterns of electoral equality before and after reviews in the annually revised Corporate Plan.

The PERs in the London boroughs were conducted with yet tighter guidelines. In other large urban areas the Commission had managed to achieve average electoral variances of around 2-3%, and believed it should be able to match or improve upon that figure in London. All authorities in the capital were advised that they should aim for perfect electoral equality, and variances above 2-3% would only be acceptable in exceptional circumstances. The previous bandings of greater than +/-10% and +/-20% were not mentioned. An officer from the Commission argued that it is easier to draw boundaries in urban areas than in rural areas. The population is large, there are fewer instances of parishes (none in London), and neither distance nor geographical features are as likely to be used in arguments about local ties and community interests.

Sparsity

At the other extreme there are wards in England, predominately in rural areas, which cover an area larger in size than some whole metropolitan or district councils. These wards often contain very small numbers of electors. As a result of the demand to make each vote of equal value, these wards may find that they are required to expand. There is nothing in legislation which allows the Commission to apply a rural weighting. However, the Commission does recognise the problem of sparsity and its effect on securing effective and convenient local government. The guidance states that, 'We will certainly be alive to the sparsity factor when considering or putting forward proposals to improve electoral balance' (Guidance, 1998: para 58). Whether and how this is done is a matter for later empirical investigation.

No local authority submission

It is made quite clear that it is the responsibility of a local authority or political or other groups within it to prepare an initial authority-wide scheme for the Commission's consideration. Where no submission is received, or the proposal supports the status quo despite the existence of significant electoral imbalances, the Commission is obliged to formulate its own scheme. The Commission does liaise with the local authority and any other interested parties in drawing up such a scheme, but without local knowledge it is difficult to draw boundaries which are sensible of local communities. The Commission's tough line has even found expression in the local press as the extract in Box 3.3 shows.

BOX 3.3 'Boundary shake-up order given'

A Midlands council has been ordered to go ahead with a boundary shake-up – despite fears that it will increase the workload of some members... 'This is not a matter of choice for the district council' said Labour opposition leader Coun Tony Lanchester (Boney Hay ward, Lichfield). 'Civil servants have been brutally straightforward in telling us that our proposals must be submitted or they will do it for us. We cannot just do nothing, but when you have reorganisation based on playing the numbers game there is never a satisfactory conclusion.'

Extract from article in the Birmingham Evening Mail, 31 January 2000

Policy making by the Commission

It is clear from our discussion so far that the LGCE has felt obliged to make its own policy where the legislation was either ambiguous or permissive. The Commission's May 1995 Consultation Paper was sent to all local authorities, as well as to local government organisations, academics, political parties and other interested parties. It sought views on fourteen main issues, including whether to use council size bandings, whether to recommend single-member wards, the acceptable level of electoral imbalance, and the length of stages within the Commission's timetable. Three-quarters of local authorities in England replied among a total of nearly 500 responses. This consultation period helped the Commission to develop its policies in preparation for the start of the PERs. The first edition of the ' Guidance and Procedural Advice for Local Authorities and Other Interested Parties' was published in March 1996. The first set of reviews started in the same month. As the Commission gained in experience from conducting reviews, Further Guidance was published in September 1996. In March 1998 and October 1999 second and third editions of the Guidance were published, each of these documents highlighting evolutionary not revolutionary change by the Commission. A fourth edition in December 2000 provided clarification about legislative changes contained in the Political Parties, Elections and Referendum Act 2000 and the Local Government Act 2000. Commissioners may discuss a policy issue amongst themselves without prejudice before they instruct officers to prepare a paper. Officer papers are not prepared without Commissioners first being sounded out by the Chairman of the Commission. Formal discussion will then take place on the issue and the policy is derived.

This was exactly the process followed when the Commission started its reviews of county councils. Some guidance for these reviews, such as that no county division should cross district council boundaries, was in place before they began (Guidance, 1998), but there needed to be changes. The Commissioners, who had already changed their policy on the phasing of county reviews, realised that they were going to be different to those in the districts and that the Review Managers and Review Leaders needed some additional direction. The main consideration was how to deal with the potentially competing criteria of electoral equality (both between the divisions and across districts in terms of the number of divisions each is 'entitled' to), council size and coterminosity. Coterminosity occurs where the boundaries of one or more district wards exactly coincide with those of a county division. In July 1998, three months before the county reviews were due to begin, the Commission started to consider its approach. Using Northumberland as a model, each Review Manager was instructed to draw up options for the county by concentrating on either a different criterion or a different balance between them. Schemes were produced based on complete coterminosity with minimal change in individual districts, on the preservation of complete coterminosity despite significant change, and on achieving good electoral equality at the expense of coterminosity. The Commission carefully watched how the early county reviews unfolded and at its January 1999 meeting, after a discussion of the officer produced options papers, revised the guidance. The Commission decided that electoral equality between divisions should be its primary objective. It would also ensure that each district received its 'correct' number of divisions according to the size of its electorate and the overall size of the county council. However, coterminosity was not forgotten,

> 'While the achievement of coterminosity will normally be secondary to the achievement of electoral equality, there may be exceptions. For example, in an urban area we may consider that an electoral imbalance in one division might be justified if it facilitated both the appropriate number of county councillors for the district and coterminosity throughout the remainder of the district' (Guidance, 1999: para 5.8).

The Commission is also guided in its policy-making by its stakeholders. At the end of every review, a survey is sent to the Chief Executive of each authority in addition to representatives of the national political parties, the local authority associations and the county associations of parish and town councils. An analysis of responses is produced each year and presented at a Commission meeting. The introduction of the Preliminary Period in the review led directly from stakeholder responses to the first survey.

Policy-making in the Commission can be flexible because the organisation is small. Staff have an important input into the process and seem to be good at raising debate on policy issues. There have been reviews of process involving all staff in July 1996, November 1996, and July 1998. The staff workshops in July 1998 had four main aims: to highlight the strengths and weaknesses of the current PER process; to ensure that the strengths are retained and built upon; to identify improvements that can and should be made; and to develop a strategy to implement the improvements identified. Commissioners believe that because it is the officers' job to run the review process on a day-to-day basis, they are the Commission's closest contact to the reviews. Interviews with Commissioners have revealed that while they have no problem following officers' advice on the development of policy if they believe it to be right, they will equally reject advice with which they are not happy. The consensus appears to be that a close working relationship between Commissioners, officers and stakeholders produces good policy exchange and shaping.

The impact of government policy on the LGCE

The Local Government Commission for England has, as a non-departmental public body, to be reactive to legislative change. During the course of our research the government has published a number of documents with potentially considerable significance for the Commission's work. The Department of the Environment, Transport and the Regions' (DETR) Consultation Paper, *Modernising Local Government – Local Democracy and Community Leadership* (1998), raised the issue of introducing annual elections in England. The White Paper, *Modern Local Government – In Touch with the People* (1998), proposed that elections should be held annually by thirds in all single-tier authorities (London boroughs, metropolitan boroughs and shire unitary districts) and by halves in alternate years in all two-tier authorities. Between the publication of the Consultation Paper and the White Paper, the Commission had no choice but to continue with its PER programme. Minutes of a Commission meeting reveal its thinking on the issue,

> 'Once the White Paper had been published, assuming a move towards annual elections and multi-member wards, it would be helpful to have a clear policy steer from the Government on the approach…[the Commission]… should take to such matters pending the commencement of any new legislation' (March 1998).

The White Paper also provoked a great deal of discussion within the Commission on council size because the government had not indicated whether it expected changes in political management to result in an increase or reduction in council size. Without a lead from the government the Commission felt itself placed in a difficult situation and spent a considerable amount of time preparing its response to the White Paper. This included holding an additional Commissioners' meeting as well as briefing meetings with the Local Government Association and the Association of London Government.

The Commission decided that it should make its response to the White Paper clear to local authorities – its stakeholders. Minutes from a Commission meeting show that there were a number of important points it wanted to get across to authorities. The Commission would be sympathetic to local authority concerns about the White Paper; authorities being currently reviewed would have the opportunity to revisit their proposed scheme in the light of the government's proposals; authorities should understand that election by halves does not necessarily mean that all wards have to be represented by two members; a change in political management does not mean that the size of the council must also change. Finally, the Commission wanted to emphasise that the actual implementation of the government's proposals would not happen immediately. Some authorities clearly heeded this advice. Scarborough, for example, proposed a predominantly two-member ward structure to facilitate 'a four year cycle of alternating elections' (Final Recommendations, 1999: para 20). A similar scheme was put forward by Shrewsbury and Atcham, although the council added as a rider in a submission to the Commission that,

> 'having based its electoral arrangements proposals on the likelihood that a two-year electoral cycle was to be introduced, [the council] is seeking strong reassurance that, should legislation to change the electoral cycle in two tier areas not be enacted, its electoral arrangements will be reviewed in order that it can put forward proposals more in keeping with elections by thirds' (Final Recommendations, 1999: para 19).

The Commission responded that it could give no such reassurance as unscheduled reviews required a direction from the Secretary of State.

After consultations with the DETR, the Commission issued a letter to all Chief Executives on 7 October 1998. It contained its interpretation of the government's proposals and advice on some of the issues discussed above. Its key substantive points are reproduced in Box 3.4.

BOX 3.4 LGCE letter to Local Authorities regarding the Government's Proposals for Changes to Local Authority Electoral Arrangements

The Government's proposals

4 In brief, the Government's proposals provide for elections by thirds – in three years out of four – for all single-tier authorities (London boroughs, Metropolitan districts and shire unitary districts), and elections by halves in alternate years for all two-tier authorities. This means that two-tier districts, whether they currently have whole council elections or elect by thirds, will move to a cycle of elections by halves, alternating with elections by halves to two-tier county councils.

5 The White Paper explains that the Commission will continue with its programme of PERs. In doing so, it will work to its current statutory criteria, as set out in the Local Government Act 1992. However, the Secretary of State intends to take a power through the new legislation to direct the Commission to have regard to a future criterion, that the number of councillors to be returned from each ward or division should reflect the authority's electoral cycle. This suggests a move over time towards a pattern of three-member wards in single-tier authorities and two-member wards/divisions in two-tier authorities.

6 Nevertheless, having said that, it is clear the Government recognises the problems associated with large electoral areas in sparsely populated rural areas. The White Paper is specific that single-member wards and divisions will continue to be a feature in many local authorities.

Implementation

7 Outside Metropolitan districts, which already have three-member wards and elections by thirds, the Government's proposals herald some radical changes to local government electoral arrangements. However, it seems clear from the content of the White Paper, and the Commission's discussions with the Department and the local authority associations, that the Government has a medium to long term time scale for achieving change.

8 While it is possible that changes to electoral cycles could be introduced reasonably shortly after the legislation has passed through Parliament, a move towards ward/division patterns which reflected those new cycles could take a longer period to achieve. As the White Paper suggests, the Commission will have a role – as part of its PER programme – in making recommendations on the pattern of warding arrangements which should be put in place. On the basis of current legislation, such a task could not be completed until the Commission's next round of PERs in ten to fifteen years' time in accordance with the statutory timetable set out in section 13(2) and (3) of the Local Government Act 1992.

Contd./

Box 3.4 continued

9 Such a situation would leave many local authorities, for some significant period, with a pattern of wards which did not reflect their (new) electoral cycle. However, it must be recognised that a move to, for example, elections by halves in two-tier districts does not necessarily mean that they must have a uniform pattern of two-member wards. Approximately a third of such districts currently have elections by thirds, yet very few have a uniform pattern of three-member wards throughout their area. There is also the White Paper's acknowledgement in relation to the continuation of single-member wards/ divisions in many authorities.

The Commission's approach

10 It has been suggested that, in the light of the Government's legislative proposals, the Commission's PER programme should be put on hold since its recommendations for changes to electoral arrangements, particularly in relation to the number of councillors returned from wards, will be quickly overtaken. However, as discussed above, this is a misconception; in most local authority areas the prevailing pattern of wards is likely to continue for some considerable period. Consequently, it is as important now as it was previously for the Commission to maintain the impetus of its PER programme, addressing the significant electoral imbalances which exist in many local authority areas.

11 In proceeding with its PER work the Commission will maintain the general approach set out in its March 1998 *Guidance*. Until such time as the Secretary of State directs otherwise, the Commission is not required to have regard to the Government's White Paper proposals. Nor can it insist that others do so. However, the proposals are clearly a consideration which it would not be sensible to ignore. Accordingly, the Commission believes it to be in the interests of local government for interested parties to PERs, particularly local authorities, to have regard to the Government's legislative intentions in the preparation of their electoral schemes.

12 Different considerations apply depending on the type of authority.

London boroughs

13 In June 1998 the Commission commenced PERs of the London boroughs. In discussions and briefing meetings with chief officers and members, the Commission has consistently advised that, in preparing their electoral schemes, London boroughs and political groups would be well-advised to have regard to the (then) Green Paper proposals for elections by thirds and three-member wards.

14 The Commission sees no reason to alter this advice. Indeed, the content of the White Paper only serves to confirm its view that, as either a first or second preference, London boroughs and political groups should consider the preparations of schemes which reflect the Government's proposals for electoral arrangements in the capital.

Contd./

Box 3.4 continued

Shire unitary districts

15 Similar considerations apply to the majority of single-tier shire districts as do to London boroughs. While in many of its electoral reviews of shire unitary authorities to date the Commission has built on, and tended to reinforce, the existing pattern of warding arrangements, single-tier districts will wish to consider and take into account the Government's proposals for elections by thirds.

Two-tier district councils

16 The Commission recognises that many authorities whose PERs have started, or are about to start, will have spent considerable time and resources in developing electoral schemes which may not accord with the Government's White Paper proposals.

17 However, as previously indicated, a move to elections by halves does not necessarily mean that all wards must return two members: a pattern of one-, two- and three-member wards is likely to be a feature in many two-tier districts for some time to come. Nevertheless, and quite understandably, a few authorities whose PERs are currently in Stage One (initial consultation phase) have requested an opportunity – and a short extension to their review timetable – to give further consideration to the schemes they intend to submit to the Commission.

18 Where this has occurred, the Commission has been prepared to extend Stage One of the review to give the authorities concerned sufficient time to consider whether they wish to modify their schemes in order to reflect the Government's proposals. However, the PERs of some or all of the districts in a county are conducted to the same review timetable. In granting any extension the Commission would wish to be satisfied that all districts whose reviews were being conducted to the same timetable were prepared to accept a potential delay in the completions of their PERs.

19 Of course, it is open to authorities whose PERs are further advanced, say in Stage Two (consideration of Stage One submissions by the Commission) or Three (Commission consultation on draft recommendations), to also consider whether to modify their proposals to the Commission. In such circumstances, the Commission would expect any modified scheme to be submitted during Stage Three. It may also agree to an extension to Stage Three should this prove necessary. However, as with any Stage One extensions, all districts whose reviews were being conducted to the same timetable would need to be prepared to accept a potential delay in the completions of their PERs.

20 If necessary, the Commission may undertake further rounds of consultation on any modified electoral schemes, either by way of a local public meeting or by publishing revised draft recommendations.

Contd./

Box 3.4 continued

Two-tier county councils

21 Under the provisions of the Local Government Act 1972, each county council electoral division may only return one member. Accordingly, until such time as new legislation is introduced and commenced, in conducting PERs of county council electoral arrangements, the Commission may only recommend one member per division.

22 In the event, it seems unlikely that the Government's proposals for two-member divisions will be a feature in other than the more urban parts of county council areas. Both the Government and the Commission recognise the particular difficulties which would arise by the creation of large two-member divisions in sparsely populated rural areas.

23 As previously indicated, the Commission can only recommend single-member divisions in PERs of county council areas. However, pending new legislation, in developing their schemes county councils are advised to at least have regard to the Government's proposals insofar as they may apply to urban areas. In practice, this means considering patterns of electoral divisions which might facilitate the creation of two-member divisions in urban areas in due course.

Conclusions

In this chapter we have examined the framework within which the Local Government Commission for England conducts Periodic Electoral Reviews. On the one hand, the 1992 Local Government Act is clear about the Commission's role and the areas of its competence; on the other, the relevant sections of the Act allow the Commission considerable discretion in setting up its own timetables and procedures, and present it with the problem of solving some potentially mutually exclusive aims. The Commission has responded by publishing further guidance about how it intends to carry out its work and interpret various aspects of the legislation. This guidance has been amended over time to take account of circumstances and experience, but it has always been drafted following consultation with stakeholders – in most cases the local authorities – and has reflected lessons learnt by the Commission 'on the job'. Such a learning process was inevitable given the limited 'corporate memory' about PERs when the Commission began its work (Chilton, 1996), and it can be seen in the implementation of incremental changes such as the introduction of the Preliminary Period, the lengthening of some of the stages of the Review, and the phasing of county council reviews.

During the course of the research the Commission, perhaps untypically, also found itself caught up in evolving government policy. At the time of writing only those changes affecting the political management structures of councils have been implemented, but the Commission has had to nurse local authorities through a period of uncertainty concerning the appropriate structure of their wards and the likely frequency of elections. In effect this meant that advice was being changed quite frequently. For example, the Commission's first edition of guidance in 1996 pointed to the advantage of single member wards, whilst at the same time acknowledging that local preferences would be respected with regard to both this matter and the issue of all-out versus annual elections. By March 1998, in the wake of the Green Paper *Modernising Local Government*, the Commission is drawing local authorities' attention to the expressed intent to introduce widespread annual elections and suggesting that 'three-member wards may create sharper accountability in authorities where there are to be elections by thirds'. Then, in October of the same year, the Commission felt it necessary to issue a letter to local authorities effectively telling them not to panic. The Commission would be sympathetic to councils which wanted a short extension of their review timetable if the White Paper had caused them to revise their thinking about their submission, but noted that although it would not be sensible for local authorities to ignore the White Paper, any legislative change was likely to be implemented only over the long term and the PERs would therefore continue as scheduled.

We now wish to move on to examine how the Periodic Electoral Review process and some of the issues it raises are dealt with in practice from the perspective both of the Commission (Chapter 4) and the local authorities themselves (Chapter 5).

Chapter 4

The Periodic Electoral Review Process – the perspective of the Commission

Conducting Periodic Electoral Reviews is not simply a matter of setting and adjusting the frameworks within which the statutory rules are interpreted. The Local Government Commission for England also has to carry out reviews on the ground and, in doing so, work closely with local authorities and others who make representations to it. In this chapter we discuss some of the practical aspects of the conduct of PERs from the perspective of the Commission. We follow the Commission at the various stages of review, using transcripts from meetings attended by the Commission in our case-study local authorities, internal Commission meetings, and interviews conducted with members of staff. We also analyse 'private' documents provided by the Commission in addition to reports in the public domain. We examine the stages of consultation and feedback, and how these representations affect the Final Recommendations. We discuss the Commission's use of public meetings and explain how decisions are taken in a Commission meeting. Finally, we relate this process to the outputs from PERs – the Commission's published Final Recommendations and the Orders subsequently made by the Secretary of State.

Staff at the Commission

According to a Commission document, the role of staff is to:

- assist the Commission in formulating its policies, procedures and programme;
- put the Commission's policies and procedures into effect, and follow the Commission's approach with respect to philosophies, objectives and values; and
- formulate recommendations within the policy and procedures established by the Commission and put them to the Commission (Memo to Financial Management and Policy Review (FMPR), 1998).

At full capacity, there is a total of 37 staff at the Commission. Twenty four of these staff work directly on Periodic Electoral Reviews, while four form the Senior

Management Team. This team, comprising the Personnel Manager, the Head of Policy, the Head of Finance and Facilities Management, and the Publications and Public Relations Manager, report directly to the Chief Executive, as do the Review Managers. It is groups of staff at the Commission (a review team) who are responsible for producing schemes for the re-drawing of boundaries in individual local authorities. There are four review teams. Each team consists of a Review Manager, a Senior Review Leader, three Review Leaders and a Review Assistant. Review Managers take responsibility for a number of concurrent reviews and ensure that acceptable re-warding schemes and accurate draft and final reports are produced. In an average week, Review Managers will spend approximately a third of their time liaising with their review team and another third reading literature and reports. The remaining time is spent handling enquiries from external sources, attending corporate meetings and external meetings with local authorities, and in general administration. Review Leaders are responsible for managing designated reviews. This means that they are in regular contact with local authorities and individuals. They examine the minutiae of every representation to the Commission, they devise the electoral scheme, and write the reports. The responsibilities of Review Assistants are primarily administrative. They provide support to the review team by maintaining the office and archiving information. They also assist in the review process by mapping and drafting reports for Review Leaders at the direction of the Review Manager.

The Commission is currently undertaking more reviews than ever before – see Table 3.1. An additional review team was formed to deal with the London borough reviews and to help speed up throughput. This brought the total number of teams to four. There appears to be quite a large turnover of review staff which does not help the smooth running of reviews. For example, of the seven staff that worked on the review of local authorities in Wiltshire in 1998, only three still worked for the Commission in the summer of 2000. The Commission states, however, that during the period of our research, staff turnover was less than 6%. Some officers have quickly achieved promotion within the organisation as experienced staff have moved on. One Review Manager started at the Commission as an administrative assistant working on the structural reviews in March 1996. One member of staff became a Review Manager after working for the Commission for only nineteen months (she joined the Commission in May 1998 and became a Review Manager in December 1999). Experienced review staff at the Commission are at a premium.

The Commission has also experienced several changes in personnel among very senior staff. Adrian Stungo was Chief Executive from July 1996 until his death in February 1998. The Commission then had two acting Chief Executives in quick succession. Both Michael Bailey (February 1998 - May 1998) and Michael Ridler

(May 1998 - August 1998) were on secondment from the Department of the Environment, Transport and the Regions. The current Chief Executive, Barbara Stephens, was appointed in August 1998. The Code of Practice for Commissioners states that,

> 'The Chief Executive has responsibility, under the Commission, for the overall organisation, management, and staffing of the Commission and for its procedures in financial and other matters, including conduct and discipline' (1998: 10).

Ms Stephens decided to become more involved in the day-to-day running of the reviews, a position previously taken by the Director of Reviews. The FMPR had concluded that staffing at the management level had to be reduced and that 'the Commission should undertake a review of the role of the Director of Reviews within the organisation'. The Director of Reviews left the organisation in March 1999. Interviews with Commissioners and officers have revealed that the new Chief Executive has helped to sharpen up review procedures and improved the time-tabling of PERs. Liaison between the Commission and the DETR (since the 2001 election, the DLTR) is the responsibility of the Head of Policy: the one member of staff who has experience of working for the Local Government Boundary Commission. Technically on long-term secondment from the DETR, he is not directly involved in the drafting of PER reports. It is the Head of Policy's responsibility to interpret new legislation and flag up issues which the Commission as a body needs to address in its guidance. He also has considerable experience dealing with legal challenges to Commission recommendations and in helping to resolve contentious re-warding issues.

The Commissioners

The responsibilities of Commissioners are to:

- determine objectives, targets, philosophies and values;
- establish and endorse policy through the published Guidance, within which staff are required to work when dealing with the detail of individual reviews; and
- determine and endorse the forward programme, provide overall quality control with respect to the Commission's approach, recommendations, values etc. (Memo to FMPR, 1998).

According to Schedule 2 of the Local Government Act (1992), there can be between five and fifteen Commissioners. At present there are seven Commissioners: Professor Malcolm Grant (Chairman), Professor Michael Clarke (Deputy Chairman), Peter Brokenshire, Kru Desai, Pamela Gordon, Robin Gray, and Robert Hughes.

Each is appointed by the Secretary of State for a three year term and can serve a maximum of two terms. There are two academics and three former local authority Chief Executives amongst the current group of Commissioners. The other two Commissioners both have extensive experience of local government. Between 1992 and 1998, Bob Scruton served as a Commissioner. He had served on a parish council in Kent since 1983 and was a Council member of the National Association of Local Councils. There is no longer an individual with similar experience and awareness of parish level local government serving as a Commissioner.

Commissioners are paid for two days work a month. The Chairman is required to work on Commission matters for one and a half days a week. The Chairman has particular responsibility for providing effective strategic leadership on electoral review matters. He chairs the Employment and Remuneration Committee while the Deputy Chairman chairs the Audit Committee. The Chairman also sits on the panel at the DETR which vets prospective candidates to become Commissioners. The appointment of new Commissioners at regular intervals helps to bring new perspectives to the review process. For example, at a Commission meeting in January 1999, each of the two new Commissioners raised the topic of electoral equality versus community identity and prompted their colleagues at least to re-examine their thinking on this key issue.

When the PER process began each Commissioner would receive detailed information on every review. Now, however, one Commissioner is designated as 'taking a particular interest' in each review and follows it through at both draft and final stage. This enables Commissioners to build up knowledge about a particular review and also to forge a good working relationship with a review team. All Commissioners seemed well-informed on the reviews in which they took a 'particular interest', but there was not a great deal of evidence to suggest that Commissioners were interested in or knowledgeable about other reviews. The relevant Commissioner is briefed by the review team early on in Stage Two. This briefing can take place by phone, by letter, by a personal visit to the Commission's offices or by a mix of all three. Officers highlight the various options in a local authority, placing emphasis on the scheme having good electoral equality and respect for local community ties. Commissioners are not asked to take a 'particular interest' in authorities in which they have recently worked, where they live, or might otherwise know well. One Commissioner told us that this was so there could be no preconceptions about an authority, and that authorities could be assured that they were being treated consistently.

Conducting PERs

Section 15 of the 1992 Local Government Act states that the Commission will follow a four stage consultation process. At Stage One, proposals are submitted to the Commission. Stage Two is the time for the Commission to deliberate on and analyse the representations received. At Stage Three, the Commission publishes the Draft Recommendations and invites responses to its proposals. During Stage Four it considers any reaction it has attracted, and then drafts and reports its Final Recommendations to the Secretary of State. In September 1997 the Commission added to this process by introducing an informal preliminary period of around six weeks during which local authorities could prepare for review. Subsequently this period has been extended to between two and three months. A summary of the roles of the LGCE at the various stages of the Periodic Review Process can be found in Box 4.1.

Preliminary period

The preliminary period serves two functions. It allows authorities more time to generate proposals and consult interested parties, and it gives the Commission the opportunity to meet with members and officers in local authorities and explain the rules of the review. In the past, the Commission offered to arrange such meetings if requested by local authorities. Now, the Commission is much more proactive in ensuring that they take place. Officers from the Commission prepare by producing background material on the current electoral (in)equality in the authority and other relevant information.

We attended a meeting between the Commission's Director of Reviews and the Chief Executives of district councils in Wiltshire in January 1998. The Director of Reviews explained the objectives of a PER and dealt with possible problem issues such as sparsity of population and the under- or over-registration of electors. Emphasis was placed on the process being open and transparent on both sides. 'The best schemes are the local schemes which have used local knowledge. The whole idea is that it is a local, participative decision-making process'(Director of Reviews). The Director of Reviews stressed that electoral equality was the key, and did not mention any resultant split of communities and local ties. Only three out of five Chief Executives in Wiltshire were present at the meeting; the other councils sent representatives. Generally, the Chief Executives did not appear to treat the meeting particularly seriously. One Chief Executive was reading a council report during the meeting. The preliminary period is also used by the Commission to publicise the review process locally. The following typical piece appeared in Wiltshire newspapers in February 1998 – Box 4.2.

BOX 4.1 The Commission's roles in the PER process

Pre-review	Determine policies and processes and programme of work Publish *Guidance* and update as necessary Notify local authorities of programme
Preliminary period	Launch meetings, brief Chief Executives, members, parish councils, press etc.; site visits to local authorities Data/map gathering from local authorities and Ordnance Survey
Stage One	**Invite submissions** Launch letters to all local and national consultees Publicity – public notice, press release, press briefings, posters/leaflets Receipt of submissions from local authorities and others
Stage Two	**Formulate Draft Recommendations** Consider evidence; develop and agree scheme; identify mapping needs Public meeting? Brief relevant Commissioner; prepare draft recommendations report Consistency and audit checks of report and mapping Commission meeting Prepare report for typesetters
Stage Three	**Publish Draft Recommendations** Despatch reports to stakeholders; publicity Maintain liaison with review staff in local authorities and others
Stage Four	**Consider Final Recommendations** Summary and analysis of submissions received Consider evidence; modify and agree scheme; identify mapping needs Public meeting? Brief relevant Commissioner; prepare final recommendations report Consistency and audit checks of report and mapping Commission meeting Prepare report for typesetters Organise publicity, notifications, despatch arrangements Present Final Recommendations to Secretary of State
Post-review	**Follow Up** Stakeholders' questionnaire Review processes and procedures Report feedback and improvements to processes to Commissioners Reflect in Commission's Annual Report

Adapted from *Quinquennial Review of the Local Government Commission* Stage Two Report (January 1999)

BOX 4.2 Example of early press notice of the review.

'Review of all boundaries'

A sweeping review which could change electoral areas across Wiltshire began this week.

The Local Government Commission wants to ensure people are fairly and equally represented, but electoral boundaries have not changed for almost 20 years in West and North Wiltshire and there is an imbalance in the ratio of councillors to the number of people they represent.

The review aims to ensure the number of electors represented by each councillor is approximately the same.

Following the review, officers may recommend changes to the number of councillors on the district councils, the number of wards, the creation of new ones and future names.

Recommendations will also be made on future ward boundaries.

Extract from article in Wiltshire Times (Bradford on Avon), Chippenham News, and Wiltshire Times, 27 February 1998

We also attended a meeting between the Chief Executive of the Commission (and one of the review teams) and Devon County councillors. This was held on 29 July 1999 in advance of the county council review starting on 24 August 1999. At a previous meeting ten days before, Commission representatives had briefed council officers. The Chief Executive explained why the review was being carried out, its aims in terms of convenient and effective local government, electoral equality and coterminosity, and the stages of the review process. She emphasised that effective consultation was important, and gave some pointers to what makes a 'good' review. County councillors focused their questions on contentious decisions taken by the Commission in the district reviews.

In attempting to set out the 'rules' of PER in a forthright fashion before the start of Stage One, the Commission does occasionally make waves. The article reproduced in Box 4.3 followed the preliminary review meeting in Brentwood.

The Commission uses a press cuttings service in order to be aware of reaction 'on the ground' in all review areas. This can prove a very useful tool as it enables the Commission to correct inaccuracies and curtail the spread of myths about the review process. In one case, press coverage alerted the Commission that a council was about to consult on a re-warding scheme drawn up months in advance of the start of Stage One and the Commission's briefings. The model proposed minimal disturbance and contained wards with electoral variances between 15% and 28%.

BOX 4.3 Example of press coverage of preliminary review meeting

'Council boundary 'shock' – Wards shake-up'

Brentwood councillors are 'in shock' following the suggestion that a major shake-up of electoral boundaries is in the pipeline.

Barbara Stephens, Chief Executive of the Local Government Commission, told councillors at a special meeting that every ward in Brentwood is at risk of changing.

The Commission is in charge of implementing the overhaul and is currently touring the country to explain the process to increasingly bewildered councillors.

Liberal Democrat council leader David Gottesmann attended the meeting and was taken aback by the conclusions.

He said: 'I think it stunned quite a few of us in council. I don't think the penny has dropped about how radical the review will be. Everyone has started to realise they could lose their ward.

Mr Gottesmann, who represents Mountnessing, has come under fire from opponents for having too few constituents. He is worried the review will break apart old communities.

He said: 'There are ways out of it but I am not sure there is a painless way. Whatever happens I will not be representing anything like the area I am now'.

The Commission will consider the number of constituents and councillors in each area and aims to create wards with a stable ratio.

The review involves a consultation process until February before a draft proposal is brought out next summer.

Any changes will come into place when the whole council is forced up for re-election in 2002.

A spokesman for the Local Government Commission said: 'Each individual case will be considered on its own merits – we have no hidden agendas concerning boundary reviews'.

Extract from article in Brentwood Weekly News, 22 October 1999

The Commission warned officers and members that this would not be acceptable and that a different scheme would be needed once the formal review began.

Stage One

The Commission relies

> '...heavily on local authorities and other interested parties to put proposals to us on how electoral arrangements within their areas might be improved. We believe that the interests of local democracy are best served by basing our recommendations on electoral schemes which are generated locally, preferably following consultation

> with local interests, address the statutory criteria, and achieve a high level of electoral equality' (Guidance, 1998: para 23).

A review is started by the Commission giving formal notice in a letter to the local authority and inviting it to publicise the review further. A copy of this letter is sent to a range of interested parties including Members of Parliament and Members of the European Parliament for the area, local parish and town councils, the national headquarters of the main political parties, police authorities, and local authority associations. The Commission issues a news release, takes out public notices in local papers, provides leaflets and posters to local authorities for display, and distributes its guidance document. It also announces and tracks the progress of each review on its web-site.

Stage One is mainly a passive stage for the Commission, as proposals and representations are being prepared. Officers are, however, involved in facilitating the work of any interested party in producing a submission. The Review Team will normally begin this process by checking all the background data (current and projected electorates) provided by the local authority for any inaccuracies or obvious anomalies. The Review Manager responds to any queries the Review Leader has received from a local authority and may attend a meeting with a parish council or similar organisation. Salisbury District Council, for example, carried out a Stage One consultation exercise on two district-wide options. Details of both schemes were sent to a wide range of interested individuals and local organisations. The council's two options were also considered in turn by its four area committees (City, Southern, Western and Northern). We attended the City Area Committee meeting on 26 March 1998 at which the Commission's Review Leader for Salisbury gave a presentation on the role of the Commission and emphasised the need to achieve good electoral equality and to guard against any gerrymandering. Thirty minutes were set aside for the public to ask questions of the Commission officer and make comments and suggestions.

Commission officers may also arrange to meet local authority officers and members to discuss the review process. A good working relationship between the review team at the Commission and the officer responsible for the review in a local authority is vital for the smooth-running of the process. During the most recent reviews in London, Commission officers arranged meetings with chief officers from every borough, and in many authorities also met members on an all-party basis. During Stage One, Commission officers respond to all enquiries from the public about the review process and the rules of the review. Submissions are usually sent to the Commission in the last few weeks.

Stage Two

This is the stage during which the Commission's proposals are prepared by the Review Leader in consultation with the Review Manager. The process begins with the Review Leader and Manager examining the council's submission. They are already likely to know what is in the submission, as contact with the authority should have been maintained throughout Stage One. In some cases, a review officer may have asked the local authority to strengthen its argument in certain places. The Commission argues that a strong council submission shows that there has been good engagement from the authority in the process. Commission officers have little detailed knowledge of the authorities being reviewed because the PER process is mostly desk-based. The Commission is reliant upon representations from the local authority, political parties and the general public. Officers from the Commission do, however, make visits to each reviewed authority at Stage Two. The Review Manager and Review Leader meet officers from the council and are given a guided tour of the area. The tour places particular focus on areas where problems may arise. It is difficult, if not impossible, to understand communities by simply visiting an authority for a day, but the visit does allow officers to give some context to boundaries which they have so far only seen drawn on a map. A comment from one response to the Commission's own stakeholder survey makes the point,

> 'We arranged two visits to the area by the Commission staff. We believe these visits are important in allowing the Commission a better understanding of local boundaries, features etc.'

The FMPR considered the idea of officers spending more time in a reviewed authority,

> '...but there would be a risk of additional exposure to unmediated lobbying. Review teams would no doubt be able to handle any such pressure, but the possibility of appearing to allow one faction more access than another could make it more difficult to demonstrate impartiality later, particularly if the Commission's recommendations turned out to be finely-balanced' (FMPR, 1999: para 5.11).

On 21 May 1998, we accompanied Commission officers on a guided tour of Swindon. Three council officers who had been working on the review began the day by briefing the Review Manager and Review Leader on the local authority's scheme. A number of maps were displayed in the council offices and these were examined by the Commission before a tour of the borough began. A minibus was used to visit a large number of wards in a journey which lasted more than an hour. On the one hand, council officers had a list of potentially contentious wards they wanted to show the Commission; for their part, Commission staff also had a list of wards they were especially interested in visiting. During the tour officers explained why the council had opted for particular boundaries. When prompted, they also offered their opinion on their favoured option in certain wards. The tour provided the Commission with information which helped in its deliberations. For example, they were able to gauge at first hand the distance and lines of communication between two communities they were minded to unite in a three-member rural ward.

Back in the office the Review Leader begins the analysis of the representations. If only a single scheme has been submitted to the Commission the electoral variances and boundaries are examined and improvements sought. Where there are two or more schemes, the first task is to identify areas of agreement and/or discrepancy. Are the same boundaries used in different schemes and where are the likely 'problem areas'? The ward electorates for each scheme are entered into a database to examine their respective electoral equalities. The schemes are then marked on to maps to compare the types of boundary used (e.g. roads, rivers etc.). The Review Leader will agree a preferred scheme with the Review Manager, and arranges what is known as a 'brain storming' session with the Director of Reviews (The Chief Executive has now taken over most of the responsibilities of the Director of Reviews in the review process). The 'brain-storming' meeting is held as soon as possible after receiving representations, but is often delayed when there are problems with a scheme. Problems could include inaccuracies, omissions or optimistic electorate projections. The Commission sees the 'brain-storming' as being a critical check in the process of drafting recommendations, and because it takes place for every review, it is another way the Commission can demonstrate that its approach is consistent. The Director of Reviews/Chief Executive acts as an intermediary between the officers and the Commissioners. S/he might suggest to the review team that if they make certain improvements to the scheme, it is more likely to be successful when it is put forward at a meeting of Commissioners. The Director of Reviews was regarded as taking a strict line on electoral equality. He often questioned the imbalances in a scheme and addressed how they could be improved. For example, during the review of Exeter, a couple of wards were proposed in urban areas with electoral variances of between 6% and 7%. The Review Manager and Review Leader were instructed to re-draw the boundaries in order to reduce the variances.

We attended one of these 'brain-storming' sessions at the Commission on 21 January 1999. The Review Manager and Review Leader discussed various options for redrawing the boundaries in the London Borough of Croydon with the Director of Reviews. The meeting began with the assumption that the Director of Reviews knew nothing about this particular review. The officers explained what had happened in the review, where the problem areas were (in this case, with the electorate projections), and summarised the submissions received. The Commission prefers a consensus to be reached at local authority level, but if there cannot be total agreement, then it at least seeks common ground between submissions on broad principles such as the size of the council and the number of members to be elected in each ward. The Review Leader placed a transparency of each borough-wide submission in turn over the current arrangements, searching for such lines of agreement on boundaries and for potential problem areas. Initially, the Review Team used the Official Monster Raving Loony Party (OMRLP) Option 1 scheme as the template from which to seek some consensus. This led to discussions about the type of housing in a particular area, the existence and distribution of major and minor roads, the relevance of distinct town centres, and the role of geographical features such as railway lines in making good boundaries. Particular attention was paid to three issues. Each submission had discussed the importance of preserving community identity, but Commission officers took the view that ward boundaries were not as important in dividing communities in London as elsewhere because people in the capital are more concerned about belonging to a place. The 'brain storming' also examined the submissions to see how they proposed councillors to be distributed between the north and the south of the borough, using Addiscombe Road as the boundary. Under the Review Team's initial proposal there would have been 33 councillors in the northern wards and 37 in the southern ones. It was decided that the scheme should be altered to improve the balance. No mention was made of the political battleground in the middle of the borough. Finally, and most importantly, the various submissions were rigorously analysed in terms of their proposed electoral equality.

We concluded from our observation of this meeting that all the borough-wide schemes received equal consideration, whether they came from the majority party or from the OMRLP. It was also clear that Commission staff place a high value on submissions or parts of submissions which back their case with evidence. In Croydon, a set of supporting photographs provided by the Labour party and the lack of evidence in other representations helped the formulation of the recommendations. Once the 'brain-storming' has taken place and any alterations have been made, the Review Leader will draft the Draft Recommendations and liaise with Ordnance Survey over mapping. The officers' draft report produced after this session was discussed by Commissioners at their February meeting. The Commission ended up using parts of all schemes.

We also followed the Commission's decision-making process at Stage Two in one of the least problematic reviews, that for Kennet in Wiltshire. The drafting of the Commission's report was helped by the fact that the council's single, 'consensus' submission was very good. The figures were accurate, there was good documentation on each new ward, there was evidence of a significant amount of consultation, and the submission paid attention to the rules regarding electoral equality and community ties. Nonetheless, Commission officers were not convinced by the whole of the council's scheme and made four changes to it. The two-way process between Commission and authority now became evident. The Commission emphasised in its Draft Recommendations that they were putting ideas forward for consultation, and were willing to respond to strong feelings from individuals and parish councils that a better option was available. For its part, the council accepted the reasoning and evidence behind one of the changes made by the Commission, but stuck by its original proposals in the other cases.

Public Meetings

Many regard public meetings as an important part of any consultation process. The Local Government Boundary Commission, as we have seen, made considerable use of public meetings in local areas to review boundary proposals and appointed Assistant Commissioners specifically for that purpose. The LGCE stated in the first edition of its Guidance that at Stage Two, 'It may also wish to hold an informal public meeting to gather further evidence to inform its draft recommendations' (Guidance, 1996: para 48). However, this sentence was dropped in the second edition of the Guidance. The Commission explains that,

> 'We have no powers to hold public local enquiries. However, we may decide to hold an informal local public meeting. From experience to date, public meetings are likely to be the exception rather than the rule' (Guidance, 1998: para 100).

There needs to be fundamental disagreement on an important issue such as council size, together with a clear feeling within the Commission that 'further evidence' is needed before recommendations can be drawn up, before a public meeting is considered. It is important, therefore, that officers can sense tensions within an authority at the earliest opportunity. If the Commission believes it has all the relevant evidence and knows the issues, a public meeting will not be necessary. Sometimes the Commission may be unsure on some minor matters. In such cases, the Draft Recommendations will state that an initial meeting will not be held, but hold out the possibility of having one at a later stage in the review process. However,

> 'Mere contention is not enough to justify a meeting as many reviews will be politically contentious: the primary determinant will be whether a meeting is likely to add sufficiently to the available evidence to justify the expense and the time involved' (Staff Manual: para 101).

The rule of thumb seems to be that any public meeting must be likely to be useful to the Commission in its work. One should not take place purely for the benefit of the local authority or a political party.

The Chairman and Chief Executive decide whether a public meeting is to be held at the beginning of Stage Two of a PER. The Chief Executive informs the Commissioners of their decision at the next Commission meeting. An Assessor is then appointed to chair the public meeting. S/he considers the representations made to the Commission, chairs the meeting, and then reports to the Commission making any recommendations. According to the first edition of the Commission's Guidance, any public meeting held during Stage Four is chaired by a Commissioner, not an Assessor. The Commission does not keep a record of the number of requests for public meetings, but says that it,

> '...received quite a number in the first year or two of the PER programme – there seemed to be an expectation that public meetings (or inquiries) should be held as a matter of course. However, this tailed off quite significantly as the Commission's approach and policies became more understood by our stakeholders' (private correspondence: 2 February 2000).

At the time of writing public meetings have been held in ten authorities: Blackburn, Bristol, Bromley, Durham, Isle of Wight, Northampton, South Hams, Surrey Heath, Taunton Deane, and Warrington. Commission officers had expected to have to hold more public meetings in the London boroughs because of the high level of party political organisation in the capital. In the event, however, a clearer exposition of the process at preliminary briefings, together with a surprising degree of co-operation between the political parties in the drawing up of local authority submissions, resulted in a meeting being required only in Bromley.

Some examples of the issues at stake and the outcomes of the meetings are given below:

Bristol (Labour controlled) – A public meeting was held during Stage Two to clarify three important issues in the review. The Commission needed more evidence on the preferred size of the council, the number of councillors that should represent each ward, and any relevant factors that needed to be taken into consideration before the boundaries were re-drawn. The Commission had received four city-wide schemes. The City Council wanted to retain the present council size of 68 with 34 two-member wards. The Liberal Democrat group also wanted a structure of two-member wards, but with a total of 35 wards and 70 members. The Conservative associations preferred a scheme of 72 single-member wards. Finally, the Labour group also suggested a 72 member scheme, but with 24 three-member wards. After a great deal of discussion, the Commission decided that the City Council would be best served by 35 two-member wards.

Bromley (Liberal Democrat led minority) – A public meeting was held during Stage Two to discuss the size of the council. Before the review Bromley was served by 60 councillors. The Conservative group on the council was in favour of keeping the same size of council. The borough council's scheme was for 23 three-member wards – a council size of 69. It argued that as Bromley was the largest borough in London by area and had one of the largest councillor/elector ratios, electors in the borough were currently under-represented. The Commission concluded that there was little objective evidence to support such an increase in council size.

Durham (Labour controlled) – A public meeting was held during Stage Two. First, there was no agreement on council size. The Liberal Democrat group on the council wanted to reduce it from 49 to 30, whereas the City Council proposed a council size of 51. Second, while both the City Council and the Liberal Democrat group wanted to retain the mixed pattern of single and multi-member wards, the Independent members on the council preferred multi-member wards only. Third, the Commission sought further evidence on how best to avoid a 'detached ward' in the authority. The existing Croxdale ward in Durham was detached in the sense that although being represented by a single councillor, it comprised two geographically disconnected parts separated from each other by another ward. The Commission recommended that the council would be best served by a council of 50 members in a mixed warding structure, but did manage to produce a scheme without a detached ward – see Box 4.4.

Isle of Wight (Liberal Democrat controlled) – The Isle of Wight was one of just two authorities where a public meeting was held only during Stage Four. The Isle of Wight's electoral arrangements had last been reviewed as recently as 1993 as part of the LGCE's structural review, and implemented in 1995. As a county council, all electoral divisions in the Isle of Wight were required to be single member. The scheme which the council put forward was backed by most representations and supported the retention of the existing boundaries as they clearly reflected local communities and had had little time to 'bed down'. However, the Commission maintained that significant electoral imbalances needed rectifying, with 30 out of the 48 divisions having variances in excess of +/-10%. The Commission therefore designed its own scheme with 47 councillors and consulted upon this at Stage Three. It received an above average number of representations (47), the majority of which argued against the proposed warding and/or splitting of parishes. These views were reinforced at the public meeting and led the Commission to make substantial changes from what it had proposed in the Draft Recommendations. In its Final Recommendations, the Commission opted to retain the existing 48 councillors and to encompass whole parishes within electoral divisions. These changes had a dramatic effect on electoral equality. There would now be eighteen divisions with electoral variances greater than +/-10% compared with four under the Commission's draft scheme. In the Final Recommendations the Commission states that it,

> '... has sought to take account of the very specific circumstances on the Isle of Wight in formulating its final recommendations. It would like to have seen an even greater improvement in electoral equality but accepts that, in the light of the evidence received, this would have been to the detriment of the interests of local communities' (Final Recommendations, 1997: para110).

Box 4.4 Redrawing boundaries in the southern part of Durham City Council

Under existing boundaries the Croxdale ward was divided into two detached parts.

Durham existing boundaries

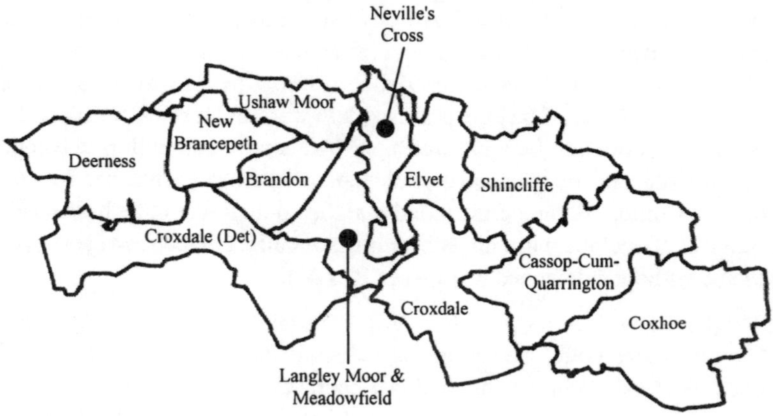

A significant revision of boundaries in the area was required to do away with the detached ward whilst at the same time achieving acceptable electoral equality.

Durham final recommendations

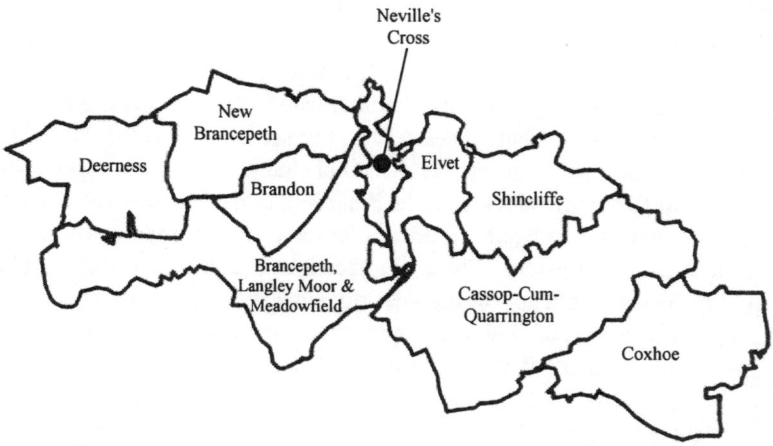

Source: based on maps published in the LGCE's Final Recommendations for Durham
© Crown Copyright

Northampton (Labour controlled) – Uniquely, two public meetings were held during the course of this review – one at Stage Two and the other at Stage Four – to seek evidence relating to differences in the three borough-wide schemes submitted. For example, the Commission wanted to investigate the reasons for the different ward boundaries proposed for the centre of town. For their part the council and the political parties wanted an open and constructive debate on re-drawing the boundaries after previous problems in the authority (the council had submitted electoral schemes in 1992 and 1994). The review was actively contested by the local parties. The Commission used the Liberal Democrats' scheme as the basis for the new electoral arrangements.

Surrey Heath (Conservative controlled) – This was the other authority where a public meeting was held only during Stage Four. The Commission needed more evidence to help it re-draw the boundaries in four wards in the Camberley area north of the M3 – see Box 4.5. At the draft stage the Commission had recommended that the boundaries follow those proposed by the borough council rather than those submitted by Surrey Heath Labour Party. During Stage Three the local Labour Party, with support from the Liberal Democrat group and the majority of representations from individuals, opposed the Commission's scheme for this area. The Labour Party argued that its proposals produced better electoral equality and used natural boundaries which reflected local communities. According to Labour, the Council's scheme, 'splits up the low density housing area into three wards, despite the obvious common interest and similarity across the whole of this area. It is an example of gerrymandering designed to exclude poorer people from proper representation on the Council' (Final Recommendations, 1998: paras 53 and 63). However, following the meeting, the Commission decided to confirm its Draft Recommendations in this area,

> 'We remain of the view that the advantages of retaining broadly the existing ward pattern outweigh the arguments for making radical changes to wards, and are not persuaded that wards should be based on socio-economic factors as an accurate reflection of communities' (Draft Recommendations, 1998: para 74).

The Commission sent a survey to the assessors who conducted the first nine completed public meetings asking for their opinion on matters including the briefing material provided by the Commission, possible improvements to the process and the function of public meetings. Given the infrequency of public meetings, the Commission subsequently decided that the surveys were of decreasing value and no longer carries them out. All assessors rated the evidence and briefing material provided by the Commission as being either 'good' or 'excellent'. A few respondents complained that they needed more time to absorb the considerable amount of detail.

Box 4.5 Redrawing boundaries in that part of Surrey Heath north of the M3 motorway

The Labour party's proposals involved re-configuring the St. Michaels and Watchetts wards so that the boundary ran roughly north to south rather west to east.

Surrey Heath existing boundaries

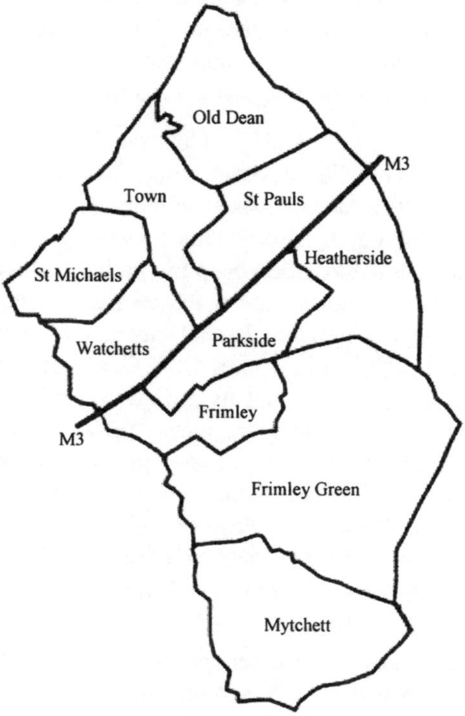

Contd./

One assessor explained,

> 'I recollect that I did find it a little difficult in the short time available to me before the public meeting to sort out from all the material what the actual issues were, what options existed and which the LGCE in principle preferred. Blackburn was not a town that I had ever visited: indeed I barely knew where it was!'.

One assessor took this problem in hand and wrote of his experience,

> 'I asked the Commission's staff to give me a conducted tour and briefing prior to the meeting. This provided essential background knowledge of the area, its

Box 4.5 continued

The Commission was not persuaded to revise the borough council's and its own original proposal and left the boundaries in this area virtually unchanged.

Surrey Heath final recommendations

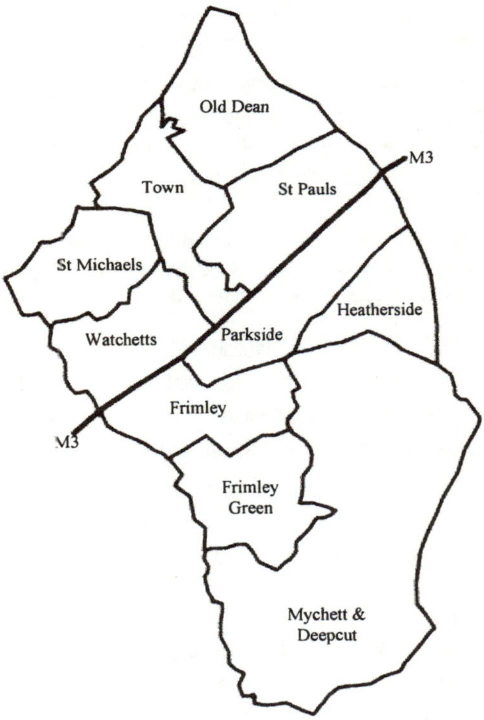

Source: based on maps published in the LGCE's Final Recommendations for Surrey Heath © Crown Copyright

topography and made some of the relationships evident. I considered it a vital part, even though it was not formally included in the process'.

The Commission asked the assessors what the organisation could have done to improve the public meeting process. Some respondents suggested that there needed to be greater liaison between assessors to share experiences,

> 'It would be interesting to hear how other assessors got on in tackling their tasks. Did they find more difficulty with urban issues than rural ones and if so, how did they resolve them?'

Another assessor believed that the Commission ought to consider the length of the meetings,

> 'Had we got involved in a detailed discussion of urban boundary issues, as well we might have done, then the time allowed (two and a half hours) would not have been sufficient. I do feel that this is something that the Commission needs to think about'.

Finally, the survey asked assessors for their overall judgement on public meetings. The feeling of assessors was very positive as the two quotations indicate below,

> 'The idea of public meetings is clearly thought to be helpful by those involved locally, and the involvement of an 'outsider' like myself underlined the impartial nature of the proceedings. I hope it was thought that the outside assessors did provide some added value, as some additional evidence of the seriousness with which the Commission received local views.'

> 'I got the local impression that everyone involved thought the arrangements added value to the process, and were entirely happy with the arrangements at the public meeting which had been widely advertised, and was well attended.'

Public meetings allow the Commission to be seen to listen, to defuse local tensions, and to help reassure local authorities, political parties and others that the process is as impartial as it is possible to be. However, such meetings remain exceptional and just two have been held since Ms Stephens took up her post in August 1998.

Commission meetings

Commission meetings are held primarily to consider Draft and Final Recommendations. They normally take place in the fourth week after the submission date in order to allow enough time to brief Commissioners and prepare a detailed scheme. Each Commissioner receives summary information on every review to be discussed about a week before the meeting. This will include an introduction to the authority and a note on its political composition, a summary of all the representations received, a map and a table showing both the existing arrangements and the proposed wards in the Draft Recommendations, a description of what has happened during Stage One, the recommendations being put forward by officers at this stage, and 'key factors which have resulted in the remaining imbalances'. The Commissioner with a 'particular interest' in a review, together with the Chairman, will also receive a copy of the draft Draft Recommendations. This is written by the Review Leader with help from the Review Manager.

We were invited by the Commission to attend two Commissioners' meetings. The first meeting on 21 January 1999 included discussion of the final reports for the

Wiltshire district authorities and the draft report for the London Borough of Richmond-upon-Thames. The second meeting on 27 July 1999 discussed fourteen reports – a mixture of Draft and Final Recommendations including the Final Recommendations for the London boroughs of Croydon and Westminster. The Commissioners used to discuss about six or seven reports in a meeting, but the accelerated work schedule has resulted in more reports being tabled. They have also speeded up the way reviews are dealt with at meetings, not only because there are more reports, but because both they and officers have gained experience of the process. On average, much more time is spent discussing the Draft Recommendations at a Commission meeting than the Final Recommendations.

Normally, the Director of Reviews (now, the Records Officer) gives an overview report at the beginning of each Commission meeting. This report sets out contextual information on the reviews in process, considers issues which have arisen from the current programme, and provides an analysis of the latest completed reviews and how far they meet the Commission's criteria. Statistics are produced on how electoral equality has been improved by the reviews and figures are compared to those produced by the LGBC. For example, the reports prepared on reviews undertaken in 1997/8 and 1998/9 clearly demonstrated not only their impact on average electoral imbalances within local authorities, but also the degree to which the LGCE had been able to reduce these averages compared with the LGBC – see Table 4.1. Information is also prepared on council size compared to electorate growth, the number and type of wards (single/multi-member), and the electoral cycle. Discussions then begin on individual reviews. These are led by the relevant Review Manager giving a five minute summary of progress and recommendations, and highlighting any problems such as areas over which there is disagreement between the representations received or where the electoral variance is high. The Commission makes it clear that,

> 'The Commissioner with a particular interest in the review is not responsible for making recommendations to the Commission. This is the responsibility of officers. Individual officers can of course raise particular issues at Commission meetings and the Commission will then make a decision as a corporate body' (Memo to FMPR, 1998).

If any Commissioner has concerns about any part of the scheme, s/he can raise it at a Commission meeting. Commission meetings are an arena where the consistency of the judgements made by the organisation can be examined. For example, is one review accepting a particular argument in allowing a high variance in a ward, when in another authority, the same argument is being rejected? One Commissioner described his role as being 'quality control'. Commissioners should cross-question officers to see if they are missing any tricks, and check that the scheme is properly thought through and consistent. In practice, Commissioners rarely change officers' reports because they will have produced recommendations which comply with the rules of the process. On the other hand, if an officer had put forward a scheme which included a number of large electoral imbalances, there would be problems.

Table 4.1 Average ward electoral imbalances within reviewed authorities, 1997/8 and 1998/9

	Before review	*After review*	*After previous LGBC review*	*N*
1997/8	15.3	5.4	10.5	33
1998/9	15.6	4.3	13.3	39

If a review is not contentious, Commissioners will quickly pass over it to concentrate on an authority where there are problems. For example, the Final Recommendations for Kennet – see above – were discussed by Commissioners for only four minutes. At the Commission meeting in July 1999, Commissioners finalised the Final Recommendations for Croydon is less than a minute. An officer explained what changes had been made to the Draft Recommendations, and highlighted the wards with the highest levels of electoral inequality. The 'lead' Commissioner then said that everything was fine and the review team had done a good job. One Commissioner told us, 'If everyone has done their job, then the Commissioners' meeting is a rubber stamp'. Perhaps one or two reviews at every Commission meeting prompt more extensive discussion. The Final Recommendations for Tower Hamlets were discussed for more than fifteen minutes. Here, the Commissioner with a particular interest did not agree with the review team in one small wedge of the borough, and his proposed amendment was accepted by other Commissioners. The majority of the time, however, was spent discussing the name of a ward – Spitalfields or Banglatown. Commissioners discussed the historical origins of the Spitalfields name, and also the argument in favour of having a name which described the Bangladeshi community now living in that area. The Commission decision was to call the ward, Spitalfields and Banglatown! (See Chapter 5 for local press coverage of this issue.) Commissioners may also consider making changes where they believe a number of representations containing good evidence have been received, but not taken sufficiently into account. When changes have been required following a Commission meeting, officers have only a few days to make them before the report goes to the printers. This re-write used to be completed without reference back to the Commissioners. However, the FMPR recommended that,

> 'The Commissioners should consider whether they are satisfied with the current arrangements for approving reports, whether they feel that their personal position

> is adequately safeguarded and whether further codification is required' (FMPR, 1999: para 5.39).

The Chief Executive of the Commission argued that there was nothing fundamentally wrong with the current system, but the Commission have now agreed a protocol for signing-off reports. This includes a clause which requires, at the discretion of the Chief Executive, clearance by the Chairman of any changes of substance.

Much general discussion at Commission meetings concerns the tensions and the need to strike a balance between the quantitative (electoral equality) and the qualitative (community interests) review criteria. Interviews have revealed that broadly Commissioners are of a common mind, insofar as they start with the aim of electoral equality and then assess the arguments relating to communities and local ties. Although one interviewee suggested that there are two clear schools of thought in the Commission regarding the rules of PERs – those who pursue electoral equality and those who have more concern for community interests, it seems that adherents of the primacy of community must make a very strong case to persuade other colleagues that they are right. One former Commissioner in particular seems to have found it difficult to accept certain Commission decisions, and twice wrote to the Chairman to explain his concerns. In an interview with us he gave an example of the kind of issue that disturbed him. Supposing there were two distinct communities, each currently represented by a single councillor and with electoral variances of +9% and –11% respectively. In its attempts to achieve electoral equality the Commission proposes that these two communities should be combined to form a new two-member ward. He would then wish to argue, from his experience 'on the ground', that people are not concerned about such precise electoral equality between wards. Rather, residents are far more interested in preserving communities which, in some instances, have been in place for hundreds of years. In practical terms too, the formation of a single two-member ward covering both communities is likely to mean that a councillor represents a large geographical area and there may be problems if it so happens that both councillors are drawn from one community. He accepted that the boundaries of a large number of wards had been agreed by the Commission as the result of community identity arguments. However, in a small number of 'outlier' cases, striking an appropriate balance between the criteria was a real issue, and he had lost more often than he had won when it came to making decisions about them.

Stage Three

Stage Three marks the publication of the Commission's Draft Recommendations and its consultation upon them. A copy of the Recommendations is normally sent to all those who received the letter announcing the start of the review and/or made submissions during Stage One, as well as their publication being announced in the local press. Copies of the report are available in local libraries and the Commission requests authorities to have copies available for public inspection. Reports can also be requested direct from the Commission, and have recently been put on the LGCE's web-site on the day of publication.

Stage Three does not usually involve Commission staff in much day-to-day work. However, occasionally there are problems to be resolved. Following the publication of the Draft Recommendations for the Wiltshire authorities, we attended a 'trouble-shooting' meeting held under the auspices of the Wiltshire Local Government Association at North Wiltshire District Council on 13 October 1998. The meeting had been arranged by West Wiltshire District Council and North Wiltshire District Council to discuss the guidance issued by the Commission on multi-member wards and annual elections following the publication of the government's White Paper. The Chief Executive of West Wiltshire, whose authority had made no submission to the Commission at Stage One, had written to the Commission on behalf of the Wiltshire LGA to suggest that the reviews be suspended pending the government's decision on electoral issues. The meeting was attended by representatives from four of the five authorities in Wiltshire. At the meeting, councillors complained that the whole PER process was a waste of money because the boundaries would have to be changed again if the government introduced annual elections within multi-member wards. The Chief Executive of the Commission explained that the Commission could not suspend the PERs because they were already running late on the statutory timetable. She advised attendees not to expect overnight change, as it could takes years for the White Paper to become an Act of Parliament, and annual elections could be achieved with the present mix of single and multi-member wards. An additional four weeks was granted to the Wiltshire authorities to reconsider their pattern of warding.

The meeting also gave local authorities the chance to complain to the Chief Executive about the Draft Recommendations. Councillors suggested that communities had been neglected for the sake of electoral equality. One Salisbury member commented, 'Villages that share a village hall have now been divided. Valleys have been completely ignored. Parishes have written letters to the Commission, but they have been ignored'. The Chief Executive of West Wiltshire District Council took the complaint a step further. He suggested that there should be a legal challenge to change the balance between electoral equality and community interests. He argued that people who work in local government understood that community is more important than numbers. Why, for example, should Warminster receive three votes and Wylye Valley only one vote on the council? He did not accept that that was electoral equality. The Commission responded that the councils should lobby the national LGA, who in turn would lobby the government, if they wished the legislation to be changed. It was put to us by sources in Wiltshire that it was significant that the two authorities which organised the meeting were the only ones in the county controlled by the Liberal Democrats. They were particularly unhappy with the Draft Recommendations and saw an opportunity to make political capital out of the review in advance of whole council elections in 1999. The Wiltshire district whose PER had caused least controversy, Kennet, believed that the new arrangements would have some currency and improve electoral equality for the time being. No representative from Kennet attended the meeting.

Stage Four

Stage Four is the final stage in the review process. All representations received following the publication of the Draft Recommendations are analysed by the review team and possible changes are discussed. In exceptional circumstances a public meeting may be held, but the Commission will not consider new authority-wide schemes at this stage of the review. The officers' proposals for the final report are then put before the Commission. It is easier for officers to produce a final report than a draft report, as the bulk of the ground work has been completed. If the Draft Recommendations have been generally accepted by the authority and its residents, there is often little for officers to change. The Commission also demands strong evidence and public support before it moves away from the draft report. Before the publication of the final report, the review team audit all the submissions made to the Commission to ensure that the views in each representation have been addressed. The same arrangements are made to advertise the publication of the Final Recommendations as the Draft Recommendations.

Following the publication of the Final Recommendations, there is a period of six weeks during which interested parties can make representations direct to the Secretary of State. During the third year of the current round of PERs (1998/9), an average of nine representations were received for each review. It is the Secretary of State's decision whether to accept or change the Commission's recommendations. However, the government has stated in Parliament that,

> 'It is important that the process for making local authority electoral arrangements should be seen to be independent. For this reason, it is the Government's intention not to modify the substance of electoral arrangements from the Local Government Commission' (17 December 1996).

Nevertheless, there are stakeholders who believe that the Secretary of State might be persuaded to overturn the Commission's decision. In Northumberland, town councillors in Morpeth were against the final recommendation of the Commission to move Morpeth Central into the same ward as Pegswood and Longhirst. The local press reported that members had raised with the Commission objections made by the public during the consultation exercise, but that they had been ignored. 'Chairman of (Morpeth) Town Council, Coun. Mrs Ann Patterson, said that the people of Middle Green were totally against it and former Chairman, Coun. Jim Rudd alleged that the recommendations were 'completely flawed'' (*Morpeth Herald*, 6 January 2000). A letter of complaint was sent to the Secretary of State, but a reply informed the local residents that it was policy to accept the recommendations of the Local Government Commission. In practice, as we shall see, the government does occasionally make minor changes to the Commission's Final Recommendations when it issues the Orders to implement the PERs.

The Commission's reports

In both the Draft and Final Recommendations the Commission attempts to demonstrate the transparency of its approach to PERs. Unlike many of their LGBC equivalents, these reports not only set out the Commission's proposals, but also explain the reasoning behind its decisions on a ward by ward basis. They also summarise all the representations received and refer to them in the text where relevant. Although it must follow the legislation and 'rules', each review is different and the Commission needs to justify the decisions it makes. The Commission argues that consistency is the by-word of the reports, although this is sometimes disputed by stakeholders. For example, during the London borough reviews, the A406 road (the North Circular) was treated differently as a boundary in two different reviews. The Commission insisted, however, that this was not necessarily a sign of inconsistency, rather a recognition that an identifiable community may breach the road in some places and not in others. The Commission always aims to leave no doubt among the readers of its Recommendations why it favoured one particular viewpoint rather than another.

Between 1996 and 1999, both the Draft and Final Recommendations were published in a high quality, glossy format. This was a carry over from the structural reviews and attracted some criticism. By contrast, the reports issued by the Scottish and Welsh Local Government Boundary Commissions are clearly produced at less expense. An assessor of a public meeting wrote in May 1997 that,

> 'Consideration should be given to produce something more basic and functional until the Final Recommendations are produced'.

In 1999 the FMPR took up the theme, calling for the Commission to,

> '... explore the potential cost savings that would arise from preparing Draft Recommendations reports in-house as desktop-published or word processed documents' (FMPR, 1999: para 5.36).

New style reports, which stylistically are mid-way between the old format and the Scottish/Welsh reports, were published for the first time in December 1999.

Orders

It is for the Department of the Environment, Transport and the Regions to decide when to publish the Statutory Instruments containing the Orders which give effect to new electoral arrangements. Sometimes there has been a considerable gap between the publication of the Final Recommendations and the Orders. In the case of the eleven districts in Surrey, for example, there was a full year between these events. Interviewees have suggested to us that the DETR had not been geared up for the increased throughput of reviews from the Commission. The Department also seemed to hold back following the publication of the government's White Paper in order to be sure that what it was recommending was going to be long lasting. The FMPR recommended that,

> 'The Department should give an undertaking that it will aim to make Orders within three months of the expiry of the six weeks allowed for representations to the Secretary of State and will let the Commission and the relevant local authorities know within a month of the expiry of these six weeks if, for any reason, it is unable or unwilling to do so in a particular case' (FMPR, 1999: para 5.50).

A further problem for the DETR has concerned when the initial elections using the new boundaries should be held. In Spelthorne, for example, the Department had initially proposed that the new boundaries would be used for the first time in 2001. This would not only have clashed with the county council elections, but would also have meant that those councillors elected in 1999 would serve only half of their expected four year term. In the event the government decided that Spelthorne will now hold elections on new boundaries in 2003. This decision has had a knock on effect across the reviewed authorities. All-out elections to determine the composition of the council following a PER are now held on the first occasion that they can co-incide with already scheduled contests in that authority. Hence the six districts in Surrey which have annual elections chose their new councils on their normal May election day in 2000, whereas the four (including Spelthorne) which have a four yearly electoral cycle must wait until their next due elections in 2003.

It is very rare for the Secretary of State to alter the Final Recommendations coming from the LGCE except where mistakes of fact have been made. Occasionally, however, the Recommendations are implemented 'with modifications', these usually involving changes to the names of wards. For example, 'The Mundens' in East Hertfordshire became 'Mundens and Cottered', and 'Macclesfield Upton' in Macclesfield became 'Macclesfield Broken Cross'. More significantly, the Commission's Recommendation in March 1997 that Purbeck should hold elections on a whole council basis was revoked by the District of Purbeck (Electoral Changes) Order September 1998, with the council being obliged to revert to its previous practice of elections by thirds. At the time this was a unique case and reflected the government's wish to prevent the number of councils with annual elections being reduced.[1]

Conclusions

We have tried in this chapter to give an impression of the work that the Commission and its staff do during the course of a Periodic Electoral Review. It is clear that the LGCE places a premium on a co-operative and constructive relationship with its 'client' local councils. For whilst it retains the legal and moral authority to insist on getting its own way, the various Stages of the review process are designed to maximise consultation and exchange between the Commission and local authorities, and between local authorities and other interested parties in their own area. Innovations such as the Preliminary Period and the designating of individual Commissioners as 'taking a particular interest' in a review help to assure local authorities that they are being given full and equal consideration as discrete individual cases. Not that the Commission always gets it right nor finds its Recommendations attracting universal approval. The correct balance between looking after the interests of communities and achieving electoral equality remains perhaps the most contentious aspect of the Commission's work. We have seen some examples of the attempts made to square this circle from the Commission's point of view. We now turn to look at PERs, and this and other issues, from the perspective of the local authorities.

---

1 In July 2000 a similar Order was made for Nuneaton and Bedworth, substituting the Commission's Final Recommendation for all-out elections with uneven election by thirds.

Chapter 5

The Periodic Electoral Review Process – the perspective of local authorities

For local authorities a Periodic Electoral Review often comes as an unwelcome, externally-driven addition to an already heavy workload. It is hardly surprising therefore that the Commission's attention can prompt irritation and resentment, and a feeling that there are more important matters to attend to than ensuring that the councillor/elector ratio in wards across the authority is as equal as possible. In an era in which it is rare for more than 4 in 10 eligible electors in any ward to vote in a local election, it is unlikely that electoral equity is a high priority among voters either. Nevertheless the PER must be faced, and in this chapter we reveal how local authorities play their part in the process. We use material gathered from the surveys of officers and councillors conducted both by ourselves and the LGCE, from detailed case studies of the review process in individual local authorities, and from monitoring local media coverage of reviews to examine the mechanics of getting from proposal to decision. The chapter covers preliminary planning, the calculation of projected electorate figures, the criteria used and the decision-making process in different councils, public consultations, and the reaction to the Commission's decisions. We also address the important question of how much PERs cost local authorities.

Preliminary planning

We explained in Chapter 4 that the Commission introduced a formal 'Preliminary Period' into the PER process in September 1997. This followed complaints from local authorities that they had been given little advance notice of the review. One authority commented that,

> 'We had no prior notice of the PER starting. The review was announced at the Association of Electoral Administrators' conference by the Home Office and started four weeks later. If I had not attended the conference, the notice would have been less. Otherwise, we would have planned for it' (North Kesteven).

The policy is now to inform local authorities approximately two to three months in advance of the start of the review. This preliminary period before Stage One allows them to plan how they are going to approach the review and to provide the Commission with information including:

- a schedule of electoral arrangements based on the current electoral register and a five-year forecast of change in electorate;
- an explanation of any significant variation between the current year's electorate in any ward and the five-year forecast for that ward;
- a map illustrating wards and polling districts in unparished areas;
- a topographical map of the local authority area illustrating parishes and parish ward boundaries, together with appropriately scaled maps(normally, but not necessarily, 1:10,000) of urban areas showing ward boundaries;
- a copy of the current electoral register for unparished urban areas;
- details of parish electoral arrangements; and
- a profile of the authority.

Before this lead in period was introduced, there was little evidence of preliminary planning before the start of Stage One. Such preparation as was carried out consisted, for example, of the formation of a review task force of councillors/chairmen of local political parties (Copeland), discussion of the PER with members and the Commission (Bristol), preliminary consultations with local town and parish councils (Congleton), analysis of existing problems/issues in terms of population (Halton), and the production of the electoral statistics (Hertsmere). It is now more common for local authorities to undertake significant preparatory groundwork. The review of Spelthorne began in September 1997. In advance of Stage One, the council had a meeting with the Commission's Director of Reviews and his staff, set up a working party, sent a report to the working party, devised three re-warding options, and showed a Commission representative around the Borough. In Exeter, the preliminary period was used to call together all councillors to formulate a strategy and to agree which officers would be assigned to the review. In Salisbury, the community were given an early chance to get involved as the council's Area Committees, which include parish councils, were alerted. In High Peak, a preparatory report was drafted for councillors on the main issues of the review; in West Wiltshire, all members of the council were asked for their preliminary views; in West Devon, meetings were held with ward members and parish councils were consulted; and in Teignbridge, a working party was set up in advance of the start of Stage One.

However, although the preliminary period was a well established part of the PER process by the time the London borough reviews began in 1998, ten of the sixteen boroughs for which we have information said that they did not carry out any preparations or consultations on the PER prior to the start of Stage One. For example,

> 'No – as Ealing was in the first tranche of the London boroughs there was little time to do this' (Ealing).

> 'No – there was insufficient time due to the very short notice of the start of the PER. The Chief Executive received advance warning of the review from the Commission, but this information was not filtered down to officers' (Harrow).

> 'No – there was no time to do so as our PER started immediately after local council elections' (Southwark).

Other boroughs explained that they did not start work on the review right away because there were more pressing council matters. Among those boroughs which did make preparations, Bexley 'pulled together' its electorate projections and Tower Hamlets 'recruited a temporary member of staff to undertake work on the review'. Elsewhere preparations included,

> 'A series of internal meetings and a meeting with Commission representatives prior to the start of Stage One. Raw data were placed on public deposit and sent to political parties in July 1998, prior to the start of the review in September 1998' (Kensington and Chelsea).

> 'Posters showing existing and proposed arrangements on display at libraries, council reception points, Neighbourhood Housing Offices with ballot paper for views. Articles and information in Council magazine delivered to each household' (Southwark).

Calculating the projected electorates

Perhaps the most important single task for local authorities involved in a PER is the calculation of projected electorates. The Commission bases its boundary recommendations on the likely distribution of electors across the authority five years from the time of the review. It is the local authority's responsibility to draw up these projections, but the Commission needs to be satisfied that they are realistic and defensible.

The method of calculating the electorate projections varies between local authorities. Some county councils prepare the projections for their lower tier councils. In Derbyshire, for example, a detailed paper was produced by the Policy and Research Division for the use of all district councils in the county. Similarly, in Shropshire, the basis for the electorate projections was agreed at county level, so all the districts worked from a common base. A wide range of information sources are used to calculate the projected electorate figures – see Box 5.1. These include the electoral register, dwelling completion forecasts, published population forecasts (including net migration figures), planning records, the Births, Deaths and Marriages Register and the County Structure Plan. The figures produced by the county council are occasionally altered by the districts who argue that they have additional relevant information on migration levels, the likely developments in the council area, and generally more specialised local knowledge than the county authority. In other cases estimates were produced by district planning departments with reference to the local plan, known/planned developments, known/anticipated population changes and the census. Once the future house building figures were calculated, they were multiplied by the average number of persons living in a household. The figure used varied between local authorities. In Hertsmere it was 2 electors per dwelling unit, in Congleton 1.89 electors, and in Three Rivers 1.75. In London the London Research Centre (LRC) was used by most boroughs to provide projections of electorate by ward. Individual boroughs then identified planning applications and other local knowledge to adjust these figures. In Harrow for example,

> 'We used the LRC's demographic projections of adult population produced at ward level. These projections take account of likely dwelling stock changes to 2003, based on information we had provided to the LRC. A ratio of electors to the adult population (based on 1997 and 1998 Electoral Registers) was applied to the projected 2003 population to provide a forecasted electorate for 2003.'

In practice, the Commission accept that projecting future electorates is an 'inexact science' and nearly always accept the figures provided by the local authorities. However one authority, which seemed to have an uneasy relationship with the Commission throughout its Review, commented that,

> 'At one stage the Commission appeared very worried by a 22 elector discrepancy in a projected electorate of 89,000 plus' (West Wiltshire).

In other cases councils highlighted problems forecasting their electorate in five years time. An officer from Peterborough wrote that,

> 'Our ability to project future electorate figures to help aid ward boundaries was fairly crude and in a growing city like Peterborough this was an issue which caused a number of problems.'

In one London borough,

> 'The forecasts were difficult to prepare due to trend information on areas smaller than existing wards. The London Research Centre had to develop new trend information to allow the process to be completed' (Barnet),

and in another,

> 'Population projections were problematic largely because it was discovered that the Council had not for some time been providing the London Research Centre with

details of new housing developments, demolitions etc. The nature of housing development in the Docklands area of the Borough where there are a large number of second homes/company properties makes electorate projections difficult' (Tower Hamlets).

BOX 5.1 Calculating electorate projections in Exeter

- Using the Chelmer housing model Devon County Council calculated that the Exeter electorate would rise from 80,612 in 1997 to 82,800 in 2003
- City Council used its own Land Availability Survey to forecast housing completions in each ward over the period 1997 to 2003
- Increase in electorate in each ward calculated as housing completions x 2 (representing 2 people over 18 per dwelling)
- Calculated increase added to 1997 electorate in each ward to produce 2003 forecast
- As total for all wards exceeded whole City estimates, figures had to be adjusted downwards. This was done by calculating the proportion of total electors in each ward in 2003 and applying that figure to the initial forecast of 82,800.

Source: Exeter City Council

Criteria used in local authority review submissions

We were interested in whether local authorities had any goals in relation to the preferred outcomes of their PERs, and the ways in which they went about trying to achieve them. Was their aim to gain an increase or decrease in council size, a re-balancing of the number of single and multi-member wards, or simply to emerge with as little as possible changed? In nearly all of our case study authorities a meeting was held in the early stages of the review to discuss the Commission's rules and procedures. In West Devon, members were informed by officers that no allowances would be made for rural areas or for sparsity of population, that they should aim for absolute electoral equality, and that if the council failed to submit a scheme the Commission would produce one of its own. In Harrow, the first meeting of the members' panel set a series of guidelines for the review. These included getting the Council's submission to be based on consensus; recasting the boundaries to have regard to natural communities and neighbourhoods, permanent geographical features, commercial centres and road patterns; using the 2003 electorate projections as the basis for the review; making no allowances for variations in registration levels between wards; and renaming wards only after the location and number of wards had been decided.

Minimal change

Many councillors and officers told us that their aim was one of minimal change consistent with achieving greater equality of representation. In West Devon they resolved, 'to get the best fit on the percentage electoral variances projected to 2003 with as little change as possible to existing wards'; in Kensington and Chelsea to cause 'least disruption to existing polling arrangements for voters'. Members often asserted that they had got to know their constituents (and local party activists) well over time and that major changes to boundaries would detrimentally affect those relationships. One councillor wrote that he wanted,

> 'Minimal change to the current warding within the acknowledged increase in population and under representation of some areas in the current ward structure' (Swindon);

another thought boundaries should be,

> 'Clearly defined, balanced, easily understood, fair geographically, historically sensible and sensitive, politically neutral: inevitably leading to minimal change' (Wellingborough).

Others put forward similar views,

> 'Our argument was that as the electoral boundaries were already quite adequate, and even the LGC acknowledged this, there was no need for any change or if change had to take place then it should be minimal' (Wandsworth);

> 'Our main criterion was to try to persuade the Commission to look at the peculiar circumstances of our district and not adhere to a merely mathematical population:member ratio. This led us to recommend the preservation of the status quo' (West Lindsey).

In some authorities there was a problem because councillors entered the review believing that if a ward had perfect electoral equality it should be left alone. In reality of course, because of the 'domino-effect' of making changes to boundaries elsewhere, a ward with perfect electoral equality may subsequently need to be altered. Despite the status quo being the admitted aim of a number of local authorities, this initial intent was often tempered by the Commission's insistence that 'no change' was not an option. Moreover, significant change was inevitable in the majority of cases simply because of the poor electoral equality figures.

Council size

Some local authorities took the view that if there needed to be changes, then an increase in the number of councillors was desirable. Two main factors seemed to account for this demand – unitary status and population growth. In Peterborough they argued that,

> 'Since the review was linked to our bid for unitary status, the authority worked on the principle of increasing its number of councillors to reflect the increase in responsibility'.

Another unitary authority (Thurrock) wished to increase the number of councillors in wards currently under-represented, while in the district of South Northamptonshire there was an assumption that population growth would lead to a small increase in council size. In Swindon, an increase in the size of the council was sought as a result of both structural change and the construction of more than 10,000 new houses –the largest single private housing development in Western Europe. Responses from only six authorities mentioned an aim of reducing the number of councillors. In South Shropshire, they wanted to reduce council size, as well as equalise representation between the urban and the sparsely populated rural areas. In Lewisham, a reduction in the number of councillors was thought to fit the new cabinet governance model. In Haringey, a councillor remarked that the review enabled the authority 'to take the opportunity to streamline councillor numbers in the light of the much reduced role for back-benchers under the 'Modernising Local Government' agenda'. A Conservative councillor in South Hams proposed reducing the number of councillors by one third, arguing that the changing nature of local government meant that there was no longer any need for the same number of councillors as in the 1970s and 1980s. In Shrewsbury and Atcham, the leader of the Conservative group tried to cover a number of bases. His criteria for the review were,

> 'Reduction of councillors from 48 to 40. Evening up of ward numbers of constituents which had become unbalanced by development. Minimal change where possible.'

Some authorities approached the same problem from the direction of the councillor/ elector ratio. One councillor wrote that the aim was to have 2,500 voters per councillor (North Somerset), while another respondent wished to achieve better electoral equality by having approximately 2,000 electors per councillor (East Hertfordshire).

Ward structures

For other local authorities the PER seemed to present an opportunity to change the structure of their wards. South Lakeland, West Wiltshire and Derbyshire Dales all had a preference for establishing single-member wards. Crewe and Nantwich, North Wiltshire, Salisbury and South Kesteven wanted single-member wards to be the norm in rural areas. Hertsmere was one of the few shire authorities explicitly to set out to achieve a maximum number of three-member wards in order to simplify the process for election by thirds. Such a stance was more common in London where it had been made clear by the Commission that movement towards a structure suitable for annual elections would be expected. Comments from officers included,

> 'As encouraged by the Commission, the Working Party opted for three-member wards' (Bexley);
>
> 'The Council accepted that it should have three member wards to allow annual elections in accordance with the Government's commitment' (Ealing);
>
> 'Preference for three-member wards as 'required' by the Commission' (Kensington and Chelsea);
>
> 'To accommodate likely move to annual elections, seventeen three-member wards were proposed' (Tower Hamlets).

The sole dissenting voice came from Wandsworth. One of the criteria used in the council's reponse to the LGCE's Draft Recommendations was,

> 'Minimal change. The Council rejected schemes based on wards with three-members in favour of a mixed two- and three-member ward scheme'.

It looked as if the Commission's interpretation of the White Paper had also been successfully fed through to councillors in London. Responses from members included,

> 'We were informed by officers that we *had* to accept that all wards would be three-member, and, therefore, that the option was simply how many' (Southwark);
>
> 'We were required to propose three-member wards, and we did so by relying on the notion of community. This borough breaks up into fairly well defined 'villages', defined by shopping centres, parks and road/railway boundaries' (Richmond-upon-Thames).

Parliamentary constituency boundaries

The relationship between local ward and parliamentary constituency boundaries is both important and symbiotic. The LGCE quite properly stated in the second edition of its Guidance,

> 'We are not required to have regard to Parliamentary constituency boundaries in developing our recommendations for new wards or changes to existing wards. Indeed, in order to address levels of electoral imbalance within a local authority area, it may be necessary to recommend a pattern of ward boundaries which does not coincide with constituency boundaries' (LGCE Guidance, 1998:14).

For its part, the Parliamentary Boundary Commission for England sets its face against proposing any constituencies which will involve the splitting of local authority electoral wards (Boundary Commission for England, 2000: 12). However, during the period between the implementation of a PER and the next parliamentary boundary review, wards can find themselves divided between constituencies. For example, the new Blunsdon ward in Swindon, which was used for the first time in the 2000 local elections, was split between the Swindon North and Swindon South parliamentary constituencies at the June 2001 general election. Several London boroughs clearly had parliamentary considerations in mind when they were thinking about their local electoral review. They looked for,

> 'Model ward options which would result in three equal Parliamentary constituencies, thus focusing on 18 and 21 ward models' (Barnet);
>
> 'Electoral equality of the Borough's three Parliamentary constituencies' (Wandsworth);
>
> 'The avoidance of boundary changes moving electors between parliamentary constituencies as far as possible' (Harrow);
>
> 'A reduced number of councillors to enable the three parliamentary constituencies to have equality of three-member wards' (Havering).

Community identity

Several authorities wished to use the review to improve the way in which ward boundaries defined the different communities and interests in the area. The aims mentioned included town centre coherence, open space unification, removing splits in coherent population (Wandsworth), giving priority to community identity and interests (Kettering), respecting identified community areas (West Wiltshire), keeping parished and unparished areas separate (Macclesfield), and removing long standing boundary anomalies (Merton).

In one London borough (Barnet), Labour members suggested that there was another reason why communities should be kept together. A councillor explained that there were wards in the borough which were very socially mixed. It became difficult to argue a case with central government for extra funding if areas were mixed and the deprivation index therefore not very high. Hence, grouping communities together would not only improve the current situation, but extra government money would benefit the whole of the borough. A participant at a public meeting in Barnet opposed the council's proposals on grouping communities together. He said that there was currently a good social balance in the north of the borough (Hadley and Arkley wards) and that the council's proposals would change this balance. For example, the new Underhill ward would consist of the Dollis Valley council estate. He argued that the council should be integrating, not dividing. The council's scheme would ghettoise the estate, and the people living in this deprived area would have less of an influence. Council officers responded to this complaint by saying that affluence was not a criterion in any of their proposals. Community identity and local ties are the guidelines. The council argued in its submission to the Commission that the proposed Underhill ward was clearly defined and that the area had an identity of its own.

The treatment of urban and rural areas was also seen as an important part of seeking to maximise community identity. A number of authorities stated that they had difficulties trying to keep the rural and urban parts apart and not combine them to improve electoral equality. In West Devon, the Liberal Democrats set out three principles for boundary revision:

- Don't bolt slices of town onto rural wards, so that town people are represented by rural members pursuing rural issues.
- Don't bolt slices of country onto towns so that rural people are represented by town members pursuing urban issues.
- Do establish a balance between the level of change and disruption (including community disruption), and the degree of equality achieved.

Party political factors

A small number of councillors who responded to our survey admitted that political motivations influenced the way in which they approached the PER. One member wanted, 'Minimal impact on the potential number of seats won (i.e. keep potential losses as low as possible)' (Chester); another mentioned 'survival' as his main criterion – we assume that this referred to his personal political survival. A councillor from Derbyshire Dales wrote of his party's criteria, 'Let's not pretend political considerations weren't there too!' In London, councillors openly admitted that they aimed to gain politically from the review. Examples of comments included,

> 'Small reduction in the number of councillors (63 to 57) in three-member wards (as at present), so as to maximise the number of winnable seats for the Conservative group' (Harrow);
>
> 'Agree to a more numerically balanced group of wards whilst attempting to consolidate/strengthen our political support within 'our' areas' (Redbridge);
>
> 'Oppose majority group's plans (Labour) to set boundaries for their political advantage' (Haringey).

We shall discuss this issue more fully in Chapter 8.

'Doing as we're told'

Some authorities, especially those whose reviews fell later in the programme, reported an almost passive approach. The review in North East Derbyshire was, 'based on criteria provided by the Local Government Commission', while in neighbouring Chesterfield they, 'closely followed the guidance notes and advice issued by the Commission'.

Drawing up submissions

The majority of local authorities set up working parties of one kind or another to formulate their PER submission. Often these were member-based, with perhaps half a dozen councillors drawn in proportion to political strength and including the party leaders. In one authority,

> 'A ward structure sub-committee of five members was set up to discuss the PER and prepare a scheme for the revision of the borough's wards' (Ellesmere Port and Neston).

In some cases the working party was given full delegated powers, while in others its proposals had to go to the Policy and Resources committee for ratification or amendment. Councillors who were not formally members of the group were sometimes allowed to attend, although they could not vote. For example, in one London borough

> 'A member level boundaries panel was set up comprising four councillors with delegated power to determine all matters except the final submission. The small Liberal Democrat Group participated in the Panel's work although not formally represented on it' (Ealing).

An officer from Derbyshire Dales mentioned that their working party meetings were open to the public and the press. Another officer told us that her authority invited the Commission to attend one of the working party meetings to set out the format of the review, the requirements and the expectations.

In other councils the boundary review working parties comprised officers who were charged with devising a selection of schemes for the consideration of councillors. In Harrow, officers prepared five different schemes. Although each was based upon strict electoral equality, they varied according to where the process of placing boundaries was begun. The schemes were then discussed formally by a members' panel. In addition, the Chairman of the panel carried out informal consultations with party group representatives aimed at reaching a consensus. In Kennet, officers formulated and presented a total of eight different schemes to a working party of members. This working party met almost monthly and discussed the minutiae of the boundary changes with individual councillors who came along to represent the arguments of their electors and parish councils. Other local authorities formed working groups consisting of both members and officers. One respondent explained that they had,

> 'An informal member/officer working group with regular, structured meetings. This comprised five councillors (political ratio, two Labour, two Liberal Democrats and one Conservative), the relevant senior officers and those who were doing the detailed work. This created a very positive 'partnership' atmosphere' (South Gloucestershire).

The other type of common arrangement adopted for formulating schemes was purely officer driven. In Lincoln, 'Two individuals were tasked to formulate (the) Council's response'; in Bristol, there was a working party of officers involved under the direction of the Electoral Registration Officer; in St. Albans, the response was co-ordinated by an officer team led by the District Secretary and Solicitor; in Merton, 'weekly or fortnightly officer level meetings took place with lead staff working on particular aspects of the review'. A key aspect of the job was liasing with and keeping 'on side' the various political parties. In Thurrock, officers negotiated directly with members, while one London borough officer told us,

> 'As the officer charged with dealing with this issue, I was given complete freedom to draft initial proposals with a view to seeing that the Commission's objectives were fulfilled and to examine the scope for achieving agreement between the main local and national parties' (Barking and Dagenham).

In another borough,

> 'No Working Party set up, but members given copies of draft proposals for them each to comment on, changes were made in the light of their comments, prior to going to committee with officers' recommendations which then became this Council's submission' (Redbridge).

Such an approach does not always meet with member approval as the newspaper extract in Box 5.2 shows. Elsewhere, officers were obliged to dance a delicate gavotte around competing parties. In Carlisle, officers advised each political grouping; and in Barnet, the Chief Executive liaised with the three political parties separately. In Havering, staff provided the parties with an outline structure based on 18 three-member wards. The council then determined that each political group could suggest its own proposals, which was precisely what all four groups did.

BOX 5.2 'Chairman blames council officers'

The chairman of Alnwick District Council has criticised its officers for taking action without consulting members. Coun. Robert Arckless, speaking at a meeting of Amble Town Council where he is also a member, criticised officers over proposed changes to electoral boundaries. He said he was not happy that officers responded to the proposals put forward by the Local Government Commission without talking to members. Coun. Ian Hinson, however, said he thought the action had been taken because there was only a short period of time in which to respond.

Extract from article in the Northumberland Gazette, 18 June 1999

The consultation process

The Commission states in its guidance that it attaches,

> '...considerable importance to obtaining locally derived proposals that have been subject to local consultation and on which there is a measure of local agreement. We look to the local authorities in each area to take the lead in this process, by developing proposals and seeking the views of local interests before they are submitted to us' (Guidance, 1998:17).

The results from our survey indicate that most local authorities do carry out a wide range of consultation. Local MPs and MEPs (or their agents) and the county council are consulted as a matter of course. Parish/town councils, local residents' associations and other interested organisations are contacted, usually by letter, and sent details about the review and the council's scheme. There can be a considerable number of such local groups and associations in an authority. In Chesterfield, for example, their consultees included Estate Committees, Townwomen's Guilds, Community Associations and Senior Citizens' Clubs – 73 organisations in total. This form of consultation was often backed up by holding public meetings in parishes at their request (Copeland), or by officers attending individual parish and town council meetings (South Lakeland). In Derbyshire Dales, meetings were held in parishes directly affected by the proposals. Two authorities took this consultation exercise with parishes a step further. In Crewe, a parish councils conference was held and in South Derbyshire, a parish forum was convened to discuss the Commission's Draft Recommendations. Kennet consulted extensively. Four months before the start of the review in February 1998, the council sent a detailed explanatory letter to all parish/town councils. Four days before the official start of Stage One, the council sent out details of two re-warding options (option X – 40 members and option Y – 43 members). More than forty parish and town councils responded to the council's consultation on the two options. A considerable number of consultees were in favour of retaining the status quo. In early April, a report of the working group advocating Option Y with modifications was sent to all parish and town councils.

Salisbury District Council used its Area Committees to consult the public about the review. Meetings were held in the four defined areas of the district (City, Southern, Western, and Northern) – see Chapter 4. The meeting of the City Area Committee did not actually focus upon the wards in the City area, but concentrated on discussing the merits of the two district-wide schemes. Support for the council's two options was broadly divided on party political lines. For example, a Liberal Democrat councillor argued that his party's scheme was opposed by Labour simply because it would not be to their political advantage. A Labour councillor countered by calling the review process 'disgusting' and the Liberal Democrat scheme 'gerrymandered'. Perhaps the most significant conclusion from this meeting was the fact that the public did not engage with the process. Only five members of the public were in attendance, and only one of them spoke. A councillor asked why the meeting was happening at all at this stage. He remarked that people in the area had not been given enough time to consider the schemes. The meeting concluded with the majority party winning a vote to confirm that their scheme was the preferred option for this area committee. Officers were directed to go away and work on making improvements to this scheme before presenting it to the Commission.

In London, where there are no parish councils, boroughs focused their consultation on local residents' associations and similar organisations. In Barnet, the consultation forum meetings did not fit within the review's timetable, so a series of *ad hoc* meetings were held in six libraries across the district. At these, the initial proposals for the borough, and the particular wards where the meeting was taking place, were presented by officers and discussed with local residents. The council scheme was also displayed at the three main offices of the council and at seventeen libraries for more than two weeks. In Kensington and Chelsea, a letter was sent to all 350 Tenants' and Residents' Associations. Another London borough gave a presentation to each of its seven Community Area Forums (local committees) to obtain feedback following the publication of the Commission's Draft Recommendations. Tower Hamlets submitted a report to its twenty-five Local Committee Forums.

Many authorities tried to solicit reaction directly from electors through media coverage or individual communication. In Exeter, local journalists were encouraged to take an interest in the review and they ran articles in the two main newspapers. Articles also appeared in the council's community newspaper with a circulation of 40,000 households. In Congleton, there was ...local media coverage throughout the various stages of the exercise, i.e. press release, local newspaper, 'The Link' and local radio and television'. In Chester there was a special newsletter; in Ellesmere Port an advertisement was placed in the local press; Vale Royal gave the PER repeated coverage in the council's free paper delivered to all households; in Kettering letters were sent to households in areas proposed for warding changes; and in Stevenage all households received an explanatory leaflet. It is difficult to gauge the success of such efforts. An officer from a London borough explained that press notices and posters in libraries were used – but no comments at all were received (Redbridge).

Local authorities were concerned to show that they had taken the process of consultation very seriously, often working against time constraints imposed by the Commission. Two London boroughs listed for us all the things they did to consult the public about the review:

> 'The publicity material from the Commission at the commencement of Stage One of the Review was placed on public deposit at the Town Hall. The local press gave reasonable coverage of the commencement of the review and the Commission also published its formal notice. All councillors received details of the proposals and these were also forwarded to representatives of all the major national and local political parties. An article outlining the purposes of the review was published in the council magazine, 'The Citizen', which was delivered free to every household in the Borough. Details were published in the public parts of the agenda for the appropriate council committees' (Barking and Dagenham);

> '(Comments relate to Stage One) Advertisement placed in local newspapers informing public of the PER and where to view proposals (the Council's draft proposals). Advert backed up by press releases. Press coverage was very good. Copies of map showing our proposals displayed in all libraries and in Civic Centre foyer. Leaflet explaining the PER and the proposals available at all display points, with Freephone tear-off slip for comments. Direct-dial hotline for telephone responses and questions' (Harrow).

The comments from Harrow are in fact slightly disingenuous. The review did not get off to a very good start because the Commission issued its press release launching the review in the *Evening Standard* rather than the local paper as planned. The council's advertisement in the local press was placed only six working days before the deadline of Stage One. Press reports discussed developments in the review but concentrated on the proposed changes to ward names. The leaflet about the review was produced with less than two weeks of Stage One left. It explained why the review was being carried out but did not include any information on the council's scheme. One press article highlighted the complaint of a resident about the time available for consultation. Only eleven representations were received as a result of the consultation, although these were taken into account at a meeting of the council. It is likely that other authorities also exaggerated the degree of consultation because of the high value placed on it by the Commission. Hackney admitted that 'consultation was difficult as the Council has no agreed position', and Watford confessed to us that it had not consulted at all.

Reaction to the Commission's proposals

Most local authorities held meetings to discuss the Commission's Draft Recommendations. Not unnaturally, reaction varied depending on the extent to which the Commission had accepted or revised the schemes submitted to it. In East Devon, for example, the LGCE made just four changes to the council's scheme. The council officer who prepared the submission suggested that the Commission took on board most of his proposals because it could not find any alternative arrangements. The changes made by the Commission were to improve electoral equality. Councillors were also reasonably happy with the draft report. They understood at the beginning of the process that the review was largely going to be a numbers game but, after reading the report, believed they had underestimated the emphasis given to numbers. It seemed to them that arguments about community ties were only accepted if there was satisfactory electoral equality as well. In Harrow, the Commission's Draft Recommendations were based on the schemes submitted by the council and the Liberal Democrats. Only one additional boundary change was added. The Chairman of the members' panel commented, 'I am delighted that the Commission has recognised the merit of our proposals, which will ensure that there are a similar number of voters in each ward' (*Pinner Times*, 18 February 1998).

In other cases local authorities persisted in trying to get their proposals accepted. Kennet District Council submitted Option Y (43 members) to the Commission. This was the only borough-wide scheme received by the Commission. 35 other submissions were made, most of them opposed to the district's scheme for a particular ward. The Commission based its Draft Recommendations on the council's scheme but made four modifications which affected seven wards. 45 further representations were received by the Commission at Stage Three. The council re-affirmed its original proposals in the case of three of the four changes made by the Commission, arguing that community ties were being broken for the sake of electoral equality. The Commission subsequently accepted one of these following supportive representations from several parish councils, three district councillors and five residents. In Swindon, the Commission had received a borough-wide scheme from the council and representations from seven parish councils. The Conservative and Liberal Democrat party groups did not make a formal submission to the Commission. The Draft Recommendations were based on the council's scheme as it substantially improved the level of electoral equality, but three modifications were made affecting the boundaries in six wards. One of these changes was to retain the existing boundary between Lawns and Walcot wards. The council had wanted to transfer the road called Chandler Close (38 electors) from Lawns to Walcot, because the properties were built at the same time as others in neighbouring Walcot and there were common community interests. However, the moving of even such a small number of electors would have the effect of pushing the electoral variance for the Walcot ward slightly beyond the Commission's +/-10% threshold. In the Commission's Final Recommendations, however, the transfer of 38 electors from Lawns to Walcot was accepted on the grounds that it 'would provide a better reflection of communities in the area' (Final Recommendations, 1999: para 51).

The media and the local PER process

As we have seen, both the Commission and the local authorities rely on the media to publicise the review process and to act as a sounding board for public opinion. At the outset local newspapers carry a press release from the Commission which gives basic information and invites representations –see Box 4.2. Once the review is up and running, stories are more common where there are competing council schemes or dissension from interested areas or groups. As the Commission experienced during the course of its structural reviews, electors are particularly liable to be upset by proposals to move boundaries with which they have become familiar and comfortable. The extracts in Boxes 5.3 and 5.4 give a flavour of the debates and some of the emotive language characteristically employed.

BOX 5.3 'Boundary Changes Infuriate Proud Osterley Citizens – Residents Win Border Skirmish'

The proud citizens of Osterley have saved four of their roads from being swallowed up by a new Heston East ward. Government Commissioners faced a revolt when they suggested excluding residents living along the west end of Jersey Road from Osterley. Petitions from horrified neighbours persuaded the Local Government Commission to spare them for 'community identity reasons'. Professor Malcolm Grant, the Commission Chairman, said: 'We concluded that our proposed boundary did not reflect community ties in the Osterley area'.

Campaigners are delighted at winning the only significant victory to reverse proposed boundary changes across Hounslow. Councillor Premila Bhanderi, one of the Tory ward councillors, said there had been strong feelings about the impending identity crisis. She said: When we told people they were horrified because they didn't want to be called Heston. We knew that would be the feeling and we told them it was going to happen unless they did something about it.

Extract from article in the Hounslow Borough Chronicle, 1 July 1999

The residents of the Claverley ward in Bridgnorth, Shropshire put up a particularly long and determined fight to preserve its identity. We followed their campaign in the local press. The overall councillor/elector ratio in Bridgnorth was 1:1,243. As Claverley had an electorate of 1,249 which was not expected to change much over the ensuing five years, it seemed as if it would be left unchanged as a perfectly sized ward. However, the two wards bordering on Claverley, Alveley to the south and Worfield to the west, had electoral variances of -20% and 38% respectively. The district council made two proposals. Its preferred option was to retain the status quo despite the electoral variances. The other option was to divide the Claverley ward between Alveley and Worfield to improve electoral equality. Claverley Parish Council opposed the division of the ward as it would not reflect community ties, but unsurprisingly the Commission came down on the side of equal numbers in

BOX 5.4. 'Burton Green in plea to Prescott'

Kenilworth may be attractive, but Burton Green doesn't want to be part of it. This is the villagers' response to the plan to move Burton Green from Stoneleigh parish into a Kenilworth ward for electoral reasons. The Burton Green Residents' Association is asking for a re-think. It has written to deputy prime minister John Prescott saying the exercise has 'given rise to feelings of bewilderment'. Members say not enough time was given for consultations and the exercise lacks 'political legitimacy'.

The residents were unable to seek views ahead of the deadline for initial consultations and were surprised that political parties were able to put forward local views without asking the people of Burton Green if they wished to be moved. But a later survey showed 71 per cent against a Kenilworth link, 16 per cent with no strong views, and only 12 per cent supporting the proposed change. The letter from chairman David Skinner and secretary Judi Hibberd said: 'Kenilworth is a very attractive and well-run town, but Burton Green is not part of it. We pointed out the long ties to a more rural area than Kenilworth, the unproven need for change, the unique nature of Burton Green, the still recent change for many from Solihull borough council, and the likelihood of great confusion through overlapping sets of boundaries'. But the residents were disturbed to see this summarised as 'no affinity' in a report.

The residents' association are telling Mr Prescott: 'Perhaps these proposals were inevitable, although as we were not consulted, we do not know.

But if the Commission's views were always going to be driven by numbers, then why consult at all?

Local media coverage has focused precisely on this point. We therefore believe: first, this recommendation should be reversed. Second, that the whole methodology of these reviews is flawed and structural reform overdue.

Far more time should be given for consultation, with residents' associations involved from the start. Door to door calling should be the norm, whether by council officers or residents' associations. Perhaps the Local Government Commission could handle more cases simultaneously, but with each spread over a longer time? The solutions lie primarily in London, not Warwickshire'.

Extract from article in the Kenilworth Weekly News, 10 December 1999

its Draft Recommendations. However, it did acknowledge that, 'The proposal for this area is likely to be the main area of contention at Stage Three, as it was during the Council's own consultation during Stage One. However, such re-warding is necessary in order to address electoral imbalances of 40% and 18% in this area' (Report to Commission meeting, 21 January 1999).

The Commission's decision attracted immediate press attention and local opposition. The councillor for Claverley complained, 'It is a sad situation – and it is hypocritical. National government asks for more decisions to be made at local level and then in the next breath tell us what to do, like dictators. Claverley has nothing to gain. It should be represented by those who understand what the local people want' (*Bridgnorth Journal*, 12 March 1999). Within two weeks, residents had started a campaign to save the ward. A leaflet entitled, 'Claverley Under Threat – a letter of protest from the parish council', was enclosed with the April edition of the church newsletter. The local vicar, Rev Simon Cawdell, said that, 'It is very important that Claverley, as a parish, receives the electoral recognition that it does at present. It is a very distinct community that can best be served by having a councillor who can recognise its individual nature. This would be lost if it is governed by neighbouring parishes' (*Bridgnorth Journal*, 26 March 1999). A week later the same newspaper reported that opposition to the change in Claverley was growing. It quoted Millennium group chairman and parochial church council secretary, Gordon Drury, 'Claverley gets its strength from being Claverley. I am very conscious that we have got a very strong community which is led by a very good parish council and I would be against anything that split this up. People from outside Claverley are probably not aware of the effort that is put in by the community here' (*Bridgnorth Journal*, 2 April 1999). By the end of April, 956 electors out of 1,249 (77%) had signed a petition protesting at the planned boundary changes. Local residents also received the support of the Bishop of Ludlow, the Bishop of Hereford, and the local county councillor. The parish council explained that there were no historic links with Alveley and Worfield, 'Claverley ward is defined within an ancient parish boundary and the local community is very aware of its heritage and its association with the centuries-old Claverley Parish Church. The economic and cultural background of the two areas is quite different to Claverley. Claverley is still largely an agricultural community, despite the presence of growing numbers of city commuters. Alveley, on the other hand, has a background of mining and light industry, which creates a rather different cultural outlook' (*Bridgnorth Journal*, 30 April 1999).

In early June, the Commission wrote to those who had made representations to it asking for further information and evidence. This letter encouraged local residents that the Commission was giving further consideration to the issue. Unfortunately for the Commission, this letter also drew some bad publicity in the local press as it had been sent to the wrong Member of Parliament. The wards of Claverley, Alveley, and Worfield all lay in the Ludlow constituency represented by Christopher Gill MP, but the Commission wrote to Wrekin MP Peter Bradley instead. Mr Gill wrote to the Commission, 'I am quite appalled to learn that, while on the one hand you are proposing to turn the electoral arrangements in Alveley, Claverley, and Worfield upside down, on the other hand you are not even aware in which constituency they are located' (*Express and Star*, 9 June 1999). In the meantime the district council reaffirmed its support for the status quo, but also produced a back-up plan which would make changes to the Alveley and Worfield wards but leave Claverley unaltered. The local furore appeared, however, to have paid dividends. In its Final Recommendations, the Commission decided to adopt the council's alternative scheme which did not split the Claverley ward because it appeared to 'enjoy a greater degree of local support' (Recommendations, Final, 1999: para 81). The Commission's U-turn was met with delight by local residents and the ward councillor. He was reported as saying, 'This is absolutely fantastic news – I am delighted. The people of Claverley will be celebrating. They have fought against these recommendations and this is something which is very important to our parish and its identity' (*Express and Star*, 7 August 1999).

Local communities can also be roused by the issue of the naming of wards. The excerpts in Boxes 5.5 and 5.6 show how it can dominate discussion and, on occasion, the review itself. Another area of contention ripe for local press coverage is if there are suggestions that boundary changes will impact on property prices! The extract in Box 5.7 is a nice example.

BOX 5.5 'Names worry of changes to boundaries'

A major shake-up of Havering borough's ward boundaries has been largely endorsed by members of the existing council from all groups. But, like many of the public, they are not happy with some of the newly suggested names of wards, which include: Corbets Tey, Wingletye, Harold Park, Suttons Farm, Bretons and St. George's. Cllr Harris, the Labour council leader, said some people had gained the impression the names had been put forward by the minority Labour administration, but claimed that it had not been responsible for some of the newly suggested names. That was despite the Labour group being behind many of the proposals adopted in draft form by the Commission which had been submitted by the Upminster Parliamentary Labour Party. He added the idea of Wingletye for the Emerson Park area had been mentioned as one case, but there had been an alternative suggested by another group proposing it should be called Nelmes. Cllr Harris said the proposed Harold Park ward should be called either Gooshays or Dagnam Park to distinguish it from the existing residential area known as Harold Park. Tory group leader, Cllr Eric Munday said it should be up to the individual parties to make suggestions on ward names.

Extract from article in the Havering Herald, 28 May 1999

BOX 5.6 'Boundary changes: It's a compromise!'

Spitalfields looks set to be renamed Spitalfields and Banglatown in a compromise set to please everyone or possibly no one. The Local Government Commission has recommended the ancient Spitalfields ward be given the new name in a report on changes to the council ward structure in Tower Hamlets.

Their report says: 'We recognise that there are strong feelings among local residents on both sides of the argument'. Senior councillors at Mulberry Place had proposed changing the name to Banglatown to reflect 'the current ethnic profile of a large proportion of the community in the area'. But strong lobbying from groups arguing both sides led the Commission to hedge their bets. Julia Mainwaring, Council leader when the borough put in its recommendations, was none the less happy saying it was a 'marvellous' compromise.

New names other than Spitalfields and Banglatown include Mile End and Globe Town, St. Dunstan's and Stepney Green, and East India and Lansbury.

Labour councillor for Lansbury, Kevin Morton said: 'The Commission's attempt to please everyone has produced several needlessly over-long and ludicrous ward names'. The borough will also lose some of the religious names for wards if the recommendations are implemented, such as St. Peter's, St. Mary's and Holy Trinity.

The report also calls for the shape of wards to change and for each one to have three councillors. The recommendations will now go to environment secretary John Prescott for final approval.

Extract from article in the East London Advertiser, 9 September 1999

A large proportion of the press coverage of the PERs focused on complaints from councillors about the Commission's decisions. Of course, this does not necessarily reflect on the Commission, but on the facts that councils and local parties have good access to the media, that it is a local news story, and that councillors are likely to use the review as a basis for trying to save their own skins, scoring political points, and putting down another public body based in London or even the government. The Commission has no public right of reply except to correct inaccuracies. The article and letter featured in Boxes 5.8 and 5.9 are good examples of the genre.

On occasion electoral reviews can even move local newspapers to take up the cudgels. The extracts in Boxes 5.10. and 5.11 show the press in west Cumbria viewing the PER as the final straw in bureaucratic interference, and the *Wembley Observer* announcing that it had made its own submission to the Commission 'on behalf of our readers'. The Commission gave the submission from the newspaper equal treatment alongside all others when the recommendations for Brent were drawn up.

BOX 5.7 'Estate change raises house price fears'

A defiant home-owner fears new voting boundaries will cost her money as her plush Longridge house becomes part of Greenstead. Under proposed changes for Colchester's electoral divisions, hundreds of homes in the Longridge area would become part of the Greenstead estate. The idea behind the review is to make local government in Colchester more democratic with each councillor representing a similar number of people. But the scheme has sparked unrest in the Longridge part of the town, where residents fear a connection with Greenstead might cause a drop in their house prices and soaring insurance costs.

Joyce Kelly, of Fulmar Close, plans to launch a petition against the new Longridge-Greenstead boundary. She said: 'When we moved from Bedfordshire 15 years ago and moved here to Longridge we did because we wanted to. If we had wanted to live in Greenstead we would have bought a house there. I have nothing against Greenstead – you have good and bad areas everywhere. The changes could affect our property or our insurance costs, it's not being snobbish. We were quite happy as we were'.

But Labour councillor Tim Young, who represents St. Andrew's, rebutted claims that property values and insurance costs would be affected, saying: 'They have always been in contact and the relationship is nearly always a good one. We who represent both areas do our best to recognise their needs'.

Colchester Council electoral and committee services officer Ray Amesbury said: 'we let as many people know as possible. They were featured in the council's newsletter, the local press and we advertised for people to come and look at the proposals'. Colchester Council's draft plans will go to the Local Government Commission where they will be scrutinised and people's views taken into account.

Extract from article in the Essex County Standard, 31 March 2000

The cost to local authorities of a Periodic Electoral Review

The Commission states in its Guidance that,

> 'The level of resources, particularly staff resources, which local authorities devote to PERs is entirely a matter for them to determine. However, the degree of officers' input required in the formulation of electoral schemes and the preparation of supporting data can be substantial, and should not be underestimated. Our officers can advise on staff resourcing in other local authorities which have been through the full PER process, or provide contacts in those authorities in order that experience can be shared' (Guidance, 1998: para 7).

We asked local authorities a series of questions in order that we could make an estimate of how much the PER had cost them in staff time and other tangible resources. In most local authorities, the PER is very much a team effort across

BOX 5.8 'Elections: County wards to change – 'Gobbledegook' plans attacked'

A re-jig of Bridgwater's county council electoral boundaries have been rubbished by councillors who have branded them as 'complete gobbledegook'.

The Local Government Commission wants to re-draw Bridgwater's political boundaries in a bid to even up the number of people councillors represent in their wards. But at a meeting of Sedgemoor's policy and resources committee councillors branded the moves as gobbledegook claiming the new boundaries left rural areas unrepresented. Angry councillor Lillian Cartwright said: 'It is just a case of evening up the numbers but it leaves councillors in rural areas to cover huge patches on their own which they cannot possibly get round. In some areas there are more sheep than people. The whole plan has been wrong from the start'...

Other councillors accused the Commission of being 'mathematicians' who were more interested in balancing numbers than representing the people's needs. Councillor John Turner said: 'Revising the boundaries is just a case of number crunching to even the electorate out'. Councillor Nobby Turner said: 'Wards have been split into two to mix urban and rural. The original district ward reorganisation was confusing enough without this on top'.

Comments of concern from councillors were noted at the meeting and will be sent to the Commission for consideration.

But councillors said they felt their worries would fall on deaf ears. Disheartened councillor David Joslin said: 'What is the point in objecting. We all know it is just a numbers game and no-one will listen to us anyway'.

Extract from article in the Bridgwater Mercury, 20 July 1999

departments plus administrative support. The Electoral Services and Planning departments are usually at the centre of the operation, and in some cases the Chief Executive or the Borough Solicitor takes a proactive personal role. Work on the review is normally in addition to normal duties. The total number of staff involved in what can clearly be a highly labour intensive task was as large as nine in the districts or even ten (London Borough of Merton). The actual number of hours spent on a review proved difficult to quantify. An officer in South Gloucestershire told us that,

> 'No separate record was kept on the time spent on the PER. Staff priorities were re-ordered to ensure the necessary work was carried out within existing resources'.

Among those local authorities that did try to answer the question, the hours claimed to have been spent on the review varied widely between 20–25 hours in Southwark to 4,025 hours in Barnet. The hours in Barnet were calculated by officers spending approximately 35 hours a week for 115 weeks on the project.

BOX 5.9 'An absurd exercise'

I found your report (March 16) on the merging of small parishes and villages into larger electoral units quite distressing for it emphasises yet again the 'Nanny knows best' attitude of the current Government. It also shows starkly a complete disregard for the ordinary man. Consider what happened. An obscure unelected quango is suddenly galvanised into action and issues an edict to every district council in England. It wants 'electoral equality on councils so that each elector has a vote of equal weight'. That quango is the Local Government Commission. To achieve that aim it announces 'virtually every ward in Sevonoaks District will change and only four will escape the changes'. This is akin to a judge sentencing a defendant before he has heard the evidence. But don't blame the quango for it is merely carrying out the behest of Government (hence the arrogance)...

Sadly, I have to say the whole exercise seems to be a waste of time and money, a farrago of absurdity.

James S Robinson

Extract from letter in the Swanley Times, 20 April 1999

In Exeter, we were told that the Principal Planner and the Planning Technician spent around 240 hours on the review, the Head of General Services 100 hours, the Electoral Services staff 60 hours, the Chief Executive 40 hours, the Copy Centre 4 hours and the Public Relations officer 4 hours – making a total of 448 hours or nearly 13 person weeks. On average, it seemed that much more time was spent on the review by officers in the London boroughs than in the district councils. Some officers complained to us that the Commission expected them to spend time on non-Council schemes and that this had increased the resource burden. For example,

> 'The Commission expect the Council to advise and respond on proposals from other organisations' (North Kesteven), and
>
> 'The Commission expected us to check figures of submissions of other parties' (Southwark).

Although the bottom line is the cost of running a PER, local authorities understandably found it difficult to calculate this. An officer from Salisbury wrote that, 'The cost was unquantifiable as all staff worked extra hours without remuneration'; another was, 'Unable to give an estimate but the costs would include staff time, the production of the booklet and maps and the publicity in the council magazine' (Barking and Dagenham). Even where estimates were made, it was clear that there were differences between authorities in terms of what had and had not been included. North Wiltshire reported spending just £500, whereas in South Derbyshire the review cost £33,100. In North Wiltshire the only costs 'claimed' were

BOX 5.10 ' COMMENT: More change – less benefit for us all!'

Can you believe the electoral boundaries are set to change again? Our corner of West Cumbria really has had its fill of such amendments ...none of which seem to have improved anything for anyone. In recent years we have had a round of pointless prodding over whether or not a unitary authority should be formed, then came changes for the borough wards and to cap it all, the Euro nonsense which lost us our local representation in Brussels. Once again officialdom is in danger of worrying too much about the statistics and not enough about the real boundaries which exist in people's everyday lives.

Schools, shopping and work are the factors which determine our areas of interest and surely electoral boundaries should follow those natural lines. Only then will the electoral areas make sense to voters. Only then might the turn-out at elections improve.

Some of the county council ward changes now proposed will leave people bewildered...

Unfortunately voters are so sick and tired of seeing their interests being placed at the bottom of the priority list, there is a real temptation that the call for comments will fall on deaf ears. Please don't let the Whitehall bureaucrats get away with any more meddling. Tell them they have got it wrong.

Extract from editorial in the Times and Star, 3 July 1999

BOX 5.11 'Carving up the boundaries'

The generals sat around the table carving up the spoils of the vanquished. The defeated German and Austrian empires were redrawn at Versailles with relish. New frontiers sliced across the map of Europe. Today, 80 years on, another map is about to unfold, but closer to home and on a far less grand a scale.

For international frontier, read ward boundary. For the Flanders trenches, read your street. For Versailles, read Local Government Commission.

Brent's 31 election wards are being replaced by 21 'super wards' each sending three councillors to the Town Hall to fight your interests. Four submissions proposing different ways to redraw your borough were received by the Commission, all vying for attention like the peace delegates at Versailles.

Labour, holding power in Brent, Conservatives and Liberal Democrats put forward their political party interests. The *Wembley Observer* made its submission on behalf of our readers on what we thought makes common sense for the communities we report on week-by-week. Labour appears to have shot itself in the foot and become the first casualty in the consultations that end on October 11, most of its proposals rejected.

Extract from editorial in the Wembley Observer, 5 August 1999

for members and catering expenses at four additional meetings. The figure for South Derbyshire, on the other hand, covered two financial years and the salaries of personnel working on the review. Other indicative estimates given to us were £800 in Southwark, £1,000 in Stevenage, £11,720 in Congleton and £75,000 in Barnet. Excluding salaries, it appears that the average cost to a local authority of a PER was £5,000 in the districts and £20,000 in the London boroughs.

Conclusions

Periodic Electoral Reviews involve local authorities in additional work which can be costly. Most prepare carefully for the review, at least attempt to consult their residents and try to make it a consensual rather than overtly party political process. Nonetheless, they routinely encounter problems varying from the calculation of projected electorates to tension between the rules set by the LGCE and their own preferred outcomes. Many begin by pursuing minimal change, especially if that will allow them to preserve the integrity of the boundaries of defined communities. However, such a policy often conflicts with the Commission's requirement of electoral equality and can lead, as we have seen, to some intense reaction from councillors, electors, the local media and other individuals and groups. Other important issues in an electoral review such as the size of the council or the structure of wards are less likely to provoke controversy, unless they too seem to threaten the representation of communities. Indeed one of the reasons why the PERs in London may have been less contentious than expected is precisely because there was less scope for urban/rural or parish/parish disputes. Even in London, though, there were clear differences between boroughs in how they approached the review, in the number and type of submissions made to the Commission, and in the reaction to them. In the next chapter we intend to use the more detailed material gathered in the course of our case studies to compare and contrast the review process in individual local authorities.

Chapter 6

Case-studies of the Periodic Electoral Review Process

A key part of our research strategy was to follow in detail the Periodic Electoral Review in a number of local authorities. Our choice for these case studies was partly determined by the LGCE's programme of work during the period of funding, but we were able to examine both rural and urban authorities, London boroughs and one county council. In each of our thirteen case study authorities – see Chapter 1 for a full list – we attended meetings, interviewed key officers and elected members, analysed media coverage of the review, and took a particular interest in how the Commission responded to submissions and representations. In this chapter we concentrate on six of the thirteen authorities – North Wiltshire and West Wiltshire district councils, Croydon, Richmond-upon-Thames and Westminster London boroughs and Northamptonshire County Council. They have been chosen to reflect both different types of council and contrasting approaches to undertaking a review. We examine each in turn using a common framework. We conclude by asking what general and specific lessons such case studies have for our understanding of the PER process. Each case study report should be read in conjunction with its accompanying Table which sets out some of the facts and figures pertaining to different stages of the authority's review.

North Wiltshire District Council (Table 6.1)

Introduction

North Wiltshire DC is based on the expanding town of Chippenham. The council has been under the control of the Liberal Democrats since 1991. At the time of the review, there were 32 Liberal Democrats, twelve Conservatives, six Labour members, and two Independents. In 1998 the electorate in the district was 94,477 and, according to projections compiled by the council's Forward Planning section, was expected to increase by more than 7% to 101,330 in five years. The district contains 59 parishes and is entirely parished. The review of North Wiltshire began on 24 February 1998. An officer from the Commission (Review Manager) visited the district at the end of

Table 6.1 North Wiltshire D.C.

Review timetable			
Last review	*Draft publ.*	*Final publ.*	*Order made*
Dec-78	Sep-98	Mar-99	Oct-99
Submissions			
No. of full submissions		*Council submission*	
1		Yes	
Representations			
	Draft stage	*Final stage*	*Public meeting?*
	8	20	No
Wards/councillors			
	Before	*Draft*	*Final*
	42/52	38/53	38/53
Ward pattern			
	Before	*Draft*	*Final*
Single member	32	24	24
Two member	10	13	13
Three member		1	1
Councillor/elector ratio (1:x)			
	Before	*Draft**	*Final**
	1817	1912	1912
Ward electorate variance			
	Before	*Draft**	*Final**
% wards >10% variance	66.7	5.3	5.3
% wards >20% variance	40.5	0.0	0.0
Worst positive % variance	119.0	13.0	9.0
Worst negative % variance	56.0	11.0	12.0
Average % variance	17.0	5.0	5.0

*after 5 years according to electorate projections

January before the official start of Stage One. Three weeks after this visit, the Review Leader was taken on a tour of the district by a council official and shown the 'problem' areas for the review.

Preparing the submission(s)

A council officer began working on the review a few months before its formal start. He produced a preliminary draft scheme with a total of 53 councillors, one more than currently, which was used for discussion purposes with members. The officer suggested that this method of working was likely to be more efficient than leaving the formulation of schemes to a group of councillors. Most councillors would be more concerned with their own ward rather than the whole council. The officer had previous experience of boundary and electoral reviews. The council's Performance Review Sub-Committee set up a formal Boundary Review Working Party on 11 March 1998 to deal with the PER process. This working party had five members and reflected the political composition of the council: three Liberal Democrats, one Conservative and one Labour. The first meeting took place on 6 April 1998 at which the officer-produced scheme was discussed on a ward-by-ward basis. The *status quo* seemed the preferred option, but as only 14 out of 42 current wards were within the +/-10% criteria, there needed to be changes. Before the review, the council consisted of 32 single member wards and ten wards represented by two members. There was strong support for maintaining single member wards, especially in rural areas, but an understanding that this would be difficult to achieve. There was also a desire to keep rural areas separate. Working party members offered various amendments while taking into account the domino-effect of making changes. The aim of the second meeting on 14 April 1998 was to produce a scheme that could go out for consultation. The biggest problem at this stage remained the fact that councillors did not want to create two-member wards in rural areas.

The council carried out considerable consultation locally. Before the review began, a letter was sent to all parish and town councils explaining the principles of the review. The letter included the officer's interpretation of the review,

> 'I have recently attended a meeting with representatives of the Local Government Commission and they are insistent that there shall be very little deviation from the mean figure of elector:councillor ratio in each district. To put it another way, they are interested in the numbers game and will not have too much regard to local community ties or geographical situations. In addition, there is no allowance whatsoever for what is known as rural weighting' (14 January 1998).

Once the projected electorates were calculated, they were passed on to all interested parties. The officer also met parish clerks to discuss whether the electorates needed adjustment in their area and to answer specific questions about the review. On 20 April 1998, the council published its preferred scheme. This scheme included three options for one area of the authority, and councillors sought the opinions of local parish councils and the general public on these. There was generally very little response to the consultation exercise. Only three out of eight parish councils in the disputed area replied and they all wanted to retain the status quo, which, as we have seen, was not an option. Meetings were held in May to confirm the single submission made to the Commission.

Interaction with the Commission

Each review team at the Commission has a different style of working. The Review Leader for this review believed a good working relationship with the responsible council officer(s) to be extremely important, and there was considerable contact between the Commission and the authority. For instance, the Commission contacted the lead officer to say that a particular ward would probably not be acceptable because of the variance of its electorate from the mean. The officer was asked for his opinion on how the council would react to an alternative arrangement. It is interesting that the Commission had no contact with the council's working party of elected members. A total of eight representations were made to the Commission during Stage One. The Commission adopted the council's scheme for the majority of wards, but proposed that a number of single-member wards be merged for electoral equality reasons. The review team admitted in the report to Commissioners that,

> 'It may look 'odd' to some that we are recommending a pattern of single-member wards in the towns of Chippenham and Calne but are putting forward two-member wards in parts of the rural area'.

The Commission expected some problems with its Draft Recommendations because the merging of single-member wards made some areas very large, and there had been no prior consultations on these new arrangements – see Box 6.1. The council's working party met on 5 October 1998 to discuss them, and reaffirmed its preference for six single-member rural wards. A letter to the Commission from the council made clear,

> 'The difficulties that would be encountered by Members in representing such a large geographical area and disparate electorate. The large wards thereby created would dilute the natural links between Councillors and the rural communities and would lessen the effectiveness of the Member's role in these areas' (11 November 1998).

Despite this, and twenty other representations, the Commission confirmed its Draft Recommendations in their entirety. It acknowledged the arguments in favour of single-member wards, but asserted that 'the level of electoral inequality that would result from single-member wards appears to be too high to justify' (Report of the Review Team to the Commission, January 1999). Moreover, if representations about community identity were accepted in one area, there would be pressure on the Commission to treat other areas similarly in the interests of consistency.

The role of 'politics' in the PER

The initial officer-produced scheme was designed with no regard to its party political impact. Similarly, the debate in the working party always overtly revolved around solving the boundary problem in the best interests of the district, even though the simple expedient of moving a few streets in an urban area such as Chippenham

Box 6.1 Redrawing boundaries in the rural north east of North Wiltshire

The electorate in rural single member wards like Ashton Keynes and Crudwell was considered too small to justify them remaining unchanged.

North Wiltshire existing boundaries

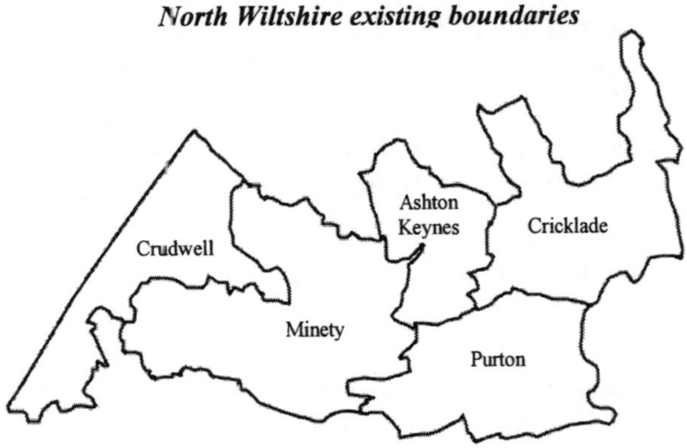

The Commission's solution was to establish two-member wards. Although this improved electoral equality, it made the area covered by each ward much larger.

North Wiltshire final recommendations

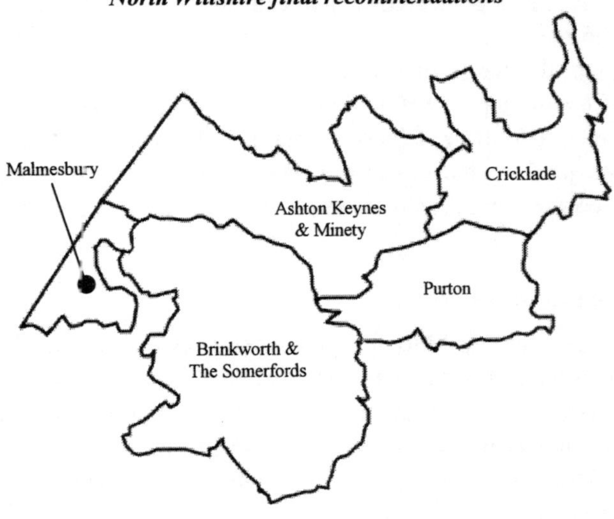

Source: based on maps published in the LGCE's Final Recommendations for North Wiltshire. © Crown Copyright

could result in Labour potentially losing seats. In fact the one significant political aspect of North Wiltshire's review process had a national rather than local origin. As discussed in Chapter 4, a meeting was held between the Chief Executive of the Commission and the Wiltshire councils in the light of the publication of the White Paper. The Commission explained that councils had to carry on with the reviews as directed until they were told otherwise. A four-week extension was offered to all Wiltshire councils so that they could consider producing a two-member scheme across the district to fit with the putative half-and-half county/district electoral cycle. Liberal Democrat councillors complained extensively in the local media about having to re-examine the scheme and the resulting waste of money.

West Wiltshire District Council (Table 6.2)

Introduction

West Wiltshire DC is located in a predominantly rural part of the county. It contains several market towns, but no single centre of population. The Liberal Democrats took control of the authority for the first time in 1991. In 1998, at the time of the review, there were 28 Liberal Democrats, eight Conservatives, four Labour members and three Independents on the 43 seat council. At 84,572 its electorate is almost 10,000 smaller than that in neighbouring North Wiltshire, but is expected to grow by 6.1% to 89,764 in five years according to council projections. The council's Chief Executive did not attend the meeting of Wiltshire Chief Executives held by the Commission in advance of Stage One. Stage One officially started on 24 February 1998. The Commission's Review Manager for the district paid a visit on 3 March 1998, but unusually did not hold a meeting with members because it proved impossible to get the council to agree a date. A council officer reported to us that they had no contact with the Commission for more than two months following the initial visit.

Preparing the submission(s)

The predominant responsibility for the electoral review in West Wiltshire rested with a single officer assisted by an administrator. The work on the review was in addition to his existing workload and he had no previous experience of boundary reviews. He contrasted this with another authority in Wiltshire where he believed that eight officers were working full-time on the review. The officer decided at an early stage that it would be possible to spend an enormous amount of time formulating schemes with which members might disagree. Before any formal or informal council discussion on the review took place, he suggested that if the council decided not to formulate a scheme and to let the Commission come up with its own proposal, then at least the council could forward information on particular

Table 6.2 West Wiltshire D.C.

Review timetable			
Last review	*Draft publ.*	*Final publ.*	*Order made*
Jun-79	Sep-98	Mar-99	Oct-99
Submissions			
No. of full submissions		*Council submission*	
0		No	
Representations			
	Draft stage	*Final stage*	*Public meeting?*
	10	30	No
Wards/councillors			
	Before	*Draft*	*Final*
	28/43	25/44	25/44
Ward pattern			
	Before	*Draft*	*Final*
Single member	16	8	8
Two member	9	15	15
Three member	3	2	2
Councillor/elector ratio (1:x)			
	Before	*Draft**	*Final**
	2513	2417	2417
Ward electorate variance			
	Before	*Draft**	*Final**
% wards >10% variance	61.9	8.0	4.0
% wards >20% variance	42.9	0.0	0.0
Worst positive % variance	83.0	11.0	10.0
Worst negative % variance	38.0	11.0	11.0
Average % variance	22.0	6.0	6.0

* after 5 years according to electorate projections

areas together with its thoughts on matters such as ward structures for the Commission to work from. He admitted that this was not a very professional way to proceed. It should also be reported that the council's Chief Executive appeared to be against planning for boundary changes until those issues relating to electoral arrangements foreshadowed in the White Paper had been resolved.

The council's Policy and Resources Committee discussed the officer's report on the review for the first time on 8 April 1998. The officer hoped that this meeting would result in staff being relocated from other departments to help with the increased workload, and in some clearer guidelines about a way to proceed with the review. At the same point in the review timetable in another Wiltshire district, Kennet, officers had produced a number of schemes, were deciding upon the two favourites and fine-tuning boundaries. A Conservative councillor started off the discussion in the meeting by emphasising the importance of the review. He said that,

> 'The PER is a very big thing for this council. It is likely to result in a big shake-up of the district, especially in rural areas. At present, we have huge variations from the average variance'.

Another councillor argued that the council must put forward its own scheme and not let the Commission impose one. He continued by saying that greater weight was likely to be given if there was a consensus between the council and the parish councils, and that there should be consultation and possibly a joint submission. The Chief Executive, who had had previous experience of a parliamentary review, explained to members that they had two options. The first was to submit a scheme based upon the Commission's criteria. The second was to talk to the Commission and explain that they could not conform to its rules because they were a rural authority. The discussion in the meeting suffered at times because members did not seem to understand the rules of a PER. On two occasions, councillors argued that there were difficulties with the review because it did not take any account of the future: one member even asserting that in a few years time, the variances would be likely to be very wide because of housing developments. Overall, there seemed to be little interest in the review: members were talking over each other and officers did not interject into the debate to correct inaccuracies.

The recommendation of the Policy and Resources Committee was to set up a working party. It had seven members, chosen to reflect the political composition of the council, and met for the first time on 12 May 1998 – seventeen working days before the deadline for Stage One. Although there was support for keeping rural and urban areas separate and for retaining single member wards, the feeling of the working party was that the council was not in a position to submit a district wide scheme. One member had attempted to formulate such a scheme but gave up as it proved to be too difficult. Members agreed that they should not put time and effort into producing a full scheme which the Commission might reject. The working party also discussed a copy of the Recommendations for West Somerset which had been sent by the Commission. That council had simply requested no change in its electoral arrangements. At the Draft Recommendations stage the Commission had proposed changes to ten of the council's 18 wards, falling to nine in the Final Recommendations. West Wiltshire councillors thought that the fact that the Commission had listened to the West Somerset council's view at Stage Three provided ammunition for their own decision to make a broad brush submission and to allow the Commission to use its experience and resources to produce a detailed scheme. The council would hold its fire until Stage Three, with the opinion being voiced that, 'The Commission have cooked their own goose'. Finally, the working party suggested that the parish councils should be given a week for consultation before the deadline. An officer mentioned that parish councils were free to make their own representations. A Conservative councillor argued that the council should not consult parishes but leave the issue to members only. The authority's area committee structure was not involved in the review.

Interaction with the Commission

The Commission became aware about a month before the deadline of Stage One that the council was not going to put forward a full submission. Nevertheless, the council did ask the Commission to have regard to its stated 'principles' when drafting Recommendations:

- Westbury should be warded;
- Two large developments in the district warranted an additional councillor;
- A preference for single-member wards;
- All wards should have identifiable geographical names;
- There should be a different elector:councillor ratio for rural and urban areas; and
- District wards should not cross identified community areas.

For its part, the Commission experienced problems liaising with officers in the district and receiving accurate electorates and other information. For example, it wrote to the council to ask for comments on its proposals. It also asked whether it had omitted any streets, where the boundary could practicably be drawn to produce equal numbers in a ward, and for electorate projections for some potential new warding arrangements. A council officer replied that,

> 'I cannot give any comments on the merits or otherwise of the proposals that have been put forward by your team. The council's policy is as confirmed to you by my letter of 12 June 1998 and as an officer of the Council I cannot signify approval to anything that would not accomplish this. Your proposals do not at the moment address the Council's stated aim of single-member wards and for this reason I have limited my replies to factual ones' (10 July 1998).

Despite this underlying tension, the issue did not appear to provoke the general public. The Commission received just ten representations from individuals and there was very little press coverage of the review. The Commission's Draft Recommendations did pay heed to a number of the council's 'points of principle'. The town of Westbury was warded for parish council purposes and its representation on the council increased from three to four. The Paxcroft ward, where significant housing developments had taken place, was given an additional member. The Commission also respected as far as possible the council's preference for single-member wards, especially in rural areas. Finally, the Commission recognised the council's case for easily recognisable ward names. However, at the special meeting of the Wiltshire LGA in October 1998 (see Chapter 4), the Chief Executive of the Commission was questioned by West Wiltshire councillors on why its Draft Recommendations had not incorporated all of the points in the council's submission. Councillor Bryant argued that paragraph 39 of the Draft Recommendations was very dismissive of the Community Areas within his authority. He asserted that the Commission did not seem to understand these Community Areas, and that if the boundaries had to change, then it should have taken account of them. The Chief Executive responded that the authority had failed to produce a district-wide scheme and she questioned whether the Commission had received a map of the Community Areas (which it had).

The Commission expected to receive a significant amount of opposition to the Draft Recommendations, culminating perhaps in the calling of a public meeting. Interviews with Commission officers revealed that they felt at a disadvantage through having no local knowledge, and that they accepted that there may be a better way of drawing the boundaries in the district than the one they were proposing. In practice, however, the Commission is reluctant to make major changes between its Draft and Final Recommendations. Thirty representations were received during Stage 3, including ones from the council, an MP, two district councillors, one town councillor, and thirteen out of a possible 48 parish councils. The council submitted alternative proposals for parishes in the southern and western rural areas of Westbury and Warminster, as well as reiterating the points which the Commission had not taken on board (especially the lack of consideration of Community Areas). The Commission endorsed its Draft Recommendations with two minor modifications.

The role of 'politics' in the PER

The review did not seem to be party politically motivated at all. Councillors wished to retain the status quo and did not look at how boundaries might be changed to bring electoral advantage. At a working party meeting one councillor commented that the PER was 'not the most important thing the council is doing at the moment' and did not 'affect the next elections'. He was, of course, correct as far as the 1999 contests were concerned but the entire West Wiltshire council will be elected on new boundaries in May 2003.

London Borough of Croydon (Table 6.3)

Introduction

The London Borough of Croydon is situated in the south of the capital. It was controlled by the Conservatives from 1968 to 1994, when Labour took control. Croydon provides an interesting case for this research because of recent instances of politically crucial disproportionality between the share of the vote and the share of the seats on the council won by the Conservative and Labour parties. In 1994, the Conservatives polled 42.3% of the vote and had 30 councillors (42.9% of the total) returned. Labour, by contrast, polled just 39.2% of the vote but elected 40 (57.1% of the total) councillors. A similar situation obtained at the May 1998 elections. The Conservatives polled an even larger share of the vote than in 1994 (47.5%) and had 31 councillors elected, while Labour received 37.8% of the vote yet retained control of the council with 38 members. Initial projections suggested that Croydon's electorate would increase by less than 1% (from 226,071 to 227,677) in the five-year period following the PER. These figures were subsequently challenged – see Chapter 7. The Commission discussed the forthcoming programme of reviews with the Chief Executives of London Boroughs at a meeting of the London branch of the Society of Local Authority Chief Executives (SOLACE) on 27 March 1998. The formal review launch letter for Croydon was sent on 20 July 1998 confirming the official start of the review on 22 September 1998. On the same day, the Commission gave a briefing on the review to officers from Croydon emphasising that they were looking for ward electoral imbalances of no greater than 2 or 3%. Before the official start of Stage One, officers from the Commission were taken on a tour of the borough. On 25 September 1998 the Commission met members of the council.

Preparing the submission(s)

The initial idea in Croydon was that a working party should be set up to deal with the PER as had been the case during the previous review in 1977. A report formalising this was scheduled to go to Committee on 21 July 1998, but the Leader of the Council (Labour) changed the report and decided against the creation of a working group. Officers told us that both major parties seemed happier with this arrangement. The local Liberal Democrats, who had a single councillor elected at the May 1998 elections, were especially content as they believed it increased their chance of getting any scheme which they proposed accepted by the Commission. In the circumstances the Chief Executive decided that it would not be desirable for the council to put forward its own submission to the Commission. He gave four principal reasons. First, that it would not be possible to have a politically neutral working party. Second, that it would not be in Croydon's best interests if he personally was obliged to stand up at a public meeting to defend a party politically driven 'council

Table 6.3 Croydon L.B.C.

Review timetable			
Last review	*Draft publ.*	*Final publ.*	*Order made*
Apr-77	Mar-99	Sep-99	Mar-00
Submissions			
No. of full submissions		*Council submission*	
4		No	
Representations			
	Draft stage	*Final stage*	*Public meeting?*
	11	44	No
Wards/councillors			
	Before	*Draft*	*Final*
	27/70	24/70	24/70
Ward pattern			
	Before	*Draft*	*Final*
Single member	0	0	0
Two member	11	2	2
Three member	16	22	22
Councillor/elector ratio (1:x)			
	Before	*Draft**	*Final**
	3230	3253	3370
Ward electorate variance			
	Before	*Draft**	*Final**
% wards >10% variance	40.7	0.0	0.0
% wards >20% variance	7.4	0.0	0.0
Worst positive % variance	27.0	7.0	6.0
Worst negative % variance	18.0	4.0	8.0
Average % variance	10.0	2.0	3.0

* after 5 years according to electorate projections

scheme'. Third, that he did not want to follow the practice in some other London boroughs where re-warding schemes were being drawn up solely by the four most senior officers. Fourth, that to ask officers to produce a scheme would inevitably involve them in political controversy and place them in a difficult position.

The borough did, however, ask Bruce Middlemass (a former Borough Secretary in Croydon who had played an influential role in the 1977 review) to produce a 'reference copy' of a submission for the council, which would be totally independent of the political parties. His scheme would not be submitted formally to the Commission, but a copy 'for information' would be forwarded. Officers in Croydon maintain that this was done at the suggestion of the Commission so that it would have something with which to compare the political submissions. The Commission insists that it did not ask the council to do this, rather advising them that it might be useful. The Director of Reviews described this as 'good management of the process'. Not only were the parties not permitted to examine Mr Middlemass' scheme, but the public were similarly given no opportunity to comment. The 'Scheme by Officers', as it was named, was sent to the Commission after the closing date for submissions at Stage One but it was used in its deliberations.

As there was no council scheme to consult upon, the discussion of the review only took place amongst those who were politically motivated. There was some coverage in the local press, but this mainly revolved around party political lines. The details of the review were placed in local libraries and an article appeared in the council newspaper, *Croydon Choice*.

Interaction with the Commission

The Commission received eleven representations during Stage One. Among these were four borough-wide schemes submitted by the Conservative, Labour, Liberal Democrat, and Official Monster Raving Loony parties. As we noted in our observation of the Commission 'brain storming' session in Chapter 4, each of these was treated and analysed rigorously. Commission officers also paid a further visit to certain potential problem areas during their deliberations at Stage Two. The Draft Recommendations reflected part of each borough-wide submission and were largely welcomed by the Labour and Conservative parties. A Conservative councillor said, 'We are 95% content with the proposals. Changes had to happen to even up the number of electors in the wards' (*Caterham and District Advertiser*, 26 March 1999). The Conservatives were, however, unhappy with the Commission's decision in New Addington and Fieldway, arguing that in other reviews the Commission had joined together areas which were both further apart and more geographically remote. The Conservatives believed that, on balance, the new boundaries would result in a gain for them of three seats at the expense of Labour. For Labour the Council Leader Valerie Shawcross said, 'In general I think they are a sane and sensible set of proposals. I'm pleased the Commission has preserved the traditional communities such as Fieldway, New Addington, Addiscombe and Waddon' (*Caterham and District Advertiser*, 26 March 1999). During Stage Three the Commission received a further 44 representations from all the political parties and a range of individual councillors and residents. As a result of these a number of minor changes were made to the boundaries within the borough, but the two two-member wards in New Addington and Fieldway proposed in the Draft Recommendations were retained within a 70 member authority.

The role of 'politics' in the PER

The disproportionate election results in Croydon in 1994 and 1998 were a direct result of unequally sized wards: the smallest being in the north where Labour support is concentrated, and the largest in the south where mainly Conservative councillors are elected. At both local government and parliamentary level it is the centre of the borough which forms the political battleground. From the outset one important bone of contention in the review concerned the boundaries in the strongly Labour New Addington (three-member) and Fieldway (two-member) wards – see Box 6.2. It was in this area that Commission officers conducted their Stage Two tour. Their inspection and the representations they received convinced them that New Addington justified retention as a *two-member* ward, but that Fieldway should not be merged with neighbouring Heathfield. The partisan consequences of any decision were clear. If the Commission was to adopt a universal three-member scheme with 72 seats in total, Labour would be guaranteed three seats in New Addington but potentially lose ground in a new Fieldway ward. On the other hand, a 70 member scheme retaining the two-member wards in New Addington and Fieldway would give Labour four seats in a smaller authority. For the parties, therefore, the issue of council size had considerable political ramifications.

Labour was well organised in Croydon and produced a full submission, together with detailed comments on the Commission's draft proposals. The party acknowledged that existing inequalities meant that boundary changes would be likely to weaken its electoral position, and focused its campaign on maintaining a 70 member council and on preserving the integrity of the area covered by the Fieldway and New Addington wards, albeit with only two councillors each. Two aspects of the party's approach can be seen as examples of 'best practice' for others in a similar situation to adopt. Labour ensured that all its ward and other branches reinforced the 'party line' in their own representations to the Commission, and that as much trouble was taken in spelling out where they agreed with the Draft Recommendations as where they did not. It is also significant that the Labour-controlled Borough Council's formal and public 'welcoming' response to the Draft Recommendations closely matched that received from the Croydon Labour parties.

The Conservatives did not receive any assistance from national party headquarters in the drafting of their submission. It was produced by one councillor in consultation with colleagues on the council, local party associations, and resident associations. He admitted to us that it was difficult keeping his own members happy because of their reluctance to lose 'their' ward and any electors. He also acknowledged that the way the boundaries were drawn was likely to have a political effect, and that this was a consideration in the 'back of my mind'. The claimed objective of the Conservative submission was to make as few changes as possible

Box 6.2 Redrawing boundaries in the south east corner of Croydon

Labour wished as far as possible to preserve the boundaries of the party's two safe wards in this area – Fieldway (two-member) and New Addington (three-member), if necessary at the expense of losing one of their total of 5 councillors. The Conservatives argued for two three-member wards with Fieldway split between New Addington and their own safe ward of Heathfield, thereby reducing Labour representation in the area to three councillors.

Croydon existing boundaries

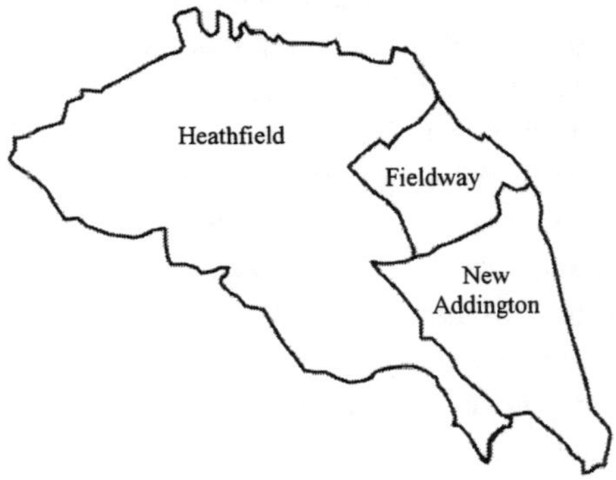

Following an inspection by officers, the Commission made only minor boundary changes in the area, albeit that New Addington became a two- rather than three-member ward.

Croydon final recommendations

Source: based on maps published in the LGCE's Final Recommendations for Croydon © Crown Copyright

because of the consequent loss of identity. It was suggested by other parties, however, that the Conservatives aimed to produce a widely altered scheme which would be completely 'gerrymandered' to ensure that they won control of the council.

The Liberal Democrats have no borough-wide organisation in Croydon. Their submission was produced by two individuals from the Croydon South parliamentary constituency and two others. The party's sole councillor was not directly involved in the review, although the ward he represented (Woodcote and Coulsdon West) was the focus of the Liberal Democrats' attention. They decided against proposing the division of Woodcote and Coulsdon West. While such a move could have resulted in their winning more seats, they felt that the change could not be justified in terms of electoral equality and did not wish to be accused of political manipulation. The Liberal Democrats were also involved in cross party discussions about the review. Labour requested a meeting with them to solicit support for its scheme of having three two-member wards. The suggestion was that such a scheme would present the Liberal Democrats with the chance of winning one ward and two more seats in the south of the borough and, together with Labour's 'guarantee' of four seats in the other northern wards, help stop the Conservatives from gaining control. The Liberal Democrats, however, were wedded to universal three-member wards and did not support the Labour scheme. On the other hand, in an attempt to get Labour support for 'their' scheme, they refrained from proposing boundary changes in one ward currently represented by three Labour councillors.

London Borough of Richmond-upon-Thames (Table 6.4)

Introduction

Richmond-upon-Thames is on the south west edge of the capital and is the only London borough bisected by the River Thames. It has been controlled by the Liberal Democrats since 1990. At the time of the review there were 34 Liberal Democrat councillors, fourteen Conservatives, and four Labour members. The council had an electorate of 125,153 in 1998. This was projected to increase to 128,096 in 2003 – an increase of 2%. The original electorate forecasts for 2003 were based on population figures provided by the London Research Centre, subsequently amended to reflect knowledge of local developments. The borough was first notified by the Commission about the PER in February 1998. In April of that year officers started work on the review and in June the process was brought to the attention of councillors. The review began officially on 4 August 1998. The Commission held briefings for both officers and members during Stage One.

Table 6.4 Richmond-upon-Thames L.B.C.

Review timetable			
Last review	*Draft publ.*	*Final publ.*	*Order made*
May-77	Mar-99	Jul-99	Feb-00
Submissions			
No. of full submissions		*Council submission*	
3		Yes	
Representations			
	Draft stage	*Final stage*	*Public meeting?*
	3	29	No
Wards/councillors			
	Before	*Draft*	*Final*
	19/52	18/54	18/54
Ward pattern			
	Before	*Draft*	*Final*
Single member	0	0	0
Two member	5	0	0
Three member	14	18	18
Councillor/elector ratio (1:x)			
	Before	*Draft**	*Final**
	2407	2372	2372
Ward electorate variance			
	Before	*Draft**	*Final**
% wards >10% variance	26.3	0.0	0.0
% wards >20% variance	5.3	0.0	0.0
Worst positive % variance	23.0	4.0	4.0
Worst negative % variance	17.0	2.0	2.0
Average % variance	8.0	2.0	2.0

* after 5 years according to electorate projections

Preparing the submission(s)

The borough set up a Review of Boundaries Sub-Committee with full delegated powers to deal with the review. This committee consisted of seven members – four Liberal Democrat, two Conservative, and one Labour. It met only three times during the review process: in August to agree the criteria for the review, in November to recommend a scheme to be sent to the Commission, and in March to endorse the Draft Recommendations. The day-to-day responsibility for the review was initially placed in the hands of two officers. This was in addition to their existing workload and they were told to involve other departments, for the production of maps for example, as required. At the first meeting of the sub-committee agreement was reached on three key aspects of the PER. First, the council's submission would be based on a uniform pattern of three-member wards (the borough had five two-member wards before the review). The Commission had advised the council that they could retain some two-member wards if they wished, but that a fall-back position of three-member wards would be wise in the light of the direction of government policy. Originally the borough had been keen to keep two-member wards because of their long historical provenance. Second, the total number of councillors to be elected to the Council should be 54, based on eighteen wards -seven on the Surrey side of the River Thames and eleven on the Middlesex side. This represented a reduction of one in the number of wards and an increase of two in the number of members. Third, the council would use the River Thames as a ward boundary. Council officers believed that the river made a good boundary because it was crossed only by two small bridges and it would be difficult to justify any ward so split. The Commission had, however, warned officers that they should not use the river as a boundary if by doing so there was an adverse effect on electoral equality. As the review proceeded, it was decided that officers should not produce a scheme of their own. Instead, the Leader of the Council (and of Liberal Democrat group) and his party colleagues produced what became the council's scheme. This was put before officers for their 'approval'. Officers were also asked to address the question: 'How will you know if the Liberal Democrat scheme is gerrymandered?' They responded that they would be content to put forward the party's submission as the council's scheme if it fitted the criteria for electoral equality and if the shape of the wards was acceptable. In the event, officers were not happy with certain parts of the scheme and the boundaries in those areas were altered. The amended scheme was then presented to the Commission as containing the council's proposals.

The borough produced a leaflet explaining the basics of the review. This was sent to more than 150 public organisations and groups. All libraries in the borough and the council offices held information on the review and posters were displayed. The council issued press releases at important stages of the review, but no other methods of consultation were used. The Community Forums were not used because the stages of the review fell outside their twice yearly meeting schedule. No public representations about the review were received at Stage One. This probably reflected the facts that the council had not put forward a scheme for public consultation and that there was very little press coverage of the PER. Although the Review Manager's report to the Commission meeting mentioned that the borough had consulted widely, we found little evidence of such consultation taking place.

Interaction with the Commission

The Commission received three submissions, one from the Liberal Democrat controlled council and one each from the Conservative and Labour groups. The council's scheme contained no ward with an electoral variance greater than +/-10% on either current or projected figures. The overall average variance from electoral equality was 2.8% in 1998, falling to 1.6% after five years. The council's submission was described by a Commissioner as a 'dream scheme' and was accepted by the Commission in its entirety. The Commission wrote,

> 'In view of the degree of consensus behind large elements of the Council's proposals we have concluded that we should base our recommendations on the Borough Council's scheme. We consider that this scheme would provide a better balance between electoral equality and the statutory criteria than the current arrangements or other schemes submitted at Stage One' (Draft Recommendations, 1999: para 46).

Following publication of the Draft Recommendations, the Commission received 29 representations including one from the Conservative party disputing the existence of a consensus. However, the only changes made by the Commission between the Draft and Final Recommendations were to the names of two wards. At this point, and arguably rather late in the day, dissatisfaction with the review outcome began to be expressed. A Labour spokesman was quoted in the local press as believing,

> '...the Commission have been fooled into thinking that there's a consensus behind them (the proposals) but they've really just come from a small committee of Liberal Democrats' (*Richmond and Twickenham Times*, 13 August 1999).

The Richmond-upon-Thames Borough Labour Party and the Richmond Park and Twickenham Conservative Associations wrote jointly to the Secretary of State to the effect that,

> 'The Boundary Commission has accepted *in toto* the partisan propositions of the controlling Liberal Party. We are disappointed by this uncritical stance by the Commission...(The proposals) were unilaterally devised by the Liberal political leadership and forced through on a majority vote against the formal opposition of Labour and Conservative parties. The political direction was clear. Certain proposals were tabled without notice to other parties by the Council Leader. The entire purpose of the proposals appears to be to preserve two wards artificially in what is called Richmond, while radically changing, or eliminating, those wards which recently elected Labour and Conservative councillors.'

The role of 'politics' in the PER

When the PER began there seemed some acceptance on all sides that Richmond-upon-Thames was safe for the Liberal Democrats. Indeed the Director of Reviews was quoted as saying at the member briefing that the review was '...unlikely to affect the balance of power in Richmond as there is such a large Liberal Democrat majority' (*Richmond and Twickenham Times*, 10 July 1998). Although the Commission was told that 'officers' initial proposals were amended by the Review of Boundaries Sub-Committee to reflect concerns regarding the splitting of some local communities', this was the reverse of what happened. Rather officers were asked to comment on drafts from the member/political side. As we have seen, the council's submission to the Commission was solely based on the scheme produced by the Liberal Democrats. The submissions produced by the Conservative and Labour parties were similar to the 'council's' in a number of areas, but there were some significant differences. The Leader of the Conservative group did not want to increase the size of the council and initially argued that 51 councillors would give better electoral equality. However, the Conservatives' scheme eventually plumped for eighteen wards and 54 councillors to avoid problems with crossing the river. Under their proposals there was one less ward in Richmond itself, the heart of Liberal Democrat electoral strength. It was assumed that Labour, as a minority party in the borough, would concentrate on fighting its own particular corners once the Commission had laid its Draft Recommendations on the table. It may well be that both Labour and the Conservatives were rather thrown by the extent and rapidity with which the Commission accepted the council (Liberal Democrat) proposals. By the time they tried to do something about it, it was too late.

London Borough of Westminster (Table 6.5)

Introduction

The City of Westminster, located in the very heart of London, has been controlled by the Conservatives since its formation in 1964. At the time of the review there were 47 Conservative and 13 Labour councillors. The electorate before the review was 125,580. Officers consulted the London Research Centre but did not use it to provide their projections. Instead, figures were produced using planning data and council knowledge about under-registration in certain areas. The high number of foreign nationals in Westminster caused some difficulties with the projections. The Commission was informed that the electorate was expected to grow by 7.5% to 134,594 by 2003. Westminster was in the third tranche of London boroughs to be reviewed, Stage One beginning on 22 September 1998.

Preparing the submission(s)

The review in Westminster was well organised. Officers began work a month before the formal start and wrote to the parties asking for their views on what criteria should be borne in mind as schemes were developed. They also provided data to all parties to enable them to design their own submissions. Two schemes were devised by officers and 'leading members' from the majority party on the basis of universal

Table 6.5 City of Westminster L.B.C.

Review timetable			
Last review	*Draft publ.*	*Final publ.*	*Order made*
Jul-77	Mar-99	Sep-99	Mar-00
Submissions			
No. of full submissions		*Council submission*	
1		Yes	
Representations			
	Draft stage	*Final stage*	*Public meeting?*
	12	60	No
Wards/councillors			
	Before	*Draft*	*Final*
	23/60	20/60	20/60
Ward pattern			
	Before	*Draft*	*Final*
Single member	0	0	0
Two member	9	0	0
Three member	14	20	20
Councillor/elector ratio (1:x)			
	Before	*Draft**	*Final**
	2093	2243	2243
Ward electorate variance			
	Before	*Draft**	*Final**
% wards >10% variance	39.1	0.0	0.0
% wards >20% variance	4.4	0.0	0.0
Worst positive % variance	25.0	3.0	3.0
Worst negative % variance	20.0	5.0	5.0
Average % variance	9.0	2.0	2.0

* after 5 years according to electorate projections

three-member wards – Option A and Option B. Both schemes had 20 wards and 60 councillors and all the wards had an electoral variance within +/-5% of the mean. Significant changes to boundaries were inevitable as Westminster previously had nine two-member and 14 three-member wards. Approximately one month after the start of Stage One the options came before the Policy and Resources Committee-appointed Members' Panel. This panel had three members, two Conservative and one Labour, and had to decide which option went out for a month long period of consultation. In fact the Members' Panel decided formally to adopt Option A for consultation and to indicate that this was the council's preference, but also agreed to circulate Option B. This was the first occasion on which any Labour representative had seen the council's schemes.

Consultation was taken very seriously in the borough. Conservative councillors suggested that both macro and micro changes were important, and that they should consider the public's ideas very carefully. One told us that he believed that consultation was important for electors and would show the Commission that there was public support for the submitted scheme. He asserted that some other authorities in London had hardly consulted at all. The council's proposals were sent to political parties and independent candidates who stood for election in 1998, amenity societies and resident organisations. A leaflet was produced by the council which explained the review and where the electorate could examine the scheme. The borough's scheme was displayed at all libraries in the borough and at the council's three One Stop Services. An item also appeared in the borough's newspaper, *Westminster Reporter*.

Interaction with the Commission

Twelve representations were received by the Commission during Stage One. Apart from the council scheme, representations were received from two Labour constituency parties, the Westminster and City of London Liberal Democrats, one councillor, and seven residents. The borough council wrote in its submission to the Commission that its proposals had been revised following representations received through its public consultation process. For example, the area of Mayfair would no longer be split between the St. James and West End wards, but remain wholly within West End. The Commission based its Draft Recommendations on the City Council's Option A scheme, but proposed adopting the 'alternative option' in the north east of the borough (the Church Street ward) – see Box 6.3. A total of 60 representations were received by the Commission during Stage Three. Fifty of these came from residents of the borough and most complained about specific changes relating to their own ward. The Commission decided to confirm its Draft Recommendations in their entirety. Unusually, at the Commission meeting which discussed the Westminster review, the political impact of changing the boundaries was highlighted. A Commission officer noted in a report to the meeting that, 'The City Council's scheme is certainly open to allegations of 'gerrymandering', as it would abolish the only Labour held ward in the north east of the borough'.

The role of 'politics' in the PER

An interview with a Conservative councillor revealed that a number of schemes had been privately produced by the Conservative group. Although they fitted the rules for electoral equality, it was acknowledged that some might be seen as obvious attempts at a gerrymander and would run the risk of being rejected outright by the

Commission. A councillor did confess that if boundary changes had been the responsibility of the borough rather than the Commission, then a completely different scheme would have been implemented. The scheme put forward by the council/ Conservative group was, it seems, tempered by rationality and the rules of the Commission. Nonetheless, the Labour member of the Members' Panel pronounced himself unhappy with a council report which stated that 'In discussion considerable consensus has been reached on appropriate boundaries for consultation purposes for most of the City' (26 October 1998). He asked fellow members whom this consensus was between, and argued that the options for change produced by the council had come from leading members with no Labour group input. One Labour councillor wrote to Lord Neill, Chairman of the Committee on Standards of Conduct in Public Life, asking him to investigate gerrymandering in the borough. The member wrote that,

> 'Over the past decade Westminster Council has been subject to a catalogue of allegations about the abuse of position for party political advantage. This appears, sadly, to be yet another example' (*Westminster and Pimlico News*, 26 November 1998).

Labour was particularly annoyed by the proposals in Option A to divide the Church Street ward. In one councillor's opinion this was a blatant attempt to get rid of Labour councillors,

> 'What arguments can be put forward to defend this option? The Church Street ward has natural boundaries including the Marylebone and Edgware roads and a railway line. It is a community in itself.'

The Church Street ward is currently represented by three Labour councillors and has been a party bastion since the 1920s. A Labour councillor who had represented the ward between 1974-90 wrote that,

> 'The proposal breaks the ward into three, and associates each part with an area with which it has little in common. Church Street ward comprises largely social housing. It scores highly on indicators of need and this can enable it to attract special funding. Such recognition can be lost when the needs of poor areas and those of wealthy areas are averaged. I have no doubt that the commonality of interest of the electors of Church Street would continue to be best represented by Councillors from a single ward, rather than being split among Councillors representing populations with different interests and other priorities' (Joe Hegarty, letter to Westminster LBC Chief Executive).

It should be remembered that the Conservative-majority Members' Panel did agree to attach Option B, which retained the Church Street ward, to the consultation package and thus made it easy for the Commission to make the amendment. This was another indication of how the party's caution balanced its desire for electoral advantage. The council had suffered a number of political embarrassments in recent

Box 6.3 Redrawing the boundaries of the Church Street ward in Westminster

One of two options submitted to the Commission by the Conservative-controlled City Council proposed the abolition of the Church Street ward and the dispersal of its electors to the Lords and Hamilton Terrace wards. This provoked controversy because it was an island of Labour support surrounded by a sea of safe Conservative territory.

Westminster existing boundaries

Contd./

years and there was a feeling that everything had to be seen as fair and above board. Interestingly, one Conservative councillor suggested the ruling party believed that Option A would not be accepted, and it would be better to have Option B than a scheme imposed by the Commission. Another revealed that some of his colleagues would probably have been happy if Option A failed because it would involve some 'social housing' being moved into their wards.

Box 6.3 continued

In the event there was little real support for this proposal and the Commission encountered scant opposition to its recommendation broadly to retain the Church Street ward.

Westminster final recommendations

Source: Based on maps published in the LGCE's Final Recommendations for Westminster. © Crown Copyright

Although there were no Liberal Democrat councillors in Westminster, that party too did try to play a role in the PER. Representatives complained in the *Evening Standard* that the Conservatives,

> '...have in effect, two bites at the cherry: they can make a party submission like everyone else, and they can also instruct officials on the supposedly impartial submission that the council itself is allowed to put forward, which would be another attempt by Westminster Tories to rig the result ...the truth is out – they are at it again' (3 November 1998).

Northamptonshire County Council (Table 6.6)

Introduction

The county of Northamptonshire, which encompasses 7 district councils, is situated in the east midlands some 70 miles from London. Labour has controlled the county council since 1993. At the time of the review the party had 37 councillors, the Conservatives 27, and the Liberal Democrats four. The council received formal notice of the review two months in advance, with Stage One beginning on 22 September 1998. Its electorate in that year, 464,368, was expected to increase by nearly 5% to 486,290 in 2003. These projections were produced by the county. In some instances the county was projecting a lower increase in electorate over the five year period to 2003 than had been forecast by individual districts in their calculations for the period 1996-2001 made at the time of their own PERs. The county was reluctant to produce projected figures for the existing county divisions as they would have to be freshly calculated on the basis of new district wards and many of the boundaries were likely to be changed anyway. Nevertheless, the Commission asked that this be done so that it could compare electoral variances before and after the review. Interviews with council staff revealed some difficulties in liaison between them and the Commission in addition to this disagreement about the utility of county division projections. For example, the Commission's Chief Executive offered to come to the council for half a day in August, but because of holidays and other commitments the meeting never took place. At a subsequent meeting in September, the Review Leader arrived on his own because the Director of Reviews had missed the train and the Review Manager could not attend. Unusually, the Commission was not represented at the press launch of the review and the council declined a meeting between members and the Commission. The Commission did, however, make another visit to the council on 9 November 1998.

Preparing the submission(s)

Officers were well prepared for the review to begin. At the end of June the county set up an *ad hoc* Working Group on the PER to prepare options for each district and to submit these to the council. This group consisted of seven councillors – four Labour, two Conservative, and one Liberal Democrat. Its first meeting, on 16 July 1998, discussed the guiding principles of the review and noted that 45 out of the existing 68 divisions in Northamptonshire had electoral variances in excess of +/-10%. It was agreed that there should be 73 county electoral divisions based, as far as possible, on the new district wards; that urban and rural areas should be kept separate; and that the scheme should adhere to the Commission's requirements on electoral variance. Some members did, however, express disquiet at the Commission paying so much attention to numerical equality when 'the electorate forecasts are

Table 6.6 Northamptonshire C.C.

Review timetable			
Last review	*Draft publ.*	*Final publ.*	*Order made*
Dec-80	May-99	Nov-99	Sep-00
Submissions			
No. of full submissions		*Council submission*	
1		Yes	
Representations			
	Draft stage	*Final stage*	*Public meeting?*
	16	49	No
Wards/councillors			
	Before	*Draft*	*Final*
	68/68	73/73	73/73
Ward pattern			
	Before	*Draft*	*Final*
Single member	68	73	73
Two member	0	0	0
Three member	0	0	0
Councillor/elector ratio (1:x)			
	Before	*Draft**	*Final**
	6825	6662	6662
Ward electorate variance			
	Before	*Draft**	*Final**
% wards >10% variance	66.2	17.8	19.2
% wards >20% variance	30.9	0.0	0.0
Worst positive % variance	172.0	17.0	17.0
Worst negative % variance	37.0	20.0	20.0
Average % variance	18.0	6.1	6.1

* after 5 years according to electorate projections

not that accurate'. The group's task was complicated by the fact that the district reviews in Northamptonshire had resulted in a great deal of change. The number of district councillors had increased from 260 to 273, and boundaries had been revised in 104 of the former 148 wards. The new arrangements for wards in the county provided little match with the existing divisions. The only district in the County where district wards and county divisions had previously coincided was Northampton. It was decided that this pattern should be maintained and that the number of divisions in Northampton should therefore be increased from 21 to 23. Elsewhere, options were drafted by officers following the principles set by the working group. The council produced two options for consultation in each district except Northampton, where the die had already been cast. Three further meetings were held at important stages of the review – on 14 September 1998 to consider responses to consultation, in early October to produce a draft scheme to take to committee, and on 24 June 1999 when the Commission's Draft Recommendations were discussed. At the beginning of the review the county's Chief Executive had floated a radical proposal for significantly reducing the size of the council. However, officers felt there was insufficient time to work on it, and councillors – with at least one eye on their own futures – took the view that they were happier tinkering with boundaries and keeping change to a minimum.

The council recognised from an early stage that consultation was a key part of the review process. It was decided in July that the county would consult with interested local groups and organisations on the criteria which should be applied to the review. For example, should there be an increase in the number of county councillors, and how important was it that county division and district ward boundaries should be either coterminous or nested? The responses to this perhaps rather hypothetical exercise were examined before the working party agreed on a way to proceed. Once the council had decided upon its actual options for each district, there was a further three week period of consultation. This included placing on deposit a package of information about the review at all district council offices and at four libraries across the county. More than 70 responses were received and the consultation was regarded as being a success. The amount of feedback varied widely across the districts. There was virtually no response from East Northamptonshire, while nearly every parish council in Corby submitted comments on the council's schemes.

Interaction with the Commission

Sixteen representations were received by the Commission at Stage One. The County Council had submitted the only county-wide proposal. This included a scheme for each district but with two options for Corby, Wellingborough and Kettering. The majority option in each case was supported by the Labour party, and the minority option was that favoured by Conservative members. The Draft Recommendations were broadly based on the minority scheme for Corby (six members) and Wellingborough, and the majority scheme for Kettering. The Commission adopted 44 out of 74 divisions proposed by the County Council. The working group were not very happy with the report because they believed that the Commission had gone too far in its efforts to achieve coterminosity. An officer told us that the Commission's new rules seemed to be, 'coterminosity first, electoral equality next, and forget community identity'. In addition, the Commission was felt to be inconsistent in its application of coterminosity versus electoral equality. The County Council wrote in response to the Draft Recommendations that,

> 'What particularly concerns the council about the Draft Recommendations is that the Commission have not argued on a consistent basis across the County. In Daventry district they have overturned a solution which they accepted achieved good equality but little coterminosity for one which had good coterminosity but worse equality. In the northern part of East Northamptonshire, the Commission have completely disregarded a solution which reflects local interests and identities for one which is coterminous but does not reflect local interests and has no better electoral equality. Perversely, in Northampton, the only part of the Council where District wards and County Divisions have been identical, the Commission recommend moving away from coterminosity despite this being opposed by authorities and all local parties'.

The Commission received 49 further representations at Stage Three. Although the County Council continued to argue for the schemes submitted at Stage One, the Commission substantially endorsed its Draft Recommendations and made only three relatively minor changes.

The role of 'politics' in the PER

It was suggested by officers that the working party had worked well on a non-political basis until a split between the Labour and Conservative members resulted in 'majority' and 'minority' options being submitted. Indeed twenty Conservative councillors walked out of a full council meeting complaining that they had not been given a chance to put forward their alternative schemes. Officers believed that although there did not appear to be too much politics in the meetings, it was likely that a great deal of activity was going on behind the scenes in the group meetings. The Commission was aware that new boundaries in Northamptonshire could have a profound impact on what was a politically marginal authority.

One area, for example, which prompted a great deal of controversy was Corby. This was the only district in the county in which the electorate had declined in the five years before 1998. Before the review it had seven county councillors. The average electorate in each division was 5,566, compared to the county average of 6,824 – a variance in excess of -20%. Given demographic trends which were likely to result in a further population decline, it seemed that Corby was over-represented and that the number of county members would need to be reduced by one. The County therefore consulted on two six-councillor options. However, Corby Borough Council disputed the electorate figures and argued that by 2003 they would be significantly in excess of the County's expectations. In turn this meant that the Borough was entitled to retain seven county councillors. The county council called the projections 'optimistic', but nevertheless voted to recommend to the

Commission seven divisions for Corby. It was clearly in the interests of the Labour majority on the county council and in Corby itself to avoid losing what would certainly have been a Labour seat. The minority (Conservative) option was for six members and, as noted above, the Commission came down in its favour.

Conclusions

These case studies provide a fascinating picture of how six different authorities approached their Periodic Electoral Reviews. All were obliged to work within the rules and framework set by the Local Government Commission, but the detail of what was done and how varied widely depending on a number of factors and dynamics internal to each council. Some chose to delegate the whole operation to officers; in others the review was seen as an intensely political process rightly the preserve of elected members. Some submitted a single scheme to the Commission; others felt it necessary to allow each party the discretion to do its own thing; and one made no submission at all. Some took care to consult widely on the review and any proposed boundary changes; among others the review took place effectively out of the public gaze. For its part the Commission takes no view on what is 'right' and what is 'wrong', but it clearly prefers to have evidence of public consultation and will be more favourably disposed to those schemes which abide by the rules *and* seem to have attracted genuine consensus. Where no schemes at all are forthcoming from an authority, it is the authority rather than the Commission that is the more likely to find that it has 'cooked (its) own goose' when the Recommendations are published. The projection of electorates provides an essential building block in the process of re-warding and is itself another potential flash point. The Commission routinely admits in its Recommendations that this is an 'inexact science' (for example, Corby, Final Recommendations, 1997: para 28) and that it is forced to rely very heavily on information provided by the local authorities themselves. Such information may not always be 'value free'.

Although all the authorities we looked at were controlled by a single political party, most at least began the process with the aim of reaching cross-party agreement. Often this did not prove possible, but even then fundamental disputes tended to revolve around particular wards and areas rather than across the authority as a whole. Perhaps that is not wholly surprising, for the need to achieve levels of electoral equality and 'shape' acceptable to the Commission severely limited the scope for 'gerrymandering'. In some councils, though, just a few wards might make the difference between the success or failure of a political party. In both Croydon and the Corby district of Northamptonshire, the then majority Labour groups were very concerned that a disadvantageous boundary change could cost them not only seats but also control of the council. The schemes they supported reflected that fear. The Conservatives' preference for Option A in Westminster had less of an urgent electoral imperative, but nonetheless could be seen as an attempt to minimise opposition strength in one part of the Borough. Faced with such circumstances, the Commission is often called upon to make a 'judgement of Solomon'. It is alive to political machinations when some of their flavour permeates the submissions it receives. However, there will be occasions when skilled party operators can disguise a scheme driven by their own electoral advantage as one about which there is widespread consensus. Certainly that was how the Labour and Conservative parties in Richmond-upon-Thames interpreted the outcome.

Case studies, of course, are only part of the story. Many more authorities underwent PER before and during the course of our research and we gathered a wide range of information about what happened to them. The next Chapter examines the Reviews from a more statistical point of view and assesses the degree to which they changed local authority electoral arrangements – and the extent to which such changes met the Commission's own criteria.

Chapter 7

The Outcomes of Periodic Electoral Reviews

In Chapter 3 we outlined the rules governing Periodic Electoral Reviews and the various aspects of local electoral arrangements with which the LGCE concerns itself. In this chapter we examine the outcomes of the PERs in all 127 local authorities which were reviewed before or during the period of our research. The aim is to measure the extent and magnitude of the changes proposed by the Commission (including any divergences between the Draft and Final Recommendations). We look in turn at the electoral cycle, the size and structure of wards both within and across local authorities, the size of the council, the calculation and accuracy of electorate projections and, crucially, the impact of review on both councillor/elector ratios and electoral equality. Finally, we calculate the degree to which ward boundaries were redrawn as a result of the reviews, and assess the consistency with which the Commission has applied its criteria over time.

Electoral Cycle

Just three authorities took advantage of the PER to propose a change of electoral cycle. Dacorum and Warrington both wanted to move from whole council elections to a system of electing a third of members annually. In Dacorum, the Commission consulted on this proposal but concluded in its Final Recommendations that,

> '...In view of the absence of consensus, we do not consider that we should propose a change to election by thirds. We consider that it would be more appropriate for the Council itself to resolve this issue, as it is empowered to alter its electoral cycle unilaterally, by a two-thirds majority, under the 1972 Local Government Act' (Dacorum Final Recommendations, 1998: para 92).

In Warrington, the Commission did not consult on the proposal to change the electoral cycle at the draft stage. The Commission wrote in the Draft Recommendations that,

> 'While the Commission has stated that it would wish to respect local preferences, on the basis of the arguments put to it at this stage, it has not been sufficiently

> persuaded that there is a case for changes to the electoral cycle' (Warrington Draft Recommendations, 1996: para 68).

Seven representations were made to the Commission on this issue during Stage Three, all supporting a change to the electoral cycle in Warrington. The council suggested that the matter had been fully debated and that the changes commanded unanimous support. As a result of these submissions, and given that there was no campaign against the change, the Commission recommended that the electoral cycle in Warrington should be changed so that councillors could be elected by thirds. Purbeck District Council proposed changing its electoral cycle the other way – from annual to all-out elections. The Commission supported this change in both its Draft and Final Recommendations, published in October 1996 and March 1997 respectively. However, with the election of the Labour government in May 1997 and the subsequent DETR Consultation Paper raising the possibility of universal annual elections, the Secretary of State used his powers to insist that Purbeck retained its original electoral timetable when the Statutory Instrument was published in September 1998.[1] Indeed, the uncertainty over government policy on local government electoral arrangements led to considerable delays in the publication of Statutory Instruments giving effect to the Commission's Recommendations for a number of authorities during this period.

In one other case some form of change in electoral cycle was inevitable. The new unitary authority of Medway Towns was created by amalgamating two districts, Gillingham and Rochester-on-Medway, which had different electoral cycles. The authority opted for all-out elections as previously used in Rochester-on-Medway. A similar decision had been made following the 1996 amalgamation of Brighton (annual) and Hove (all-out) district councils, which had been carried through without an accompanying electoral review.

Council structure

Table 7.1 shows the impact of PERs on the number and type of wards in the reviewed authorities. Although the total number of wards fell only modestly from 3,059 before the review to 2,937 after the publication of the Final Recommendations, the composition of those wards changed more dramatically. Following review there were 213 (or 20%) fewer single-member wards and four fewer two-member wards. By contrast there were 95 (or 9.1%) more three-member wards. No fewer than 82 of these were in London where, as we have seen, the Commission issued strong guidance about the desirability of creating wards to allow for the future implementation of annual elections. The table also indicates the degree of change

[1] A similar case arose in Nuneaton and Bedworth in July 2000.

between the draft and final stages. A total of 36 wards were added, with the balance of change favouring a move back to single member wards. In no case did the Commission support the creation of a ward with more than three members.

Table 7.1 The structure of wards in local authorities

	Number of wards	*Single-member*	*Two-member*	*Three-member*	*N*
Before	3,059	1,063	955	1,041	127
Draft	2,901	810	968	1,123	127
Final	2,937	850	951	1,136	127

Detailed reading of Commission reports suggests that much of the fall in the number of single-member wards was a result of ward electorates having become too small in the long period since the previous electoral review. The solution was either completely to abolish them or to amalgamate them with parts of other wards to bring the total electorate up to the average authority councillor/elector ratio. The 40 extra such wards created following the Draft Recommendations reflect local authority success in persuading the Commission to respect existing local ties even at the cost of some reduction in overall electoral equality. Further evidence of such a trend will be presented later in the chapter. The Commission's substantive decisions on council structure also show it moving away from its initially expressed support for single member wards (Guidance, 1996: para 26). For example, a change from multi- to single-member ward schemes with acceptable electoral equality was submitted to the Commission and rejected in favour of multi-member solutions in both Stevenage and Taunton Deane. In each case it appears that there was reluctance to embrace the necessary radical alteration of boundaries and its associated upheaval, despite interested parties reiterating their support for such a change during Stage Three. More recently, the Commission has found a pattern of uniform single-member wards 'to be incompatible with our statutory criteria and the achievement of good electoral equality. We have yet to receive a...scheme which gave good reflection of community identity and good electoral equality' (Private correspondence from Chief Executive, June 2001).

Council size

Given that the Commission started its programme of reviews with the assumption that the current number of members in a council was already producing effective and convenient local government, it is not surprising to discover that most changes in council size amounted merely to incremental adjustments following the redrawing of ward boundaries. Specifically, the Commission tests that the correct proportion of the total number of councillors is allocated to any geographically distinct parts of a district, for example urban and rural areas or areas on either side of a significant barrier such as a river or a motorway. Table 7.2 shows that there was a total increase of just 56 councillors from 6,086 before the review to 6,142 at the publication of the Commission's Final Recommendations. The smallest authority in our sample in terms of council size was and remains Purbeck, whereas Ealing was supplanted by Medway Towns as the largest. In 44% of local authorities the PER resulted in an increase in size, in 23% a decrease, and in a third there was no change. One of the greatest increases (from 68 to 80) was in Medway Towns. Here a directed electoral review was conducted against the background of an Order giving effect to the Commission's own structural review. This established the electoral arrangements for the new unitary authority by disregarding imbalances in electorates and decreeing that each existing ward in the two districts that were being merged should elect two members. However, wearing its PER hat, the Commission felt obliged to take into account both the need to balance representation between Gillingham and Rochester-on-Medway, and the fact that the new council would be taking on previous county council responsibilities. Before the review there was one councillor for every 1770 electors in Gillingham and one for every 2117 in Rochester-on-Medway. The councillor/elector ratio in Medway Towns was proposed to be 1:2219. The 80 elected members was still 27 fewer than the total number of county and district councillors before reorganisation. The London borough of Lewisham saw the greatest reduction in the number of members (the size of council fell from 67 to 54). The authority had linked the electoral review with the government's proposals for modernising councils and argued that 'the proposals for streamlining councils, separating the political executive, representative and scrutiny roles mean that we should move towards a smaller sized council' (Lewisham Draft Recommendations, 1999: para 25).

Table 7.2 The number of councillors in local authorities

	Mean	*Total*	*Min*	*Local auth.*	*Max*	*Local auth.*	*N*
Before	47.9	6,086	22	Purbeck	71	Ealing	127
Draft	48.3	6,134	24	Purbeck	80	Medway Towns	127
Final	48.4	6,142	24	Purbeck	80	Medway Towns	127

The Commission had made clear that, 'Proposals for increases in present council size will need to be justified in full' (Guidance, 1996: para 17). Just because the population in an authority has increased, it does not mean that the size of the council also has to increase. However, as we have seen, the Commission accepted that there might be 'small' increases in the size of the new unitary authorities as a result of them taking on some county council responsibilities. There are fourteen such councils in our database – the eight directed reviews plus Bath and North East Somerset, Bristol, Isle of Wight, North Somerset, South Gloucestershire, and Swindon. In nine cases there was an increase in the number of councillors, ranging from two additional members in Blackburn, Bristol, and North Somerset to 12 more in Medway Towns. A total of 53 extra council seats were created in this way. The factors which the Commission considered to be important when adjudicating on an increase in council size can be seen in the cases of Southend-on-Sea, not part of our statistical database, and Bromley. In Southend, a cross-party working group sought an increase in council size from 39 to 51. The authority carried out an effective advertising campaign and provided good evidence of having consulted its residents on the most effective way of managing the council. The Commission recommended the change. In Bromley, there was no consensus on the size of the council and no evidence of public involvement. Bromley Borough Council wanted to increase the size of the council from 60 to 69, but the other borough-wide submissions from the Conservative group on the council and from a resident favoured retaining the current membership. The Commission supported the *status quo*. In all, slightly more than half (53%) of authorities whose whole council scheme was included in full in the Draft Recommendations proposed a (usually very modest) increase in council size. On the other hand, few councils saw any reason to offer up a reduction in size. Such a move may have found favour with some Chief Executives, but for members it would be a case of turkeys voting for Christmas. In fact just 7% of authorities put forward schemes which would leave them with fewer members. The uncertain status of the Commission's size bandings was reinforced by the fact that several authorities remained 'below size' even after their PER. Before the current round of reviews, five councils in our sample, Purbeck with 22 councillors, Corby (27), Berwick-upon-Tweed (28) and Alnwick and Oswestry (29 each), fell below the minimum size of 30 for shire districts. Although all except Oswestry were given additional members, only Alnwick was brought 'up to size'.

The generally small adjustments to council size made as a result of PERs should not come as a surprise. The Commission's guidance contained a presumption against granting significant increases, and proposals for large reductions were unlikely to be accepted by councillors. For most authorities alterations in council size were a knock on effect of the boundary changes made inevitable by electoral reviews rather than at the core of the process. The one development that might have caused them to alter their approach, the government's modernisation agenda on political management, was fully articulated too late in the day. Even in London most boroughs – Havering and Lewisham were exceptions – took the pragmatic view of retaining the *status quo* until the implications of any change were known. However, it is now clear that diversity in the structure and organisation of councils is to be encouraged and that future electoral reviews are likely to find that questions about council size which were not asked in the past are centre stage.[2]

Electorate projections

The average electorate before review in the 126 authorities for which we have complete data was 90,621.[3] The smallest electorate was 19,681 in Teesdale and the largest 291,749 in Bristol. According to local authority projections the average electorate five years after review was expected to grow to 93,721 – an increase of 3.4%. However, figures for the initial years suggest that such growth is unlikely. The 1999 electoral register showed an increase of only 0.34% in the number of electors compared with the situation at the time of review between one and three years previously. By the time the 2000 register was published this figure had risen to 0.43%. Authorities would argue that it takes time for the developments which they took into account to work through, but it seems fair to conclude that many over-estimated their likely electorates. Some 35 councils in our database – including 9 of the 22 London boroughs – which had predicted an increase in five years time actually had smaller electorates in 2000 than at the time of their review. The most serious disparities are outlined in Table 7.3. One explanation may be that the canvass for the 2000 register was poor because, with no general election in the offing, residents were indifferent to whether or not their names appeared. Indeed, when the 2001 register was published, Barnet recorded an additional 27,000 names, Barking and Dagenham 9,000 extra and Richmond-upon-Thames 6,000 more.

Table 7.3 Early disparities between current and projected electorates in London

	1999 electorate	*2003 electorate (projected)*	*Electorate change(%) (projected)*	*2000 electorate*	*Electorate change (%) 1999-00*
Barnet	227,425	234,145	2.9	198,093	-12.9
Barking and Dagenham	114,004	121,620	6.3	107,055	-6.1
Richmond-upon-Thames	125,153	128,096	2.4	120,893	-3.4

We decided to check the accuracy of the projected electorates provided to the Commission more rigorously by concentrating on the 52 local authorities whose reviews had begun during the currency of the 1996 electoral register and whose projections were therefore calculated for 2001. In Table 7.4 we compare those projections with the 2001 register.

2 Recent reviews in some unitary councils show evidence of support for radical reductions in council size. See Draft Recommendations for Brighton, February 2001 and Draft Recommendations for Medway Towns, May 2001.

3 Blackburn did not provide the Commission with a projection.

Just one council, Allerdale, had expected its electorate to fall in five years time – from 75,867 in 1996 to 74,989 in 2001. The 2001 electoral register shows that the electorate in Allerdale has fallen since 1996, but by a smaller margin than expected – to 75,611. A further 7 out of 52 authorities – Dacorum, East Northamptonshire, Eden, Isle of Wight, South Kesteven, South Lakeland, and Telford and the Wrekin – appear to have under-estimated the increase in their electorates. In five cases the disparity is marginal, but in the Isle of Wight and Telford and the Wrekin the electorate in 2001 was almost 2% above projection. The remaining 44 local authorities over-estimated their five year electorate growth, eight of them by in excess of 5%. In a small authority like Alnwick, an over-estimation of just over 2,000 electors equates to an 8% difference between projected and actual figures. In Halton, the Commission's recommendations were based on projected electorates which proved to be nearly 5,000 electors out. Two authorities, Daventry (12.7%) and South Northamptonshire (15.5%), reported to the Commission that they expected their electorates to increase by more than 10% by 2001. The Commission accepted both claims. Daventry explained to the Commission that it had difficulty projecting future growth, especially in the town of Daventry itself, because although substantial development was planned it was not certain when it would take place. The 2001 electoral register shows that the electorate in Daventry had increased by 8% to 54,803, two-thirds of the growth projected. The Commission reports for South Northamptonshire give no special explanation for the large expected increase from 55,283 to 63,857 electors. The Draft Recommendations simply report that, 'The District Council has estimated rates and locations of housing development with regard to structure and local plans, and the expected rate of building over the five-year period' (South Northamptonshire Draft Recommendations, 1996 : para 35). In its Final Recommendations the Commission does no more than reiterate the standard formulation that, 'Reasonable estimates have been made of the changes in electorate that will arise. The Commission accepts that this is an inexact science and, having given consideration to projected electorates, is content that they represent the best estimates that can reasonably be made at this time' (South Northamptonshire Final Recommendations, 1997: para 34). By 2001 the electorate in South Northamptonshire had risen by 7.6% to 59,490, less than half way to its projected level.

There are occasions, however, when the Commission disputes the electorate projections provided by an authority. In Oswestry the council submitted figures to the Commission which predicted its electorate to increase by 10.5% from 28,259 in 1998 to 31,233 in 2003. At the draft stage, the Commission asked the council to re-consider their projections and asked for further representations on the matter. One parish council, Llanymynech and Pant, had already questioned the amount of population growth projected for two wards within its boundaries. At the end of Stage Two, after discussions between the borough council and the county council,

Table 7.4 Rank order of disparities between 2001 electorate projections and actual 2001 electorates

	1996 electorate	*Projected 2001 electorate*	*Projected %ch 1996-01*	*Actual 2001 electorate*	*Actual %ch 1996-01*	*%diff. projected-actual*
Alnwick	24,740	27,198	9.94	25,171	1.74	8.19
Wansbeck	48,568	49,666	2.26	45,751	-5.80	8.06
South Northamptonshire	55,283	63,857	15.51	59,490	7.61	7.90
Lincoln	63,707	66,930	5.06	62,455	-1.97	7.02
Three Rivers	59,372	63,972	7.75	60,389	1.71	6.03
Corby	39,101	41,456	6.02	39,241	0.36	5.66
Halton	92,972	97,031	4.37	91,809	-1.25	5.62
Barrow-in-Furness	54,913	55,400	0.89	52,612	-4.19	5.08
Mendip	75,883	79,374	4.60	75,832	-0.07	4.67
Wellingborough	52,636	56,083	6.55	53,665	1.95	4.59
Daventry	50,645	57,075	12.70	54,803	8.21	4.49
Peterborough	109,011	114,080	4.65	109,460	0.41	4.24
Macclesfield	122,065	125,581	2.88	120,604	-1.20	4.08
Purbeck	34,273	37,019	8.01	35,647	4.01	4.00
Warrington	145,466	152,217	4.64	146,728	0.87	3.77
North Kesteven	66,604	72,723	9.19	70,269	5.50	3.68
Blackpool	115,891	116,054	0.14	111,961	-3.39	3.53
Carlisle	80,557	82,001	1.79	79,419	-1.41	3.21
Berwick-upon-Tweed	21,826	22,509	3.13	21,835	0.04	3.09
Medway Towns	177,551	186,545	5.07	181,099	2.00	3.07
Hertsmere	68,871	71,192	3.37	69,191	0.46	2.91
Thurrock	98,310	106,136	7.96	103,548	5.33	2.63
West Lindsey	61,692	64,635	4.77	63,024	2.16	2.61
Stevenage	57,255	61,002	6.54	59,525	3.96	2.58
South Hams	64,245	67,981	5.82	66,446	3.43	2.39
North Hertfordshire	88,602	92,390	4.28	90,389	2.02	2.26
Taunton Deane	76,356	80,364	5.25	78,759	3.15	2.10
Welwyn Hatfield	71,831	73,342	2.10	71,848	0.02	2.08
Boston	42,913	44,534	3.78	43,706	1.85	1.93
Isle of Wight	101,852	102,802	0.93	104,702	2.80	1.87
South Somerset	115,970	121,179	4.49	119,141	2.73	1.76
East Hertfordshire	93,466	99,873	6.85	98,233	5.10	1.75
Copeland	54,693	55,110	0.76	54,174	-0.95	1.71
Northampton	141,161	148,300	5.06	145,920	3.37	1.69
Telford and the Wrekin	109,992	114,347	3.96	116,172	5.62	1.66
Sedgemoor	78,998	83,443	5.63	82,146	3.98	1.64
Broxbourne	63,380	65,085	2.69	64,183	1.27	1.42

Contd./

Table 7.4 continued

	1996 electorate	*Projected 2001 electorate*	*Projected %ch 1996-01*	*Actual 2001 electorate*	*Actual %ch 1996-01*	*%diff. projected-actual*
Castle Morpeth	38,967	39,959	2.55	39,406	1.13	1.42
South Lakeland	82,091	83,421	1.62	84,403	2.82	1.20
West Somerset	27,603	28,133	1.92	27,817	0.78	1.14
Kettering	60,843	64,986	6.81	64,293	5.67	1.14
South Kesteven	91,408	95,972	4.99	96,708	5.80	0.81
Eden	38,037	39,341	3.43	39,644	4.22	0.80
East Northamptonshire	53,696	57,935	7.89	58,347	8.66	0.77
Watford	57,645	61,240	6.24	60,892	5.63	0.60
South Holland	57,807	61,883	7.05	61,539	6.46	0.60
Tynedale	45,829	47,230	3.06	46,963	2.47	0.58
East Lindsey	97,342	101,514	4.29	100,964	3.72	0.57
Allerdale	75,867	74,989	-1.16	75,407	-0.61	0.55
Dacorum	103,252	104,976	1.67	105,529	2.21	0.54
St. Albans	98,340	100,348	2.04	99,956	1.64	0.40
Blyth Valley	62,527	63,338	1.30	63,183	1.05	0.25
Mean	**74,460**	**77,764**	**4.67**	**76,046**	**2.17**	**2.81**

officers agreed that they had over-estimated the number of housing completions expected over the next five years. After a number of amendments had taken place to both the existing electorate and the projections, the council suggested that their electorate would likely increase from its revised 1998 level of 28,312 to 30,117 in five years time – an increase of 6.4%. The Commission reported in the Final Recommendations, 'We were content that these revised forecasts formed a more realistic assessment of growth patterns and accepted them' (Oswestry Final Recommendations, 1999: para 26). According to the 2001 electoral register, the electorate in Oswestry has so far increased from 28,312 in 1998 to 28,928 – a growth of 2.2%. Elsewhere, Commission meeting minutes show that it

> '... expressed reservations over Lambeth's five-year projections for Bishop's ward, particularly in relation to the estimation of the number of resident electors to be occupying some of the converted residential developments which are currently in progress or are planned' (Minutes of meeting on 15 December 1998).

The council had projected the ward's electorate to rise by over 40% – from 7,880 in 1998 to 11,104 in 2003. The Commission decided to publish its Draft Recommendations using these figures but noted that, '...given the uncertainty over the figures, particularly in the north of the borough, we wish to seek the views of all interested parties on this issue (including further evidence if appropriate) during Stage Three' (Lambeth Draft Recommendations, 1999: para 41). All three political groups of the council supported the electorate projections in the borough at Stage Three. Although there was some opposition to the figures from local councillors, the Commission did accept the projections in its Final Recommendations. By 2001 the electorate in Bishop's ward had risen to 8,166 – an increase of less than 4%. Another London borough, Croydon, also experienced problems with its electorate projections. As Croydon was one of our case-study authorities – see Chapter 6, we were able to follow the intricacies and political issues that surrounded this important area of an electoral review. The story is told in Box 7.1.

The data we have examined would suggest that the calculation of electorate projections is one of the less satisfactory aspects of the PER process. Willfully or unintentionally optimistic estimates (and most councils err in that direction) can undermine the integrity of the Local Government Commission's work. They may lead to the preservation of wards whose current electorate has fallen too low, or to the establishment of new wards to the advantage of a particular political party. At worst they call into question the methodology of an electoral review. Although the Commission strives long and hard to achieve electoral equality within local authorities, all too often the figures on which its calculations are based never reflect the reality on the ground. The ideal of one vote, one value thus becomes a mirage forever disappearing over the horizon. Since we began this research the Commission has itself established a ward level database of electorates which will enable it to check the accuracy of the projections it has accepted and worked with. The Head of Policy at the Commission has acknowledged that such an analysis is likely to confirm that electorates have consistently been over-estimated. Nevertheless, it has been decided to leave individual authorities to continue to calculate these figures in consultation, where relevant, with county councils on the grounds that they alone have the necessary local knowledge and information.

Councillor/elector ratio

We might have expected that the average councillor/elector ratio would have fallen as a result of the review. Our reasoning for this was two-fold. First, as the representations to the Commission from councils and political groups were likely to have been devised or at least influenced by existing members, it would be irrational for them to submit schemes which would make their task of representing their electors more difficult. Second, given that the *status quo* was judged unacceptable by the Commission, stakeholders would be likely to opt for an increase rather than a decrease in council size. In fact, in the same way that the average size of councils was hardly affected by review, so the councillor/elector ratio remained largely unaltered. In 46% of authorities councillors now represent, on average, a smaller number of electors; in 26% more electors; and in 28% there has been no change. The precise figures for the councillor/elector ratio at different stages of the review

BOX 7.1 Compiling Electorate Projections in Croydon

The London Borough of Croydon has the largest population of the 32 London boroughs. At the time of the review in 1998 it had an electorate of 226,071, projected to increase by 1% to 227,677 in five years time. This was calculated by estimating future development in the borough. Members decided, however, to request the Commission that the borough be allowed to revise the base figure (1998 electoral register) because they believed that it under-estimated the true size of the eligible electorate. In its Guidance the Commission says that it,

> '...will take claims of under-registration into account for the purposes of five-year forecasts where credible evidence is provided, both of the existence of under-registration, and of steps being taken which are very likely to increase registration in a particular area' (Guidance, 1998: para 46).

The council suggested to the Commission that it would carry out a number of initiatives to improve the level of registration. These included setting up registration points in places people regularly visit such as train stations and supermarkets, and enlisting the help of ethnic minority community centres to deal with language problems, to display posters and distribute information, and to set up registration points. Taking into account estimated future development and an improvement in the accuracy of the register produced a new projected electorate of 237,991 in five years time – an increase of nearly 4% on the initial figures. The Commission used both the original and revised figures in its Draft Recommendations and asked for further evidence.

It seemed likely that the request to the Commission to accept the higher projected electorate figure had a party political motivation. Conventional wisdom had it that Labour was harmed by under-registration, and that any campaign to increase the numbers on the register would benefit that party. Certainly the minority party groups in the borough were unhappy with the revised electorate figures. The Conservatives suggested that there was no way that the council could find the extra people claimed and thereby increase the size of the register. For its part the LGCE was aware that under-registration is most apparent in Labour held wards and that electorate revisions are therefore a sensitive issue. By the time the Commission came to draft the Final Recommendations the council had adjusted its projected 2003 electorate down to 235,884, still a sizeable increase from the original position. This figure was accepted, not least because the 1999 electoral register showed an increase of nearly 5,000 electors over 1998 to 230,922. This was seen as acceptable evidence that the campaign to improve registration levels was reaping dividends. In 2001, however, the electoral register in Croydon had dropped back to 229,142 electors!

process are set out in Table 7.5. Before the review one councillor represented an average 1,804 electors. This figure falls marginally to 1,788 in terms of current electorates in the Commission's Final Recommendations, with a projected increase over 5 years to one councillor for every 1,855 electors.

However, there remains very considerable variation in councillor/elector ratios between authorities. Using data for current electorates from the Commission's Final Recommendations, there is a range of 3,553 between 1:615 in Teesdale and 1:4,168 in Bristol. In other words a councillor in Bristol represents, on average, nearly seven times more electors than a councillor in Teesdale. Similar, if less dramatic differences, can also be found between authorities of the same type. Among the shire districts Teesdale's councillor/elector ratio of 1:615 varies from that of Northampton (1:3,003) by a factor of almost 5. In London, there is one councillor for every 1,877 electors in Kensington and Chelsea, but one too for nearly twice as many (3,611) in Barnet. The Commission had previously stated that the ratio of councillors to electors should be around 1:4,000 in the Unitary authorities (Consultation, 1995: para 29). Bristol alone of the unitaries in our sample seems to approximate this. Most of the other councils have councillor/elector ratios of about half that size including Thurrock (1:2,166), Peterborough (1:1,912) and Blackburn (1:1,639).

Table 7.5 Councillor/elector ratios before and after the review process

	Mean ratio	*Min ratio*	*Local authority*	*Max ratio*	*Local authority*	*Range*	*N**
Before	1,804	635	Teesdale	4,290	Bristol	3,655	127
Before (+ 5 years)	1,871	642	Teesdale	4,352	Bristol	3,710	126
Draft	1,790	615	Teesdale	4,168	Bristol	3,553	127
Draft (+ 5 years)	1,856	622	Teesdale	4,228	Bristol	3,606	126
Final	1,788	615	Teesdale	4,168	Bristol	3,553	127
Final (+ 5 years)	1,855	622	Teesdale	4,228	Bristol	3,606	126

* One council, Blackburn, did not produce projections of its electorate

The Commission's attitude to such disparities is ambiguous. On the one hand, it rejects the system of 'banding' used in Scotland and, less successfully, Wales for ensuring that similarly populated and structured councils have similar councillor/elector ratios (see Chapter 3) and states in its public documentation that it does not make comparisons between districts. On the other hand, the minutes of a Commission meeting held on 28 January 1998 note a decision being made on the basis that,

> 'Although Elmbridge had a council size which was at the top of the Commission's indicative range band, its councillor/elector ratio was not excessive when compared with those of other Surrey districts.'

However, whilst such considerations may have been taken into account in Surrey, they seemed less relevant in Devon where two of the eight councils in our database had post-review ratios of more than 1:2,000 and three ones of less than 1:1,300. The single most important factor determining the councillor/elector ratios recommended by the Commission for authorities of all types appears to be what they were before the process started. The LGCE has made very little attempt to rationalise or standardise them and to that extent can be accused of ossifying a pattern of local government originally designed for an earlier age. In particular, while rejecting arguments that rural areas within local authorities should have more generous representation, the Commission is effectively preserving a system that provides a more generous councillor/elector ratio throughout sparsely populated councils.

Electoral equality

There can be little doubt that the Commission's prime aim is to comply with Schedule 11 of the 1972 Local Government Act and ensure that 'the ratio of the number of local government electors to the number of councillors to be elected shall be, as nearly as may be, the same in every ward in the district'. Indeed the whole point of the PER process is to correct imbalances which have grown up in the period since an authority's last electoral review.

i. Before the review

Table 7.6 shows that there were no fewer than 1,627 wards among our sample authorities which had an electoral variance greater than +/-10% from the average at the time of review. In the mean local authority 13 wards (more than half the total number) fell into this category. The range varied between one ward out of 20 in the London borough of Wandsworth to 90% of all wards in Northampton, where the electorate had increased by 35% since the boundaries were last reviewed in 1978. Left unchecked there would have been a further increase to 1,680 in the number of wards with such a variance in five years time. In 739 wards the electoral variance actually exceeded +/-20%. The mean local authority had six wards (23% of the total) with a disparity of this magnitude, although 13 councils had no such cases. At ward level the largest positive electoral variance before the review began was in Orton Waterville ward, Peterborough. Its 1996 electorate was 6,663 compared with an authority average of 2,271, a disparity of no less than 193%. The population of Peterborough had increased by 35% since the last PER and new developments had centred on particular parts of the area. The Commission noted that, 'Peterborough has a greater degree of electoral imbalance than any other principal local authority in England' (Peterborough Draft Recommendations, 1996: para 16). At the other extreme the single member ward of Edmondsley in Chester-le-Street had just 472 electors compared with a district-wide councillor/elector ratio of 1,310 – a variance from the mean of -64%. In the Commission's Final Recommendations, the majority of this ward was combined with two neighbouring wards to form a new three-member Edmondsley and Waldridge ward.

Table 7.6 Patterns of electoral variance within local authorities before the PER

	Mean no.	*Mean %*	*Min no.*	*Min %*	*Max no.*	*Max %*	*N*
1,627 wards >10% variance	13	52	1[1]	5[1]	33[2]	90[3]	127
1,680 wards >10% (+5 yrs)	13	54	2[4]	9[4]	32[2,6]	86[5]	126
739 wards >20% variance	6	23	0 (13 cases)	0	17[7]	57[7]	127
823 wards >20% (+5 yrs)	7	26	0 (8 cases)	0	22[8]	71[5]	126

[1] Wandsworth [2] S Lakeland [3] Northampton [4] Blackpool [5] Stevenage [6] Isle of Wight [7] E Hertfordshire [8] Salisbury

ii. Draft Recommendations

Analysis of the Commission's Draft Recommendations shows a dramatic improvement in electoral equality compared with the pre-review pattern. Only 349 wards (an average of three per council) had a variance from the authority mean of more than +/-10% – see Table 7.7. This number was set to fall to just 200 after five years according to the projected electorates, the benchmark against which the Commission works. It was expected that by this time 51 councils (40% of the total) would have no wards with variances of this size. The one exception to this trend appeared to be Warrington, where electoral variances were calculated as likely to get worse over the projection period. It would be surprising if we do not find that the Commission had addressed this anomaly by the time it published its Final Recommendations for the authority. In terms of wards with an electoral variance beyond the +/-20% figure, the published Draft Recommendations sanctioned just 53 of them falling to16 after five years. Corby had the highest proportion of wards in this category (2 out of a total 13), but the Commission acknowledged that these were rural and geographically large areas for which no alternative configuration would comply with its criteria.

Among individual wards the proposed (and unchanged) Welland ward in Kettering (Northamptonshire) had the highest initial positive electoral variance of 29% worsening to 34% after five years. The Council maintained that, 'Although fully part of the Borough, this community is distinctly different even from the other rural areas of the Borough' (Kettering Draft Recommendations, 1996: para 78). The ward contains eight parishes, has Market Harborough (Leicestershire) postcodes, and the nearest major settlements are Market Harborough and Corby (both outside the Borough). For its part the Commission stated that any changes to the boundaries in Welland would have a detrimental effect on the electoral equality in neighbouring wards. Potentially the worst case of electoral under-representation seemed likely to arise in the Brompton ward, Medway Towns. Although the ward was perfectly sized in terms of current electorates and was to remain unchanged, the planned Chatham maritime developments within its boundaries presaged an electoral variance after five years of +45%. Declining to change its Draft Recommendations the Commission argued that, 'Revising current arrangements to reflect such growth would have a significant adverse impact on present electoral equality. The Commission wishes to avoid this, given its general approach to the review.' (Medway Towns Final Recommendations, 1996: para 144). A local councillor put to the Commission the idea that the ward should be split in 2000 to create a new single-member ward, which in time, either in 2003 or in 2007, could become a two-member ward. The Commission responded that the projected imbalance in Brompton would best be dealt with by a future PER after the development had taken place.

Table 7.7 Patterns of electoral variance in the Commission's Draft Recommendations

	Mean no.	*Mean %*	*Min no.*	*Min %*	*Max no.*	*Max %*	*N*
349 wards >10% variance	3	12	0	0 (32 cases)	12 [1,3]	36 [2]	127
200 wards >10% (+ 5 years)	2	7	0	0 (51 cases)	10 [4]	42 [4]	126
53 wards >20% variance	0	2	0	0 (91 cases)	4 [5]	23 [6]	127
16 wards >20% (+ 5 years)	0	1	0	0 (113 cases)	2 [6,7,8]	15 [6]	126

[1] S Lakeland [3] Mendip [5] N Somerset [7] Telford & Wrekin
[2] Owestry [4] Warrington [6] Corby [8] W Somerset

The clearest example of negative electoral variance or over-representation among the Draft Recommendations was in the new Abbey Meads ward, Swindon. In 1998 there were only 992 electors in this proposed three member ward. This meant that it had a councillor/elector ratio of 1:331 compared with an authority mean of 1:2,300 – a disparity of 86%. In five years time, however, the electorate was expected to reach 6,860 and the councillor/elector ratio to be spot on the average. The council had explained that the 'largest single private housing development in Western Europe' would mainly be contained within this ward. By contrast the unchanged Deeping St. Nicholas ward in South Holland was expected to have a greater variance in 2001 (-41%) than at the time of review in 1996 (-37%). The Commission explained that,

> 'The ward raises the most difficult issues in relation to the Commission's statutory criteria. It is a distinctive linear fenland settlement with most housing situated on the Peterborough to Spalding road, and has poor communication links with neighbouring parishes. The ward is some 6,685 hectares in area (which is larger than 25 of the 32 London boroughs)' (South Holland Draft Recommendations, 1996: para 44).

Despite considering a number of alternative arrangements it decided that the ward was 'exceptional'.

iii. Final Recommendations

Our examination of the Commission's Final Recommendations shows that more wards with electoral variances in excess of +/-10% were proposed at the final stage than at the draft stage – see Table 7.8. 430 wards had such disparities following review, falling to 258 after five years. A larger number of wards (74 reducing to 29) also fell into the greater than +/-20% category. Part of this increase would appear to be the result of the Commission bowing to further representations from stakeholders about the importance of preserving 'local ties' in already existing wards. In other instances, for example in South Holland and Teesdale, geography imposes constraints on the options for drawing 'effective and convenient' boundaries. In the Isle of Wight the Commission was bound by a statutory requirement that as a 'county' it must be comprised entirely of single-member electoral divisions. It has argued that such high electoral variance is unavoidable if warding arrangements are to reflect that and other criteria. The Wootton ward in the Isle of Wight has the highest positive electoral variance of 37% based on current electorates. Wootton was changed at the draft stage, but after visiting the area and meeting local interests, the Commission modified its view. In Warrington, although the Final Recommendations contained fewer wards with large variances than did the Draft ones, the level of electoral inequality was still projected to increase over time. The Commission argued that this was 'unavoidable, given substantial ongoing development in parts of the borough and the inherent difficulty of making further changes whilst respecting local ties and maintaining identifiable boundaries' (Warrington Final Recommendations, 1998: para 97). It also pointed out that as this was a 'directed' review, it still had a duty to undertake a periodic review at a future date. Such a review was flagged as part of the Commission's 2000/01 PER programme (Corporate Plan, 2000).

Table 7.8 Patterns of electoral variance in the Commission's Final Recommendations

	Mean no.	*Mean %*	*Min no.*	*Min %*	*Max no.*	*Max %*	*N*
430 wards >10% variance	3	14	0	0 (30 cases)	18[1]	47[2]	127
258 wards >10% (+ 5 years)	2	8	0	0 (48cases)	18[1]	4[3]	126
74 wards >20% variance	1	2	0	0 (82 cases)	8[1]	23[4]	127
29 wards >20% (+ 5 years)	0	1	0	0 (105 cases)	8[1]	17[1]	126

[1] Isle of Wight [2] Teesdale [3] S Holland [4] Corby

iv. Overall impact

The overall impact ofPeriodic Electoral Reviews on the pattern of electoral equality within local authorities can be gauged from Table 7.9. Despite small increases between the Draft and Final Recommendations stages in the number of wards with large electoral variances, the Commission's proposals – based on current electorates – amounted to a reduction of 74% in wards with a variance in excess of +/-10% and to one of 90% in wards with a disparity greater than +/-20%. When ward electorates are projected five years into the future, the improvement in equality is even more marked. It should then be the case that only 8% of wards will vary from the mean by more than +/-10% and just 1% do so by more than +/-20%.

Table 7.9 Changing patterns of electoral equality through the review process

Stages of PER	*No. of wards greater than +/-10%*	*% of wards greater than +/-10%*	*No. of wards greater than +/-20%*	*% of wards greater than +/-20%*
Before	1,627	52	739	23
Before (+ 5 years)	1,680	54	823	26
Draft	349	12	53	2
Draft (+ 5 years)	200	7	16	1
Final	430	14	74	2
Final (+ 5 years)	258	8	29	1

Table 7.10 examines the changes in electoral variance at the local authority level. A mean figure has been calculated using every ward in an authority and a comparison is made between the position before the review and that at the Draft and Final Recommendations stages. Before PER the average variance was 15%, worsening slightly to 16% in five years time. The council with the lowest variance was Haringey (5%) which had experienced no significant changes in either the size or distribution of its population since it was last reviewed in September 1977. It had only two wards with variances greater than +/-10% before the review started and none where the disparity was more than +/-20%. In Peterborough, on the other hand, the average electoral variance was 32%, with 13 out of 22 wards exceeding +/ -10% and one being +193% away from the mean. The Commission's Draft Recommendations bring a sharp reduction in variances. Based on current electorates the local authority mean falls to 5%, ranging between 1% in Spelthorne and 11% in South Derbyshire and Corby. The publication of the Final Recommendations results in only marginal change to the overall pattern. The three London boroughs of Haringey, Havering and Hounslow each have a mean variance of 2%, and Bexley continues to be projected to have exact electoral equality five years after review. As might be expected following our discussion above, the Isle of Wight joins the 'outliers' on 11%.

Table 7.10 Changing patterns of electoral equality at the local authority level

	Mean variance %	*Std Dev*	*Min variance %*	*Local authority*	*Max variance %*	*Local authority*	*N*
Before	15	5.3	5	Haringey	32	Peterborough	127
Before (+ 5 years)	16	5.9	6	Blackpool	33	Peterborough	126
Draft	5	2.0	1	Spelthorne	11	S Derbyshire	127
					11	Corby	
Draft (+ 5 years)	5	1.8	0	Bexley	10	South Holland	126
Final	6	2.1	2	Haringey	11	S Derbyshire	127
			2	Havering	11	Isle of Wight	
			2	Hounslow	11	Corby	
Final (+ 5 years)	5	1.9	0	Bexley	10	South Holland	126

Redrawing ward boundaries

The evidence we have examined so far suggests that while PERs have had little impact on the overall size and structure of councils, they have led to a considerable improvement in the level of electoral equality within local authorities. Such an outcome could only have been achieved by moving electors between wards. We have used the electorate figures for each ward at the different stages of review, together with a textual analysis of the published Draft and Final Recommendations, to calculate the degree to which ward boundaries were redrawn.

On average, only 18% of existing wards in each local authority were unchanged between the start of the review and the publication of Draft Recommendations. The least upheaval was proposed for Wellingborough (last reviewed in May 1979), where the council had strongly supported minimal change and where nine of the fifteen wards (60%) were left untouched. In four other authorities half or more wards were proposed to stay the same – Blackpool (last reviewed in September 1996) and Purbeck (October 1996) with 50%, and Eden (December 1975) and West Devon (February 1977) with 57%. At the other extreme, eighteen of the 127 authorities in our database found that all their ward boundaries were likely to change. These were the seven districts of Chesterfield (Oct 1977), Ellesmere Port and Neston (Nov 1975), Hertsmere (Dec 1975), Runnymede (July 1975), Spelthorne (Aug 1975), Stevenage (Feb 1976) and South Derbyshire (Aug 1976); Peterborough unitary council (Nov 1975); and ten London boroughs – Ealing (May 1977), Hackney (July 1977), Havering (May 1977), Hounslow (April 1977), Islington (May 1977), Lewisham (April 1977), Merton (Aug 1977), Richmond-upon-Thames (May 1977), Southwark (April 1977) and Tower Hamlets (Aug 1977). The large number of London boroughs in the list reflects not only population movement and migration over the last twenty-plus years, but also the Commission's strict guidelines on the level of electoral equality achievable in the capital.

As we have already noted, however, Draft Recommendations can be changed. Indeed the Commission explicitly states in each of its individual local authority reports that,

> 'Because we take this consultation very seriously, we may move away from our draft recommendations in the light of Stage Three responses. It is therefore important that all interested parties let us have their views and evidence, *whether or not* they agree with our draft recommendations.'

It appears that these are not merely placatory sentiments. For while 73% of ward boundaries were left unchanged between the Commission's Draft and Final Recommendations, only in sixteen authorities were the two reports identical. These were Amber Valley, Barking and Dagenham, Blyth Valley, Broxbourne, Derbyshire Dales, Derwentside, Eden, Erewash, North Wiltshire, South Holland, Surrey Heath, Tandridge, Torridge, Waverley, West Devon, and Westminster. Some of the amendments made were quite significant, with eighteen councils having more than half the wards proposed at Draft stage revised. In Kettering, for example, the Commission retained just four of the twenty-three wards (17%) recommended at Draft. Before the review began, the electoral equality in Kettering was poor. Fifteen out of the existing twenty-two wards (68%) had variances greater than +/-10%, and six of these fifteen wards had variances greater than +/-20%. Although the Draft Recommendations proposed a substantial improvement in electoral equality, Kettering Borough Council argued that they '...sought electoral equality at the expense of the statutory criteria' (Kettering Final Recommendations, 1997: para 18). The council re-examined its original proposals and, after consultation, put these forward to the Commission. The Final Recommendations commended to the Secretary of State 'much of the council's Stage Three proposals' (Kettering Final Recommendations, 1997: para 40), even though eleven of the twenty-three wards (48%) had a current variance greater than +/-10% and three had 'exceptional' variances of more than +/-20%. In the case of the proposed Barton ward, the Commission acceded to the Borough's reiteration of its own proposal even though this had the effect of increasing the electoral variance from 1% to 22%. The Final Recommendations acknowledged 'the significant boundary created by the Southern By-pass, and the impact that the trunk road has had on community identities' (Kettering Final Recommendations, 1997: para 75). In the London borough of Lewisham the Commission itself appeared confused over the extent of changes being made. On the one hand it writes in Lewisham's Final Recommendations that, 'We have substantially confirmed our draft recommendations, although some modifications have been made' (Lewisham Final Recommendations, 1999: v), then later in the same report claims, '...we have decided to substantially modify our draft recommendations in response to local views: we propose that 14 of the 18 wards included in the draft recommendations be modified to reflect the Labour group's proposals and local concerns' (Lewisham Final Recommendations, 1999: para 136). Our analysis confirms that only four out of eighteen wards (22%) were unaltered between the Draft and Final reports. The Commission had noted at Draft stage that,

> 'We recognise the improved electoral equality which would be achieved by the Borough Council's scheme, compared to the existing arrangements. However, the electoral equality is not as good as we would expect to achieve, particularly in urban areas such as Lewisham' (Lewisham Draft Recommendations, 1999: para 49).

In a rare example of the possible impact of ward boundaries on parliamentary constituencies being taken into account, it seemed that one sticking point for the Commission was the fact that the electorate in the Lewisham Deptford constituency would be relatively under-represented (11%) on the Borough Council while electors in Lewisham East would be relatively over-represented (16%).

A more common explanation in the event of big changes between the Draft and Final Recommendations seems to be that the Commission was persuaded to restore a number of the wards which were in existence before the PER began. Table 7.11 lists those councils where the total proportion of wards left unchanged increased by 10% or more between the two stages. In Alnwick, for example, only four out of seventeen initially proposed wards remained unchanged between the Draft and Final Recommendations, and the number of existing wards preserved increased from one to six. The council had been unhappy that the Commission had produced a draft scheme that had broken local ties. They argued that,

> ' ...in several instances, it appears that these aspects (presumably due to an understandable lack of local knowledge) appear to have been sacrificed for the purposes of electoral equality' (Alnwick Final Recommendations, 1997: para 21).

In its Final Recommendations the Commission conceded that,

> '... any further improvements to electoral equality may be at the expense of the statutory criteria, namely the need to reflect community identities and secure convenient and effective local government' (Alnwick Final Recommendations, 1997: para 92).

Even councils such as Wellingborough and Blackpool, which already were facing relatively little upheaval, managed to achieve a further increase in the number of unaltered wards. A further two authorities in addition to the five noted earlier, Teesdale (53%) and Tynedale (56%), ended up with more than half of their wards being exactly the same as before the review.

Table 7.11 Existing wards left unchanged in the Draft and Final Recommendations

	% (No.) wards unchanged (Draft)	*% (No.) wards unchanged (Final)*	*% (No.) difference*
Alnwick	5.9 (1/17)	35.3 (6/17)	29.4 (5/17)
Wellingborough	60.0 (9/15)	80.0 (12/15)	20.0 (3/15)
Castle Morpeth	28.6 (6/21)	47.6 (10/21)	19.1 (4/21)
Guildford	19.1 (4/21)	38.1 (8/21)	19.1 (4/21)
Tynedale	37.5 (12/32)	56.3 (18/32)	18.8 (6/32)
Blackpool	50.0 (11/22)	63.6 (14/22)	13.6 (3/22)
Spelthorne	0 (0/15)	13.3 (2/15)	13.3 (2/15)
S. Gloucestershire	18.4 (7/38)	29.0 (11/38)	10.5 (4/38)

The process of consultation and reassessment between the publication of the Draft and Final Recommendations had the effect of restoring at least one of their currently existing wards to a quarter of all local authorities. In Spelthorne, for example, the reinstatement of two wards removed that authority from the list of those whose ward structure was wholly revised. Spelthorne's place was taken by Harrow (last reviewed in Feb 1996) and Reigate and Banstead (Oct 1977), which were among the just one in ten councils that had such wards stripped away. Overall, the average proportion of wards left unchanged by PER rose from 18% at the Draft stage to 20% in the Commission's Final Recommendations. This mirrors the drift in the achieved level of electoral equality between those two stages to which we have already referred, and the similar movement noted between the provisional and final recommendations of the Parliamentary Boundary Commissioners (Rossiter *et al.*, 1999: 170-1). It is difficult to avoid concluding that, to some extent, the Commission uses its Draft Recommendations to test the water, and is prepared to back down quite readily in the face of well evidenced local representations for it to protect community ties and thus to restore some of the *status quo ante*.

In one important respect our measurement of the extent of alterations to ward boundaries may even over-estimate the amount of change brought about by PER. The situation is analogous to that following parliamentary boundary reviews. In 1995 we calculated that although 486 out of 651 (75%) existing constituencies had experienced boundary changes, in 129 cases these involved the transfer in or out of less than 10% of the total electorate (Rallings and Thrasher, 1995). Moreover, whereas whole wards have to be moved in the process of building parliamentary constituencies, local government boundary changes can often involve moving just a couple of streets and a handful of electors. Although the Commission's reports simply note whether a ward's boundaries have been changed or not regardless of whether 10, 100 or 1,000 electors are affected, it is clear that in many cases only marginal adjustments were made to ward electorates in order to achieve the necessary improvements in electoral equality. It is impossible fully to track the movement of voters, but an example from the review in Kettering provides a flavour. Although only 3 of the original 22 wards were left unchanged following PER, a number of other wards were scarcely affected. Just 13 electors, less than half of one per cent of the total, were moved between the St. Michael's and Wicksteed wards with everybody else left where they were. That may be one reason why PERs attract so many fewer public representations than do proposals to alter the administrative boundaries of local authorities.

The changing outcomes of PERs

Officers from the Commission admitted to us in interviews that they were very much 'finding their way' when the programme of Periodic Electoral Reviews began. It was expected that higher electoral variances would be an identifiable outcome of the early as opposed to the later reviews. The Commission's 1998 Annual Report made this precise point,

> 'The key distinction between the reviews undertaken in 1997/8 and those undertaken in our first year is that there is now a much better understanding of our requirements for good electoral equality, having regard to the statutory criteria' (Annual Report, 1998: para 58).

Another respondent suggested that some of the variation in the early reviews reflected the type of authorities being considered. For example, in a rural authority like Tynedale (Final Recommendations, March 1997) a boundary change affecting a small number of people could make a large difference to the percentage variation between ward electorates. With a councillor/elector ratio of just 1:881 moving 100 people between wards would change the electoral variance by 11%. Equally, it was in such authorities that geographical factors were most likely to limit the Commission's scope for manoeuvre.

The figures in Table 7.12 do provide some support for the claim that electoral variances were higher in the earlier reviews than the later ones. The first 29 Final Recommendations published in either December 1996 or March 1997 projected a mean local authority variance of 6.7% five years following review. After that it never exceeds 5.8%, and is below 5% on nine of the fourteen other occasions when tranches of Recommendations were published. The very low mean figures for June, July and September 1999 reflect the reports on 22 London boroughs which had been given informal, yet clear guidance by the Commission that they should produce schemes in which neither individual ward variances nor the authority average exceeded 2-3%. Table 7.12 confirms two other facets of the review process to which

Table 7.12 Current and Projected Local Authority Electoral Variances by date of publication of Commission's Final Recommendations

		— Before —		— Draft —		— Final —	
Date of final report	***Number of councils***	***Mean variance (current)***	***Mean variance (projected)***	***Mean variance (current)***	***Mean variance (projected)***	***Mean variance (current)***	***Mean variance (projected)***
Dec '96	8	16.0	18.4	6.0	6.1	6.4	6.7
Mar '97	21	17.4	19.0	7.0	6.2	7.6	6.7
Jun '97	1	17.0	18.0	6.0	5.0	11.0	5.0
Nov '97	12	14.5	14.8	6.6	6.1	6.8	5.8
Feb '98	10	15.6	17.7	6.0	4.6	5.9	4.6
Mar '98	9	15.2	15.7	5.7	4.8	6.0	4.8
Jun '98	1	21.0	22.0	5.0	4.0	5.0	5.0
Sep '98	11	13.1	14.1	4.5	4.1	4.9	4.6
Oct '98	7	17.6	18.3	5.1	4.4	5.3	4.6
Nov '98	8	16.0	17.9	5.6	4.1	5.8	4.1
Jan '99	7	14.7	15.9	4.7	4.4	5.0	4.7
Mar '99	5	20.2	24.8	7.4	5.4	7.6	5.6
Jun '99	8	7.4	7.9	3.0	1.9	3.3	2.0
Jul '99	4	7.0	8.0	3.0	1.5	3.3	1.5
Aug '99	5	15.4	16.0	5.6	5.4	6.0	5.6
Sep '99	10	9.5	10.4	3.4	2.1	3.7	2.4

we have drawn attention. First, that the mean variance tends to be greater at the Final than at the Draft Recommendations stage. Second, that because the Commission is required to take future electorate changes into account when devising new ward boundaries, electoral variances based on projected figures are the same or lower than those derived from current electorates in all but one case.

Conclusions

This analysis of our database has provided powerful evidence that the different interests and approaches of the Local Government Commission and of the local authorities it is reviewing come together to influence the overall outcome of PERs. Local councils are interested in the minimal possible change to their existing arrangements, not least because it is those who currently run the authority who are responsible for devising its submission(s) to the Commission. The Commission is empowered to recommend alterations to the size and structure of councils, but tends to concentrate on that aspect of its statutory duties which requires it to seek electoral equality between the wards of individual authorities. As a result it is relatively rare for the Commission to receive submissions which argue for a radical re-think of a council's electoral cycle, ward structure or overall size, and even rarer – except when prompted by central government – for it to initiate such proposals. In those areas the preferences of local authorities are considered to weigh heavily. This recipe for relative stasis is compounded by the fact that the Commission makes its judgements about electoral equality within rather than between local authorities. Thus the councillor/elector ratio prevailing before the review tends to approximate that after the review, and the interaction between Commission and councils focuses on various schemes for the moving between wards of such electors as necessary to achieve the holy grail of electoral equality.

That PERs do have a significant impact on electoral equality cannot be doubted. We noted dramatic reductions in the number of wards with electoral variances in excess of +/-10% and it is clear that this is a performance indicator of some importance to the Commission itself, albeit that it routinely notes that this 'improvement in electoral equality…must be balanced against our [other] statutory criteria' (Corporate Plan 2000, para 24/25). For their part, local authorities often complain that mathematical exactitude is being pursued at the expense of respecting local communities and ties. However, it does appear that the Commission listens to local representations, whether from councils themselves or other interested parties, between the Draft and Final Recommendations stages. Across a range of measures we found the Commission latterly proposing changes which had the effect of reinstating previous boundaries even at the cost of worsening average electoral equality. Yet we have unearthed evidence that casts some doubt on the accuracy of the Commission's work. For the purposes of published Recommendations electoral variances are calculated not by reference to current figures, but to those which the local authorities have projected for five years hence. The Commission admits it has no way of questioning the veracity of such projections except in the most blatant cases, and we have clearly shown that local authorities consistently tend to over-estimate their future electorates. It may be that the precision on which the Commission prides itself rests on rather shifting sands.

It has been relatively straightforward to set out the consequences of the Periodic Electoral Review process in terms of the electoral arrangements of local authorities. However, all boundary changes are about more than simple geographical delineation. The electors being moved to and fro have votes, and changing boundaries can affect the balance of those votes between the parties. In Chapter 8 we turn to ask whether local government electoral reviews are perceived to have a party political dimension, how such a dimension may be expressed, and whether there is any evidence that they have resulted in a political advantage for one side or another.

Chapter 8

Party Politics and the Periodic Electoral Review Process

Assessing the impact of changing ward boundaries on the electoral fortunes of the political parties is the 'dog that doesn't bark' of the Periodic Electoral Review process. All sides accept that party advantage (or disadvantage) can accrue, but the Commission is officially blind to such considerations and expects local authorities to be as well. However, there is clear evidence from studies of parliamentary boundary reviews that political parties have strategies for maximising their gains and minimising their losses, and that they have learnt to do this by using the niceties of apolitical criteria such as 'community interest' and 'local ties' to greatest partisan effect (Rossiter *et al.*, 1999). In this chapter we examine the party political dimension of local electoral reviews from a number of different perspectives. We consider how the Commission attempts to guard against being persuaded to accept politically biased schemes and whether it believes these to be an endemic problem. We gather evidence from our survey of both officers and members to see how far they believed party politics intruded into the review process in their own authorities and whether it had any effect on the final outcome. Finally, we use the results of local authority elections before and after the review to conduct an empirical analysis of how far boundary changes can help explain any change in the number of seats won by the different parties.

The Commission and partisan schemes

The Commission, like its predecessors at the LGBC (see Chapter 2), is fully aware that the review process makes it quite possible for any political party or group, whether or not it holds a clear majority in a local authority, to ensure that any scheme submitted for consideration is one that will bring it potential electoral benefits. However, recognition of the problem is a far cry from having systems in place to prevent such gerrymandering. Nonetheless, both officers and Commissioners take the view that the experience which they collectively possess, and the enquiries which they routinely make about any proposed scheme, enable them to uncover blatant attempts at partisanship. All new staff are given an induction at which they are taken in detail through two or three example reviews and have pointed out to them the sorts of factors which might indicate political interference. A number of review managers had previously worked on the much more contentious structural reviews and have found this valuable in detecting where party politics might be driving the review process. Commissioners are also experienced in the ways in which local authorities work. Three current Commissioners are former Chief Executives – Peter Brokenshire (Epping Forest and Greenwich), Robert Hughes (Kirklees), and Pamela Gordon (Hackney and Sheffield), and both the Chairman and Vice-Chairman – Professor Malcolm Grant (University of Cambridge) and Professor Michael Clarke (University of Birmingham) – are academics with a background in providing legal and policy advice to councils and other public bodies.

It is probably fair to assume that the Commission has become more attuned to weeding out partisan schemes over time. Both Commissioners and officers admitted to us that they sometimes found it difficult to spot any political motivations in the early reviews, but soon began to 'find their feet'. A number of factors militate against crude attempts at gerrymandering being successful. The primacy accorded to electoral equality and the fact that proposals tend to take existing ward boundaries as their starting point both restrict the scope for radical, partisan driven change. Local authority officers will often alert the Commission to what is happening 'behind the scenes', especially if they feel that their professional integrity is being compromised. In addition, all schemes put forward by political parties *qua* parties are examined in great detail, and the opportunities to make representations to the LGCE mean that it is rare for the Commission not to hear local cries of 'foul' from opposition groups and others. As a result, or so the Commission argues, it soon became clear that 'biased' schemes would not be accepted and that any local authority or political party tempted to put one forward was wasting its time.

That is not to say, of course, that the outcome of all reviews is politically neutral. With a first past the post voting system the very act of moving electors around from one electoral unit to another can make a difference, whatever safeguards are in place. For its part, the Commission is bound by the rules. If a scheme has good electoral equality, the boundaries reflect local communities, and there is local support for the changes, it cannot be concerned that the changes may help a political party. Indeed such 'help' may very properly be a consequence of re-drawing existing wards in which the supporters of that party did not receive due value for their votes. For example, Commission officers understood that their recommendation to re-package the Dartmouth and Kingswear wards of South Hams district was likely to produce a safe seat for the Labour party. Nevertheless they stood by it as the best solution according to the published criteria. On occasion, though, the Commission does find itself in danger of being ensnared by politics. During the review of the London borough of Westminster it detected potential gerrymandering in the council's proposal to divide up the traditionally Labour Church Street ward between two strongly Conservative wards, Lords and Hamilton Terrace – see Box 6.3. Having visited the area and considered the interests of residents, officers recommended rejecting the scheme. At the Commission meeting to discuss and ratify this recommendation, the partisan implications were mentioned and the desirability of the residents continuing to be represented within a socially homogeneous ward rather than being dispersed into more prosperous ones formed part of the argument. It could be argued that the Commission was straying very close to the bounds of its remit.

In general, though, Commissioners and officers both reported that the PER process in local authorities seemed surprisingly apolitical. Cross-party support for schemes was common, and even where a number of alternatives were submitted the differences between them were more often than not only in the detail. It could indeed be argued that it is the presence of the Commission that has had this effect. For although local authorities are responsible for their own submissions, they are aware that the umpire will be keeping a sharp eye out for any possible infringement of the rules. The more the Commission develops a reputation for being hard to deceive, the fewer will be the attempts to hoodwink it. One Commissioner was so confident of his ground that he told us he doubted if any minority group leader could stand up in a court of law and say that a gerrymandered scheme had been allowed through.

The role of national political parties in PERs

The scope of local boundary reviews is so large and the practical problems of acquiring relevant, detailed knowledge so daunting that the national political party organisations appear to get involved with PERs only in the most general way. Their formal contact with the Commission has been limited to a meeting in February 1999 to discuss its approach and timetable. Their contribution to individual reviews has scarcely ever proceeded beyond ensuring that their members on the ground have received some general notes of guidance about what to do.

The Labour party produced its guidelines in time for those areas affected by the first wave of the re-warding in 1996. This document explained that the aim should be to secure the best possible outcomes for the party from the review process. 'Re-warding does not only affect the winnability of certain wards, or the whole council, but also the winnability of parliamentary constituencies. Following re-warding, the parliamentary boundary commission will revisit the area, to ensure the new constituencies are contiguous with the new wards. This will affect the general election due in 2001/2' (Labour Party internal document, 1996).[1] The listed objectives for the review are:

- To maximise the number of winnable parliamentary constituencies and reinforce our parliamentary boundaries strategy (wards are the building blocks for constituencies).
- To maximise the chances of an overall Labour majority of councillors.
- To ensure a party consensus throughout the review process.
- To aim, wherever the option exists, for annual elections, with retirements by thirds.
- To put forward schemes that both meet the Commission's criteria and are capable of winning widespread public support.
- To aim at the best starting point in terms of the electoral registration base.

Labour councillors are advised to follow a strategy in their approach to re-warding. The factors which need to be considered, by whom and at what stage in the process are discussed and there is a warning that representations to the Commission 'should never be promoted in a party political manner'. Councillors are also provided with advice on how to marshall local opposition to other schemes, on how to support arguments about community and local ties, and on whether any press or letter-writing activity would be helpful. The rather ambitious objectives set out in the guidelines, significantly published in the wake of Labour's triumphant campaign during the Fourth Periodic Review of parliamentary boundaries, do not appear to have been matched with assistance on the ground. A party representative told us that although the progress of reviews is tracked, and questions and requests for information answered, there has been no further national involvement in reviews outside London.

The Conservative party has also produced guidelines for its local parties on how to conduct a review. The third edition of the booklet *Boundary Changes* was distributed to Conservative associations and council groups in October 1997 and took into account comments received about and experiences gained from the current reviews. It concentrates on the practical side of the review process, covering what needs to be done at each stage and how to comply with the guidance issued by the Commission. It emphasises that good organisation, good evidence, good argument and popular support can have a positive impact on the Commission's recommendations. Unlike the Labour party, however, no overt mention is made of

---

1 This statement was not accurate. Under the provisions of the Boundary Commissions Act 1992 the earliest date at which any of the Parliamentary Boundary Commissions are able to produce their reports on the Fifth Periodic Review is February 2003.

the potential political gain from a review. A party spokesman suggested to us that the national co-ordination of PERs would have been impossible. The party did not have the manpower for such a project, and only local party members (if then) would understand the political effect of moving boundaries and have sufficient knowledge of communities and local ties. Moreover, it was probably the case that outside the towns there was little scope for electorally significant change. Area Campaign Directors were, however, charged with overseeing the reviews on their patch, with ensuring that queries about the process were answered or passed on, and with emphasising how important it was to make a separate Conservative representation in every authority. It appears that the Liberal Democrats similarly limited their national role to the provision of general information.

Against this background it is perhaps not surprising that only 28% (28 out of 100) of councillors who responded to our survey recalled receiving advice from national party headquarters, and very few mentioned party briefing meetings. Most saw it as technical rather than political information about the process. A Labour councillor from Derbyshire Dales described it as, 'Assistance with information on the mechanics of the process'. For some this information was, 'very helpful' (Thurrock) or 'moderately useful' (Bristol), while others thought it, 'not directly relevant' (Alnwick). Only one Labour councillor in the districts seemed to have caught the underlying message. He told us, 'information was received which was aimed to minimise adverse impact and seek maximum advantage' (Chester). In London, reaction was similarly varied. One respondent claimed he had been effectively told,

> 'we haven't got the staff or local knowledge to help, so do it yourself' (Wandsworth),

whereas another noted,

> '[the] attendance of Regional Officers at all internal discussions in local party. This was all very useful' (Hackney).

The information and advice given to Conservative councillors met a similarly mixed reception. In Chester, one Conservative councillor wrote that they,

> 'received information on how to present our case, what would be acceptable and what pitfalls to avoid. The advice was very helpful.'

A colleague from Welwyn Hatfield noted the detail given on issues such as the preferred size of wards, the maximum number of councillors, respecting the wishes of local residents, adherence to localities, communities and parish boundaries and the importance of consultation. A councillor in North Somerset called it a 'very good booklet', and one in Vale Royal said there had been 'regional and county meetings which were very useful to gauge an overview'. On the other hand, a respondent from Redbridge wrote that they were, 'general guidelines and warnings – of no great value in our particular circumstances', and a councillor in Three Rivers that the information provided was too nationally orientated and did not really meet the requirements of the district. Conservatives in Harrow actually complained that they had been misled by national party headquarters. They had based their scheme on guidelines written by the Commission in 1992 (and passed on by the party) which suggested that an optimum number of electors per councillor was 2,800. On this basis they had proposed that Harrow be split into 19 three-member wards. In the event they discovered that such a councillor/elector ratio was 'not relevant' in London and claimed that the bad advice 'deflected us from proposing a more radical reduction in size (to 42 or 45 members (from 63))'.

The Liberal Democrats fared no better than the other two main parties on this issue. A Southwark councillor wrote that, 'general information was received – some use but not especially', and one in Haringey called it 'background information on the process and experiences from Boroughs done before [us]'. However, one of the problems which the parties faced was encapsulated by a comment from West Devon. Our respondent took the view that,

> 'the guidance should have proceeded from regional organisation down and should have been more flexible (i.e. less centralised/Whitehall decreed criteria)'.

He appeared to be blissfully unaware that local authorities were being obliged to take part in a nationally determined and judged review of their electoral boundaries, and that the scope for local or political 'flexibility' was deliberately very small.

The role of local political parties in PERs

The evidence we have looked at so far suggests that the Commission believes that the review process in most authorities is not characterised by excessive partisanship, and that political parties at the national level accept the significance of PERs but make little effort to direct or oversee how their local branches respond. Nonetheless, just under three quarters (73/100) of respondents to our survey reported that their local party had drawn up a review scheme for discussion by the council and/or submission to the Commission. The cases where this did not happen were often 'hung councils' where the parties agreed at an early stage to co-operate. These party schemes were mostly produced by holding internal meetings between executive committee members and councillors, often in the form of a working party which produced proposals for wider discussion and ratification. The situation in Harrow was typical,

> 'A working party of activists prepared draft proposals which were circulated to representatives of the party in each ward. Their comments were incorporated in the

final proposals. The working party also submitted comments on the Council's and other parties' proposals'.

In some instances the responsibility for the review fell into the hands of one person, although usually with a remit to consult on the emerging proposals. Some respondents thought that this method was best suited to the job in hand. The individual is able to evaluate all the possible options for their party and only then lay the plans open for the input of their colleagues. This is likely to be more efficient than a group of councillors all pouring over a map, while at the same time keeping an eye on their own interests. Several respondents recognised that public as well as party support was desirable for any schemes sent to the Commission. Opposition parties can find this difficult when the party which controls the council has a monopoly of the means and methods of consultation. A Liberal Democrat councillor from Chesterfield complained that he,

> 'gave our proposals to the party in power at the Town Hall for general public comments, but only the official proposal was advertised (not ours)'.

Almost all local parties accepted that the rules of the Commission had constrained their thinking about re-warding. Sometimes this took a benign form. In Wellingborough they 'were not constrained because we were all agreed on minimal change', and in Wandsworth, 'our proposals followed their rules – so we were constrained but 'accepted' the rules and have no complaints'. In other cases the rules, especially the requirement for electoral equality, posed a number of problems. Comments from councillors included,

> 'To work out a satisfactory scheme, keeping communities and estates together, with wards of equal numbers all with three-members was really difficult. In particular, the Commission apparently tightened up the +/- limits so we had to go back and tighten up all our figures. It is not easy without officer help' (Southwark).

Many respondents argued that if there had been more leeway over the numbers in a ward, it would have been possible to keep some communities together. By which, of course, they might have meant areas which had a habit of strongly supporting their party. We were told that in Swindon, for example,

> 'The loss of a councillor representing the rural part of the borough was particularly unpopular with the Liberal Democrats. This was a direct result of the councillor/elector parity rule which is fixed and not varied for rural areas.'

Parties also commented that they found the requirement to assess electoral equality on the basis of projected electorates an additional complication. For the Haringey Liberal Democrats,

> '[the] main problem was the Commission's insistence on using projections for the electorate which have a very mixed record of accuracy, but which they think can be used to fine-tune boundaries.'

In London especially a further constraint was the apparent advice from the Commission to produce schemes based on three-member wards in anticipation of the introduction of annual elections. A councillor in Haringey commented,

> 'The Commission made it clear that they only wanted to see three-member wards to allow for Annual Elections as per the Government's modernising agenda. This was a straight-jacket. It was subsequently surprising to find that they have accepted two-member wards elsewhere',

and a Liberal Democrat from Harrow noted that,

> 'The indicated wish of the Commission for three-member wards throughout the Borough to facilitate future Annual Elections was a major limitation. Our view was that a mixture of two- and three-member wards would have made it easier to identify ward boundaries with natural communities.'

Overall responses from the parties indicate that they felt very constrained by the Commission's criteria in formulating their representations. Many would have been likely to submit a very different scheme given a freer hand. The rules have been designed so that a fair system of local government is the outcome of a Periodic Electoral Review: where one person's vote is equal to another's within a local authority. If the parties did not feel constrained by such rules, then schemes could easily have been drawn up which were aimed to benefit a particular political party. One councillor in Thurrock made this honest observation,

> 'We were very much constrained. Our strategy was to ensure we gained maximum benefit in terms of increased numbers of councillors so long as it was consistent with the objectives of the Commission, which were very tightly drawn. Only a limited number of options were therefore available' (Thurrock).

We were also interested in the extent to which parties had been successful in getting their own schemes, however constrained, adopted as the local authority's submission. The key variable here tended to be their strength of numbers on the council. In Crewe and Nantwich, for example, a Labour councillor wrote that the party was, '100% successful – although we accepted a few non-partisan suggestions from other parties'. Another councillor from a Cheshire district, this time a Conservative, commented that they were,

> 'Very successful. The entire rural area submission was our plan and we impacted very strongly on the submission for the urban area' (Chester).

In West Devon, a Liberal Democrat councillor was entirely satisfied with the outcome as the 'official' council recommendations matched his party's, and in Havering, 'the majority party carried a vote for their views to be put forward as those of the Council'. Box 8.1 contains an example of the local press coverage following the adoption of the majority party's plan in Braintree.

BOX 8.1 'Labour electoral plan branded 'dictatorship''

Braintree councillors were in angry mood last week as members fiercely debated options for a radical shake-up of wards across the district.

The electoral review is carried out periodically by the Local Government Commission (LGC). Its main aim is to even out the electoral vote to ensure that each ward councillor is represented by an equal number of voters. Though any group or party is free to make a submission, an agreed district council proposal for the re-drawing of the ward map has to be in the hands of the LGC by February 28.

And there was outrage from opposition parties as Labour pushed through its own proposals as the district council's official submission to the LGC. Labour's radical submission suggests cutting the number of district councillors from 60 to 52 and reducing the number of wards from 33 to 25. Malcolm Fincken (Lab, Halstead Trinity) said it retained the integrity of urban and rural areas, giving an equal number of voters without the need to split parishes.

Opposition members said unlike submissions from council officers and other political parties, Labour's submission had not been open to public consultation.

Parish councils from Cressing through to Panfield, Coggeshall and Earls Colne feared the consequences the proposed ward boundaries would have on their communities. David Finch (Con, Stour Valley Central) said: 'There has been no consultation with the parish councils. Devious and underhand is one way it has been described to me. We are very close to moving from democracy into dictatorship.' James Abbott (Green, Witham, Silver End) added: 'This cannot be called the view of Braintree District Council.'

But Mr Fincken said there had been no underhandedness in Labour's approach and the final decision would be made by the LGC. "It was not possible for consultation in the time available", he said. 'The parishes and district council will have a further opportunity to be consulted and comment before the final order is made'.

Extract from article in Braintree and Witham Times, 24 February 2000

On the other side of the coin, however, opposition parties felt powerless. In Crewe and Nantwich it was felt that the 'controlling Labour group imposed its proposals en-bloc'; in Stevenage a respondent wrote that the Liberal Democrats were, 'totally ignored by the Labour majority who controlled what the officers were allowed to do'; and in Macclesfield,

> 'the majority [Conservative] group used its power to ensure their ideas went forward as the authority's submission. All opposition members voted against the proposal.'

The situation in London was no different. In Southwark, a Liberal Democrat explained that, 'the majority (Labour) party put forward their scheme as the Council's. We voted against it and put our own in, in conjunction with the Conservatives'. A Conservative councillor from Haringey wrote that,

> 'We submitted a very detailed proposal in concert with the Liberal Democrats and the Greens but separate from the controlling Labour group. Labour had ignored our views, and we felt, would not be trusted not to gerrymander the proposals.'

However, even in councils where one party had an overall majority, it was not always the case that it dominated the review process against protests from the opposition parties. For instance, a Liberal Democrat councillor in Swindon wrote that,

> 'The council's working party worked effectively on a cross-party basis. I was able to feed in our group's suggestions which were largely agreed by the other two groups.'

In Ellesmere Port and Neston, a councillor reported that 'the Conservative opposition eventually backed the Labour controlling group', and in South Kesteven (where no single party had a majority) there was complete cross party support. In South Somerset the Liberal Democrats were 'the controlling party [and] therefore our ideas formed the basis for the submission. There was a high degree of consensus by all parties on the submission despite this'. More frequent were the reports of individual suggestions and proposals from minority groups being included. In Kettering, for example, a member told us that, 'we managed to get some wards enlarged and another three-member ward split into half to make it two two-member wards', while in Harrow the Conservatives,

> '...secured a few minor changes to the Council's proposals. Modifications proposed by us and supported by the Liberal Democrats to a number of ward boundaries were adopted as the authority's submission.'

Where no consensus could be reached parties submitted alternative schemes to that put forward by the local authority. Sometimes there were fundamental differences between them,

> 'Labour wanted elections by thirds, Tories wanted all single-member wards, while the Liberal Democrats kept changing their view to try and protect their Leader's vulnerable seat' (North Somerset).

In neighbouring Bristol the Liberal Democrat and City Council schemes were broadly similar 'least change' options, while the Conservatives wanted single-member wards and Labour three-member wards. Sometimes it was specific areas or wards that were at issue. In Chester, consensus was reached on 48 of the 60 seats, but for three parts of the urban area each of the political parties made separate representations.

In North East Derbyshire, the sticking point was the political effects of the boundary changes. A councillor wrote that,

> 'There was a dispute with respect to two large communities (Dronfield and Wingerworth) which make up approximately one third of District Council wards. These also represent the main area of the opposition parties!'

On occasion we could not even be certain that our informants were describing the same process. A Liberal Democrat from Harrow was clear that,

> 'The Labour party's final submission was the council's submission. Only the Independents fully accepted it. We indicated our disagreement on a few of the boundary proposals. The Tories disagreed completely and submitted their own proposals with six fewer councillors and major boundary changes.',

while the chairman of the panel which produced the council's scheme insisted that,

> 'At every opportunity, compromises were agreed for the sake of the common good. Each party set aside its political clothing and calmly set down to work out the best situation for the borough. The process has shown that, with understanding, the old tribalism can be forgotten for the sake of the community' (quoted in *Harrow, Stanmore and Kingsbury Times*, 8 July 1999).

For the record, the LGCE received three full schemes for Harrow – one each from the Borough Council, the Liberal Democrat group, and the Conservatives' Electoral Review committee.

Unsurprisingly, the satisfaction expressed by local party politicians with the outcome of the PER tended to depend on how successful they had been in getting their preferred scheme adopted by the Commission. Comments from respondents included, 'satisfied, as the Commission agreed with 98% of our proposals' (South Northamptonshire); 'satisfied, apart from the boundaries of one ward' (Harrow); 'perfectly satisfied since they are largely our proposals' (Northampton); 'very successful, the Commission accept that many of their recommendations came from our submission' (Wandsworth); 'very successful. Over 70% of our suggestions were wholly or largely accepted by the Commission to the chagrin of the Labour controlled group' (High Peak); 'almost completely satisfied. The Commission accepted our rather than the majority group (i.e. the Labour party) proposals' (Southwark). It is significant though that not all these cases of 'success' involved the Commission agreeing with the council or majority party scheme. Where parties were not completely satisfied with the outcome, the argument was often over a small part of the authority. For example,

> 'Fairly satisfied – as it largely followed our proposals. However, our proposals that one ward should be split into two to allow it to grow with a proposed housing development was rejected. We saw this as short-sighted – especially as it could have benefited our party to a small extent.' (St. Albans), or

> 'The final decisions taken by the Commission were, in the main, sensible and workable. One or two were a trifle bizarre and we were left with the feeling of 'Why did they do that?" (Halton).

Those who were unhappy usually chose to tilt at the Commission and its rules. The commonest complaint was about the emphasis on electoral equality at the expense of community. Councillors asserted that,

> 'We believe our scheme was a more efficient scheme for the Council and was able to be more responsive and accountable to the electorate. In addition, our wards reflected local characteristics in their geographical make-up' (South Hams), or

> 'Unnatural wards have been created which make the job of encouraging the public to vote in local elections even harder. In addition at a time of taking high housing allocations we object to the principle that builders and developers effectively now determine the need for ward boundaries' (West Lindsey).

In Bristol there was discontent that the Commission, which had after all received four complete submissions from the city, had retained a system of two member wards with annual (and therefore partial) elections. A Labour councillor wrote, 'it is a mess...We are left with another ten years of confusion'. In Macclesfield there seemed to be some misunderstanding about the status of the government's White Paper on local government. We were told,

> 'The Commission's proposals were contrary to recommendations in Government's consultation document which suggested two-member wards' (Macclesfield).

Other councillors thought that the Commission had been 'lazy' in adopting one political party's scheme 'as a basis for their own recommendation – without challenging statements which reduced the whole process to a mathematical exercise' (Bexley). A Wandsworth Labour councillor said his colleagues were so disappointed with the outcome and the part played by the Commission, that they were taking legal advice about challenging the decision. In the event no such challenge materialised.

On rare occasions party respondents did acknowledge that the review had produced a fair outcome, even if not always to their partisan taste. A councillor in Redbridge was,

> 'On the whole politically satisfied. As a better, democratic division the new arrangements are far more equitable than its outdated predecessor',

and in Welwyn Hatfield,

> '[although] not everything was to our liking...we could see the sense and justice in their submissions and final decisions'.

Perceptions of 'politics'

Officers

Having examined some of the detail of political party involvement in electoral reviews, we wish now to make a general assessment of the extent to which officers and members believed that partisan politics played a role in the process in their own authorities. This is not simply a question of looking for differences in approach and perception between councils but, perhaps too, an opportunity to discover differences in interpretation between the elected and non-elected participants. In several authorities officers insisted to us that there was no 'politics' involved. Mostly this was the case where officials had been charged with preparing the authority's submission. Comments included,

> 'I prepared the draft proposals and little was changed by the members' (Stevenage).
>
> 'It was accepted that this was an officer prepared scheme' (North East Derbyshire).
>
> 'The officers went to great lengths to pursue the Commission's criteria and produced options accordingly' (Salisbury).

Similar remarks were reported from Vale Royal, Copeland, West Wiltshire, South Northamptonshire and Chesterfield. The role of politics was even downplayed in two electorally competitive London boroughs. In Redbridge,

> 'The Strategy Committee unanimously supported officers' recommendations',

and in Ealing,

> 'Politics did not come into the PER to any great extent, there were no political differences. In Ealing, there is a tradition of members of different groups working effectively together. There was no overt political manipulation of the process' (Ealing).

The feeling in a number of local authorities is nicely summed up by an officer in Derbyshire Dales. She wrote that,

> 'Members appreciated that electoral equality for the district wards was paramount and that community identity should be maintained wherever possible. Politics did not become an issue – not even through contacts with our party agents etc. – achieving what was best for Derbyshire Dales and its residents was foremost. The comments from political parties were helpful'.

However, there is no doubt that party politics was at the heart of the review process in many local authorities. Sometimes the pursuit of party advantage will have been successfully cloaked behind apparent adherence to the Commission's criteria. For instance, an officer from Crewe and Nantwich wrote that, 'Each of the three political group submissions were clearly minded of their own interests, but were all well reasoned', and from Thurrock we were told, 'The process was driven by politics but tempered by a realistic view of what would be acceptable'. In other cases partisanship was more overt. Comments from respondents included, 'A great deal of politics. Schemes suggested were drawn on political lines' (Bexley); 'Politics was a major part' (Amber Valley); 'Politics came into the process in a big way! (Durham); ''Politics' was an overriding feature of the review due to the particular circumstances of the Borough' (Southwark); 'Politics entered into the process in a significant way' (Exeter). Several officers saw it as perfectly rational for the parties to engage in such behaviour. For example,

> 'Members regarded the process as very much an exercise of politics. Each group naturally sought to maximise the benefit for them from the exercise' (Havering), and

> 'It is inevitable that political opinions will form the basis of PER. All the political parties made an active and at times strong representation of their views' (Northampton).

There is, however, a danger that such an emphasis on pursuing partisan goals could pose problems for the authority. We received two contrary views on this from London boroughs.

> 'Obviously, the local political parties were looking for a favourable outcome, but no pressure was bought to bear on officers in drawing up proposals for formal consideration by members' (Tower Hamlets).

> 'Both political groups, by submitting proposals, ensured that the PER process in the Borough was conducted on a partisan basis and it left the Council open to the allegation that its submission was influenced by the interests of the majority party on the Council' (Wandsworth).

Officers clearly had different perceptions of the presence or desirability of party politics in the Periodic Electoral Review process. We have no reason to believe that they were not telling us the truth as they saw it, but we need to be aware that interpretations of seemingly similar circumstances can vary. One respondent provided an interesting – and perhaps more widely applicable – observation drawn from experience in his own authority,

> 'The PER is the kind of issue that parties think they have different views about. In reality, they were more or less in agreement' (Lewisham).

Members

We expected that councillors would be more attuned than officers to the potential political ramifications of electoral reviews, and would treat the process accordingly. In some authorities the stakes were high,

> 'As the political balance on the Council is very fine, small changes to the boundaries could change control of the Council' (Hackney);

in others rather lower,

> 'Labour's political dominance was such that it was difficult to discern whether any party gained an advantage from the review' (Ellesmere Port and Neston).

However, the majority of respondents to our survey did admit to seeing if there was any way party advantage could be secured. A member from Haringey asserted that 'all parties tend at least to try to shuffle good/bad roads in/out of marginal wards', and one from Derbyshire Dales – interestingly an authority where officers noticed little 'politics' – commented, 'of course [we looked for political gain] – we live in the real world'. From Bristol, there was cross-party agreement. A Conservative representative wrote that, 'All parties are 'political' – so this is inevitable'; a Liberal Democrat councillor commented that, 'I don't believe any party would put forward proposals that would damage their election chances'; and the Labour leader of the Council told us, 'Entirely – the schemes were based on maximising party advantage, but dressed up as community identity'. Some councillors felt the need to justify their approach by arguing that they were tackling imbalances in the current warding. A Labour respondent from Wandsworth wrote that, 'The 1975 arrangement was one that artificially benefits the Tories and now we hope to come out more evenly.' Party colleagues in Barnet suggested to us in an interview that the borough was gerrymandered at the last review. Their goal was to redress the resultant anomalies. For a Liberal Democrat in Southwark equitable treatment was also at issue,

> 'In fairness the present system disadvantages us greatly as there is one Liberal Democrat ward with an electorate of 15,000 and one Labour ward with an electorate of 3,000. Obviously, we tried to submit a scheme which would not disadvantage us, but I think it would have been difficult to do otherwise in view of the above.'

We even came across a case of politicians launching a pre-emptive strike about the unfairness of existing boundaries more than a year before a PER was due – see Box 8.2.

For others though, the PER was a game which they could win and gain from politically – or at least not lose, if they played to the rules and were aware of what their opponents were doing. The Liberal Democrats in Northampton, for example, sought more winnable seats by supporting the splitting of wards in some instances and arguing for additions to the core electorate in others. In Salisbury, where officers seem to have believed they were drafting a scheme in an atmosphere of neutrality, an Independent councillor noted an intense battle between very different Labour and Liberal Democrat district-wide schemes, each reflecting that party's electoral self-interest. Such manoeuvring more commonly takes place over the drawing of boundaries in small but crucial parts of an authority. The future of the Childs Hill ward in Barnet, from which the Liberal Democrats drew half their entire representation on the council, provoked a bitter inter-party dispute which resulted in the Commission performing a *volte face* between its Draft and Final Recommendations. As a Liberal Democrat councillor from the area put it,

> 'We were rather reluctant to see areas of strength (i.e. where we are known and appreciated for hard work) being removed.'

BOX 8.2 'Tories look to border change'

Worcester's Blue Brigade thinks that a boundary change in the city could prove a shot in the arm. Coun Robert Rowden feels the Tories are hard done by in Worcester, and is eager for anything that could lead to the Labour party, which has controlled the city for 19 years, releasing its grip.

He has pointed an accusing figure at the People's Republics of Holy Trinity and St. Barnabas, two wards which are Labour heartlands. Despite having fewer than 4,500 voters, they each return three city councillors.

It's because of this that the Tories have been moaning about the fact that the vast St. Martin's ward – which covers Warndon and Warndon Villages – returns three councillors but has 11,778 voters…

'A periodic review by the Local Government Commission for England is scheduled for 2001-2002' said Coun Rowden. 'It can only be to our advantage. Local Tories are currently disadvantaged by the unequal sizes of wards in Worcester'.

Whatever the eventual outcome, I'm sure the Tories – who dominate the southern side of Worcester anyway – have their eyes fixed on the commuter belt of Warndon Villages, where rich pickings are to be had.

Extract from article in Worcester Evening News, 29 November 1999

The motivation of 'hanging on to what we hold' was important for all the parties. Labour in Richmond-upon-Thames lamented,

> 'From 1978-1994 we had no councillors at all, so we were concerned only to retain what we had. The opportunity for much more gain in this Borough is very limited' (Richmond-upon-Thames),

and a Liberal Democrat in Stevenage wrote, 'To be precise, it was 'survival' rather than 'gain'. In Havering, preserving boundaries was not only about party,

> 'Where we had a strong local residents' association we were reluctant to see it broken up' (Havering).

However, about a third of responding councillors denied that they saw the PER as a way to benefit politically. Some had thought about it and rejected the idea,

> 'We considered producing a political scheme but decided it was not realistic' (St. Albans).

> 'We discussed the issue at length and finally discarded the potential for short term

> gain in favour of long term acceptability based largely on community of interest.' (High Peak),

whereas others claimed different priorities,

> 'The Committee dealing with the issue were more concerned to strike a reasonable balance with the laid down criteria of the Commission' (Halton).
>
> 'Getting our larger wards reduced in size so that they became more manageable was the priority' (Shrewsbury and Atcham).
>
> 'Political gain was not a relevant factor. We were concerned with minimal change and keeping the status quo' (Westminster).
>
> 'Our proposals were broadly neutral as they had to be if we were going to influence the Commission' (Elmbridge).

One fascinating aspect of the replies to our survey was the extent to which politicians denied that they had acted 'politically', but imputed to their opponents the basest of motives. In Alnwick, for example, a Labour member replied to our question about whether politics featured strongly in the review process by saying, 'this was very unlikely in our district'. A councillor from the Rural Alliance (consisting of nine Independents and two Conservatives), on the other hand, said that although politics had not come into their decision-making, it had been a substantial influence among the other parties '...especially from the Liberal Democrat and the Labour groups'. Similarly, in Crewe and Nantwich, a Liberal Democrat councillor denied that his party had tried to achieve party political gain except in being 'determined not to allow our existing area of strength to be fragmented', whereas the Labour leader of the Council suggested to us that 90% of the Liberal Democrat scheme was politically motivated, but was disguised as 'common sense'.

A detailed example of how a PER may be seen from different political perspectives came from Stevenage. While the Labour leader of the council wrote that politics didn't enter into the process at all, the leader of the opposition Liberal Democrats complained bitterly. He set the scene and then interpreted the situation from his standpoint,

> 'Stevenage Borough Council in recent years has been Labour (38), Liberal Democrats (1) – now it is Labour (37), Liberal Democrats (2). The Liberal Democrats are confined to one ward, 'Mobbsbury', which has since 1982 been exceptional in often electing Liberal Democrats councillors. At Stage One of the review, Labour got Stevenage Borough Council officers to draw up a plan which took hours of officer time and resources. Surprise, surprise, it involved tinkering with most wards a bit, and splitting only one ward exactly in two – that being the 'Mobbsbury' ward. This was gerrymandering of the highest order i.e. abolishing the only opposition ward! Our small local party were denied access to officer time/resources for any alternative plan and couldn't match this ourselves. The Local Government Commission (to

> save them work) swallowed it wholesale. Subsequently despite protests nothing changed. The whole thing has been stitched up by Labour to squeeze us out.'

The Commission use Stevenage as an example of 'best practice' in the way that the authority consulted the public. The scheme, therefore, was said to reflect local preferences. The Commission write,

> 'Stevenage Borough Council, in Hertfordshire, undertook extensive local consultation on its Stage One proposals prior to their submission to the Commission. This included:
>
> - distribution of an information leaflet to each household in the Borough via free newspapers;
> - presentations to the public at each of the Council's six local committees;
> - depositing the submission for public inspection at the main council offices and all housing offices; and
> - circulating the proposals for comment and information to a wide range of interesting parties, including political groups and associations, community associations, the local M.P. and M.E.P., and the local media and press.
>
> The Council's proposal provided for a high level of electoral equality within the borough, and the Commission adopted it in its entirety, without amendment, as its recommendation' (Guidance, 1999: para 22).

It is also worth remembering that an officer in Stevenage told us that he had prepared the draft submission and that this had been little changed. Our Liberal Democrat informant is implying that he and his colleagues were working under instruction.

There were other cases of opposition parties asserting that the council and the controlling group had worked hand in hand on drafting proposals. A councillor from North East Derbyshire, for example, concluded that the 'initial District Council proposals (and final proposals) appeared designed to retain Labour party representation'. However, there were also occasions where it appears that officers were required to rescue politicians from the pit they had dug. In Harrow, all sides initially accused the others of seeking partisan advantage. Yet, later, the Conservatives accepted that 'blatant gerrymandering in Labour's initial ideas were largely removed and their final proposals were objectively justifiable as well as slightly advantageous to them', and the Liberal Democrats concurred, 'the Labour proposals in their final form seemed to be heavily dependant on officer advice. Apart from one boundary they did not appear to have made any 'political' decisions.' Something similar also occurred in one of our case study authorities, Swindon. At the outset party politics dominated. Before each Electoral Review working party meeting the ruling Labour group met to discuss its favoured scheme, and the officer detailed to work on the review was briefed by Labour members about the likely contentious areas in this preferred scheme in order that he could answer any potentially 'tricky' questions from opposition councillors. However at one meeting, under challenge from the Liberal Democrats, a Labour councillor conceded that improvements needed to be made and claimed to want the process to be as apolitical as possible. Officers were now instructed to take away from the meeting changes suggested by all parties and to ensure that the council could defend its boundary proposals to the Commission. Another Labour councillor subsequently admitted to us that initially Labour members were trying to manoeuvre to protect their position, but then realised what they had to do – design boundaries according to strict electoral equality.

In only about half a dozen authorities were all sides agreed that there was no politics involved in the PER process. A councillor from West Somerset suggested that,

> 'We are a 'non-political' Council. We do sometimes vote on party lines and there is some party rivalry over Chairmanships, but we have no party with an overall majority and no important votes are conducted on party lines',

and in another west country rural local authority we were told that there was a 'minimal amount of politics'. However, even independent councillors are not beyond pursuing self-interest. In Kennet, for example, we found that boundary changes were often discussed in terms of their impact on personalities rather than parties. When it comes down to a question of whether a councillor's ward will be changed or even disbanded, it is perhaps inevitable that there is a degree of personal preservation as well as political manoeuvring involved.

The political effects of local boundary reviews

So far we have used information gathered from surveys, face-to-face interviews and press reports to assess the degree to which participants in periodic electoral reviews believed the process to be influenced by party political motivations. These sources suggest that although some political parties may attempt to produce boundaries which bring them electoral gain, there are a number of factors which act as constraints on their ability to do this successfully. The most important constraint is that provided by the role of the Commission. Although the rules to which it works might be thought to be ambiguous, there can be no doubt that its obligation to secure 'effective and convenient local government' whilst reflecting 'the identities and interests of local communities' cautions it against sanctioning either radical changes in boundaries or the creation of wards with outlandish geographical shapes. Both being likely to be proposed by those attempting a gerrymander. Partisans are also likely to find their room for gaining advantage limited by housing patterns. In many towns and cities in Britain the type of housing stock changes incrementally across a given area. Public housing will often be adjacent to low-cost housing, which itself will abut slightly more expensive housing and so on. Given the continuing relationship between socio-economic circumstances and party preference, together with the fact that adjustments to wards often involve the relocation of a few contiguous roads or streets, it becomes easy to see how unusual it might be for boundary changes to bring in their wake large political changes. The situation is different to that pertaining at Parliamentary boundary reviews, where whole wards are the building blocks and where the exchange of just one or two wards can profoundly alter a constituency's character and thus likely political loyalties. At local level, perhaps the situation in which parties stand to gain or lose most is where there has been a rapid increase or decrease in electorate in relatively homogeneous localities. The Commission will rightly adjust boundaries to redress any electoral imbalances which such developments have caused and any consequent amalgamation or sub-division of wards might significantly impact on party strength.

It now seems appropriate to try to conduct an empirical test of the party political effects of re-districting. This is routinely done when parliamentary constituency boundaries are changed (BBC/ITN, 1983; Rallings and Thrasher, 1995; Rossiter *et al.,* 1999), but presents a more difficult problem in terms of local boundary reviews. The reason for this is that whereas socio-economic and local electoral data can be used to provide robust estimates of the character of wards being moved between constituencies, there is no readily available way of determining either the social or political make-up of those individuals or streets which find themselves in different wards following a PER. The methods that we have been obliged to adopt are crude and at best only indicative, but they do allow us to bring some evidence to bear on this crucial issue.

We can illustrate our approach by considering the three electoral reviews which have taken place in Welwyn Hatfield over the past 25 years. The first two were conducted in 1975 and 1989 by the LGBC (see Kelly, 1996), the most recent was completed by the LGCE in 1998. The council was under Labour control on all three occasions. In each case we have examined the last local elections under the old boundaries and the first under the new ones. Given that the boundary of the local authority itself remained constant, our fixed points of reference are the share of the authority-wide vote gained by each party at each election and the changes recorded over time. For example, we can note that the Conservative share in Welwyn Hatfield rose from 39.9% in 1973 to 53.6% in 1976, an increase of 13.7% – see Table 8.1. However, to estimate the impact of the electoral review we need to discover both how the old wards might have behaved in 1976 if there had been no changes, *and* how the new wards might have behaved in 1973 if they had then been in existence. In order to achieve this we calculated notional results for each ward. The 1976 notional results are calculated by applying the percentage change in the local authority-wide share of the vote for each party between 1973 and 1976 to its actual share in each ward at the 1973 election. For example, the Conservatives received 22.2% of the vote in the Haldens ward in 1973. Between 1973 and 1976, their overall share increased by 13.7%. Therefore we add 13.7% to the original 22.2% (35.9%) to determine their notional result for 1976 if the boundaries had not been changed. This procedure is repeated for each party in every ward, and the number of notional council seats 'won' can be tallied on the basis of which party topped the poll. The 1973 notional results are calculated in exactly the same way except the process is reversed. Here, the inverted percentage change in the vote for each party is applied. In the 1976 election, the Liberals received 15.6% of the vote in the Handside ward. To calculate the notional result for 1973, we apply the inverse of 2.5% (change in Liberal share of the vote between 1973-1976) to the share of the vote in the ward election (15.6% -2.5% = 13.1%). And so on.

We are now ready to measure the partisan impact of boundary changes. Table 8.1 displays the number of seats won by each party at the actual elections in 1973 and 1976 and the number notionally won given the above assumptions. It appears from this that the boundary changes that took place prior to the 1976 election were worth three extra seats for the Labour party and cost three for the Conservatives. The 1976 notional results reveal that if the old boundaries had remained in place the Conservatives would have won 28 seats as compared with the 25 the party actually won. Similarly, Labour would have won 15 seats compared with an actual 18 in 1976. Examining the position in reverse, we find that the Conservatives would have won 16 rather than 19 seats in 1973 if the new boundaries had then been in place, and that Labour would have returned 27 rather than 24 councillors. The boundary changes had no impact on Liberal representation. The boundary changes which came into effect in Welwyn Hatfield between the 1990 and 1991 local elections had a less consistent impact on party fortunes, not least because the total number of seats rose from 43 to 47. Table 8.2 shows that if the 1990 boundaries had been used for the 1991 elections, the notional results suggest that the Conservatives would have won 16 seats. With the new boundaries in place they actually won 20 seats. Conversely, if the new boundaries had been in place for the 1990 election, the Conservatives would have won a single additional seat whereas Labour would have gained an extra 3 members. The difference looks as if it might be accounted for by the new and then marginal Panshanger ward which 'changed hands' between Labour and the Conservatives in line with their average fortunes across the borough.

Table 8.1 Actual/notional election results, Welwyn Hatfield 1973 and 1976

Authority-wide shares of the vote	*Con*	*Lab*	*Lib*
1973	39.9	53.7	5.1
1976	53.6	38.8	7.6
% change 1973-76	**13.7**	**-14.9**	**2.5**

	— 1973 Actual —			— 1976 Notional —		
Ward	*Con*	*Lab*	*Lib*	*Con*	*Lab*	*Lib*
B'Mans Park & Little Heath	Con unopposed					
Haldens	22.2	47.5	24.7	35.9	32.6	27.2
Handside	65.2	34.8	0.0	78.9	19.9	0.0
Hatfield Central	21.2	48.6	30.2	34.9	33.7	32.7
Hatfield East	54.5	45.5	0.0	68.2	30.6	0.0
Hatfield North	33.1	66.9	0.0	46.8	52.0	0.0
Hatfield South	43.3	56.7	0.0	57.0	41.8	0.0
Hollybush	22.3	77.7	0.0	36.0	62.8	0.0
Howlands	22.4	77.6	0.0	36.1	62.7	0.0
Northaw	Con unopposed					
Peartree	18.6	68.3	0.0	32.3	53.4	0.0
Sherrards	51.0	49.0	0.0	64.7	34.1	0.0
Welham Green	39.6	60.4	0.0	53.3	45.5	0.0
Welwyn East	75.3	24.7	0.0	89.0	9.8	0.0
Welwyn West	63.2	36.8	0.0	76.9	21.9	0.0
Seats won	**19**	**24**	**0**	**28**	**15**	**0**

	— 1976 Actual —			— 1973 Notional —		
Ward	*Con*	*Lab*	*Lib*	*Con*	*Lab*	*Lib*
B'Mans Park & Little Heath	71.3	8.5	20.3	57.6	23.4	17.8
Haldens	31.7	48.9	19.4	18.0	63.8	16.9
Handside	59.1	25.3	15.6	45.4	40.2	13.1
Hatfield Central	42.6	57.4	0.0	28.9	72.3	0.0
Hatfield East	66.0	34.0	0.0	52.3	48.9	0.0
Hatfield North	46.2	53.8	0.0	32.5	68.7	0.0
Hatfield South	45.0	43.0	12.0	31.3	57.9	9.5
Hollybush	35.2	64.8	0.0	21.5	79.7	0.0
Howlands	37.7	43.0	19.3	24.0	57.9	16.8
Northaw	70.7	13.0	16.3	57.0	27.9	13.8
Peartree	46.8	53.2	0.0	33.1	68.1	0.0
Sherrards	63.1	36.9	0.0	49.4	51.8	0.0
Welham Green	50.6	49.4	0.0	36.9	64.3	0.0
Welwyn East	74.0	26.0	0.0	60.3	40.9	0.0
Welwyn West	71.7	28.3	0.0	58.0	43.2	0.0
Seats won	**25**	**18**	**0**	**16**	**27**	**0**

Table 8.2 Actual/notional election results, Welwyn Hatfield 1990 and 1991

Authority-wide shares of the vote	*Con*	*Lab*	*Lib*			
1990	37.1	46.3	12.0			
1991	42.3	38.3	17.5			
% change 1990-91	**5.2**	**-8.0**	**5.5**			
	— 1990 Actual —			— 1991 Notional —		
Ward	*Con*	*Lab*	*Lib*	*Con*	*Lab*	*Lib*
B'Mans Park & Little Heath	72.8	13.4	13.8	78.0	5.4	19.3
Haldens	26.5	58.6	8.4	31.7	50.6	13.9
Handside	39.3	21.9	31.0	44.5	13.9	36.5
Hatfield Central	21.7	64.3	14.0	26.9	56.3	19.5
Hatfield East	41.9	43.9	14.2	47.1	35.9	19.7
Hatfield North	29.2	53.7	12.1	34.4	45.7	17.6
Hatfield West	30.5	55.8	13.7	35.7	47.8	19.2
Hollybush	20.6	70.7	0.0	25.8	62.7	5.5
Howlands	25.7	60.8	8.6	30.9	52.8	14.1
Northaw	74.7	14.7	10.5	79.9	6.7	16.0
Panshanger	did not exist					
Peartree	15.4	71.8	7.5	20.6	63.8	13.0
Sherrards	32.5	53.0	8.9	37.7	45.0	14.4
Welham Green	31.8	45.8	10.2	37.0	37.8	15.7
Welwyn North	64.2	20.2	8.9	69.4	12.2	14.4
Welwyn South	58.9	24.9	16.2	64.1	16.9	21.7
Seats won	**13**	**30**	**0**	**16**	**27**	**0**
	— 1991 Actual —			— 1990 Notional —		
Ward	*Con*	*Lab*	*Lib*	*Con*	*Lab*	*Lib*
B'Mans Park & Little Heath	74.5	6.5	19.0	69.3	14.5	13.5
Haldens	22.4	44.4	20.2	17.2	52.4	14.7
Handside	46.1	15.5	38.4	40.9	23.5	32.9
Hatfield Central	23.6	56.1	20.3	18.4	64.1	14.8
Hatfield East	44.8	39.0	16.2	39.6	47.0	10.7
Hatfield North	31.8	49.3	18.9	26.6	57.3	13.4
Hatfield West	35.4	44.4	20.2	30.2	52.4	14.7
Hollybush	30.7	69.3	0.0	25.5	77.3	0.0
Howlands	34.6	51.3	14.2	29.4	59.3	8.7
Northaw	76.7	10.8	12.5	71.5	18.8	7.0
Panshanger	46.2	36.9	16.9	41.0	44.9	11.4
Peartree	23.0	62.1	0.0	17.8	70.1	0.0
Sherrards	39.2	45.8	15.0	34.0	53.8	9.5
Welham Green	41.3	43.3	15.4	36.1	51.3	9.9
Welwyn North	62.2	15.2	22.7	57.0	23.2	17.2
Welwyn South	58.0	22.6	19.4	52.8	30.6	13.9
Seats won	**20**	**27**	**0**	**14**	**33**	**0**

Our third example for Welwyn Hatfield comes from the most recent boundary review enacted between the 1998 and 1999 local elections. This comparison is particularly interesting because although the number of seats was increased once again from 47 to 48, the shares of the vote recorded by the various parties at the two elections were very similar – see Table 8.3. Our analysis suggests that the Conservatives won two fewer seats in 1999 and Labour three more than would have been the case if there had been no boundary changes. Similarly, if the 1999 changes had been in place in 1998, the Conservatives would have won one fewer and Labour two more. This suggests that the boundary changes proved a modest benefit to Labour, with their advantage stemming from the creation of the Hatfield South ward mainly from the more Labour inclined parts of the Welham Green and Redhall ward. The genesis of this change is interesting. The initial submission to the Commission by the Labour controlled district council, endorsed by the Welwyn Hatfield Constituency Labour party, argued for minimal change within the existing wards. Rather it was Hatfield Town Council, also Labour controlled, which argued for the division of Welham Green and Redhall on the grounds that it contained 'two physically separate communities divided between two parishes' (Welwyn Hatfield Draft Recommendations, 1998: para 38). The Commission adopted this proposal in its own Draft Recommendations and found it supported by the Conservatives and other groups. Thus, a change that served to increase the number of 'safe' Labour wards emerged without controversy and attracted bi-partisan endorsement.

We repeated the kind of analysis done in Welwyn Hatfield for 36 of the 58 local authorities that had elections on new boundaries in either 1999 or 2000. Councils excluded from the analysis included those dominated by Independents, those with very uneven patterns of party competition, and those whose electoral cycle meant that more than one ward had no contest scheduled at the final round of pre-boundary change elections. Table 8.4 summarises the impact of re-districting both overall and in each individual authority. It appears that the Conservatives won 11 more seats on the new boundaries in 1999/2000 than they would have done if no re-districting had taken place that year, with the Liberal Democrats registering an even greater number of 'gains' (21). By contrast Labour took 25 fewer seats. Looked at from the reverse perspective, if the 1999/2000 changes had been in place at the previous elections in each authority, the Conservatives would have won 4 extra seats and the Liberal Democrats a massive 39 more. Once again Labour seems to be the loser from the periodic electoral reviews, with 23 of the seats it actually won at the pre-review elections likely to have been lost if the new wards had operated at those contests. The pattern of gains and losses varies between authorities, but there is little sign of political parties being able consistently to reap a bonus from having control of the council at the time of PER.

Table 8.3 Actual/notional election results, Welwyn Hatfield 1998 and 1999

Authority-wide shares of the vote	*Con*	*Lab*	*Lib*
1998	43.3	40.3	15.6
1999	42.8	40.0	16.1
% change 1998-99	**-0.5**	**-0.3**	**0.6**

	— 1998Actual —			— 1999 Notional —		
Ward	*Con*	*Lab*	*Lib*	*Con*	*Lab*	*Lib*
B'Mans Park & Little Heath	71.0	14.7	14.3	70.5	14.4	14.9
Haldens	22.8	62.2	15.0	22.3	61.9	15.6
Handside	50.3	23.9	25.8	49.8	23.6	26.4
Hatfield Central	19.3	52.2	28.5	18.8	51.9	29.1
Hatfield East	45.7	39.8	14.5	45.2	39.5	15.1
Hatfield North	29.0	57.4	13.6	28.5	57.1	14.2
Hatfield South	did not exist					
Hatfield West	30.7	51.3	18.0	30.2	51.0	18.6
Hollybush	20.2	66.7	13.0	19.7	66.4	13.6
Howlands	29.4	57.9	12.7	28.9	57.6	13.3
Northaw	65.2	12.0	9.1	64.7	11.7	9.7
Panshanger	54.1	29.4	16.5	53.6	29.1	17.1
Peartree	19.5	66.6	13.8	19.0	66.3	14.4
Sherrards	46.8	39.9	13.4	46.3	39.6	14.0
Welham Green & Redhall	45.0	43.3	11.7	44.5	43.0	12.3
Welwyn North	64.4	20.8	14.8	63.9	20.5	15.4
Welwyn South	65.2	21.4	13.4	64.7	21.1	14.0
Seats won	**26**	**21**	**0**	**26**	**21**	**0**

	— 1999Actual —			— 1998 Notional —		
Ward	*Con*	*Lab*	*Lib*	*Con*	*Lab*	*Lib*
B'Mans Park & Little Heath	73.4	14.1	12.5	73.9	14.4	12.0
Haldens	22.5	60.8	16.7	23.0	61.1	16.2
Handside	52.6	23.7	23.7	53.1	24.0	23.2
Hatfield Central	21.9	43.6	34.4	22.4	43.9	33.9
Hatfield East	46.0	40.5	13.5	46.5	40.8	13.0
Hatfield North	29.6	51.8	18.7	30.1	52.1	18.2
Hatfield South	25.9	61.2	12.9	26.4	61.5	12.4
Hatfield West	38.6	44.2	17.2	39.1	44.5	16.7
Hollybush	24.2	68.8	7.0	24.7	69.1	6.5
Howlands	27.6	60.7	11.8	28.1	61.0	11.3
Northaw	56.8	12.8	13.1	57.3	13.1	12.6
Panshanger	44.0	38.2	17.9	44.5	38.5	17.4
Peartree	19.1	67.8	13.1	19.6	68.1	12.6
Sherrards	44.0	43.1	12.9	44.5	43.4	12.4
Welham Green	59.2	28.7	12.1	59.7	29.0	11.6
Welwyn North	64.0	19.6	16.4	64.5	19.9	15.9
Welwyn South	58.8	26.7	14.5	59.3	27.0	14.0
Seats won	**24**	**24**	**0**	**25**	**23**	**0**

Table 8.4 Comparing election results before and after re-districting

Authority	*Control/ largest party*	*Seat change*	*Post-review. cf 'old' wards*				*'New' wards cf. pre-review*			
			Con	*Lab*	*LD*	*Oth.*	*Con*	*Lab*	*LD*	*Oth.*
Barrow	Lab	0	-3	0	0	3	3	-2	0	-1
Bath & NE Somerset	NOC(LD)	0	2	-1	-3	2	3	-2	-3	2
Blyth Valley	Lab	3	0	-2	0	5	0	-6	3	6
Boston	NOC (Lab)	-2	-1	0	2	-3	2	-5	1	0
Bristol	Lab	2	2	-9	9	0	0	-1	3	0
Broxbourne	Con	-4	-4	0	0	0	-7	3	0	0
Copeland	Lab	0	-1	2	1	-2	-2	2	1	-1
Corby	Lab	2	1	2	-1	0	-1	4	-1	0
Dacorum	Lab	-6	-3	-7	4	0	-4	-5	8	-5
East Hertfordshire	NOC (Con)	0	-3	6	-5	2	2	6	-5	-3
E. Northamptonshire	Lab	0	5	-5	0	0	3	-3	0	0
Kettering	Lab	0	-2	0	2	0	0	-2	2	0
Lincoln	Lab	0	-3	3	0	0	0	0	0	0
Mendip	NOC (LD)	3	3	3	-2	-1	-2	-3	11	-3
Northampton	Lab	4	2	-1	3	0	4	1	-1	0
North Kesteven	NOC (Lab)	1	0	-1	0	2	1	-3	0	3
North Somerset	LD	2	-2	5	0	-1	-7	7	3	-1
Reigate and Banstead	NOC (Con)	2	6	-2	-2	0	2	0	0	0
Runnymede	NOC (Con)	0	6	-3	-3	0	6	-3	-3	0
Sedgemoor	NOC (Con)	1	6	1	-3	-3	2	4	-2	-3
Sefton	NOC (Lab)	-3	3	-3	-3	0	0	-3	0	0
South Hams	NOC (Con)	-4	-2	2	0	-4	-1	2	0	-5
S. Northamptonshire	NOC (Con)	2	0	-2	1	3	7	-4	-3	2
South Gloucestershire	NOC (Lab)	0	-1	-1	4	-2	-3	2	3	-2
South Somerset	LD	0	1	0	-5	4	-1	0	-1	2
St. Albans	LD	1	2	-3	2	0	-1	-3	5	0
Stevenage	Lab	0	3	-3	0	0	3	-3	0	0
Swindon	Lab	5	0	1	5	-1	1	1	4	-1
Taunton Deane	LD	1	1	-3	2	1	3	-3	-2	3
Three Rivers	NOC (LD)	0	-2	-1	3	0	0	-3	3	0
Vale Royal	Lab	-3	-2	-3	3	-1	-2	-5	5	-1
Wansbeck	Lab	-1	0	-9	8	0	0	-4	3	0
Watford	Lab	0	-2	1	1	0	-1	0	1	0
Wellingborough	NOC (Lab)	2	1	3	0	-2	-1	5	0	-2
Welwyn Hatfield	Lab	1	-2	3	0	0	-1	2	0	0
West Somerset	NOC (Ind)	-1	0	2	-2	-1	-4	1	4	-2
Totals		**8**	**11**	**-25**	**21**	**1**	**4**	**-23**	**39**	**12**

Table 8.5 shows that Labour 'lost' more seats in those places where it ran the council than where it was a powerless minority, and that the other parties were only moderately successful in protecting their own interests. Indeed, once account has been taken of the increase or reduction of seats in each authority, only in 14 of our 36 cases did a political party gain or lose the equivalent of more than a single ward (3 seats) from the review process. Even where the exchanges between parties were of a greater magnitude, factors other than pure political manipulation can usually explain the outcome. For example, although the new boundaries in Mendip looked as though they would have delivered the Liberal Democrats 11 more seats than they actually won if they had been in force in 1995, they were insufficiently partisan to withstand the swing against the party experienced between 1995 and 1999. In fact, given the level of support they attracted in 1999, the Liberal Democrats would actually have been 2 seats better off if there had been no boundary changes. In Wansbeck, on the other hand, the Liberal Democrats benefited from a Labour council-inspired re-districting scheme by the simple expedient of fielding candidates and winning in wards which the party had previously left uncontested. One of the few cases of the party running the council unambiguously benefiting from the PER was in Runnymede. Despite only a modest change in vote share between the pre-and post-review elections in 1999 and 2000, the Conservatives appeared to have carved out an additional 6 seats. Moreover, the Commission's Final Recommendations are littered with statements such as 'we noted that the Conservative group's proposals...would achieve marginally better electoral equality' and 'we endorsed the Conservative group's proposal for the boundary between these wards' (Runnymede Final Recommendations, 1998: paras 63 and 84). However, even here all is not as it seems. The party can take credit for proposing and getting accepted a boundary change which tipped the balance in its favour in one marginal ward, but the other three seats came thanks to a Labour intervention in a ward where previously there had been a Conservative/Liberal Democrat straight fight. The effect of this was to split the anti-Conservative vote and allow the party to win despite polling a lower share of the vote.

Table 8.5 Comparing election results before and after re-districting – by controlling party

	Net Seat Change	*Post-review cf. 'old' wards*				*Pre-review cf. 'new' wards*			
		Con	*Lab*	*LD*	*Oth.*	*Con*	*Lab*	*LD*	*Oth*
Lab/largest party	5	-3	-29	38	-1	2	-25	32	-4
Con/largest party	-5	3	4	-10	-2	9	8	-13	-9
LD largest party	7	5	0	-3	5	-5	-7	16	3

The impact on election results of such factors as party competition and turnout shows how limited is the Commission's ability, beyond its own statutory remit to ensure evenly sized electorates, to reduce any 'bias' favouring one or another party. In previous work we have shown how such bias – defined here as differences in the allocation of seats to parties when they have equal shares of the votes cast – can be disaggregated into a number of elements (Rallings, Thrasher and Johnston, 2002). These include variations in electorate size, the impact of abstentions, the number of votes cast for a third party, the effect of victories by a third party, and the efficiency with which the votes cast for each party are distributed. Here we examine the degree to which each of these factors favoured or disadvantaged the parties at the elections before and after PER.[2] Our primary aim was to discover how much of any overall bias was accounted for by variation in electorate size and how far this changed following electoral review. We added an extra dimension to this by controlling for the political party that had most seats on a local authority at the time of review.

Table 8.6 shows that there was a bias to the Conservatives on Conservative-dominated councils at the elections both prior to and after the PER. The element of this accounted for by unequal ward electorates reduced from 15 seats to 9 seats once the boundary changes had been implemented, but the Conservatives did appear to benefit from their vote being more efficiently distributed at the later elections. It is at least possible that this was a consequence of the way the new ward boundaries were drawn. In councils where Labour was the largest group the party consistently won more seats than it was entitled to, but it was actually more disadvantaged by variations in ward size after electoral review than before it. Equally, it had a reduced benefit from the way its vote was distributed (efficiency). Labour's bonus instead came from winning large numbers of seats with relatively few votes because of low turnouts (abstentions), and from the success of the Liberal Democrats in winning seats that might otherwise have been Conservative (third party victories). In those authorities where the Liberal Democrats held the whip hand, the party suffered less bias after the review because of variations in ward size but also saw its previous advantage from efficient vote distribution disappear.

Our analysis suggests, therefore, that elements of the electoral system over which the Local Government Commission for England can have little direct effect have a greater role in producing biased electoral outcomes than does the geography of ward boundaries. The success of the Commission in redressing uneven councillor/electorate ratios, which we demonstrated in Chapter 7, is reflected in an overall reduction in the bias produced by variations in ward electorates, but even before

---

2 Technical details of the method employed can be found in Johnston *et al.*, 1999.

PER this was never the most important variable in accounting for disproportional results. It could be argued that astute local parties would be able to draw, and get the Commission to accept, boundaries that allowed them to distribute their support most efficiently. However, only the Conservatives appear to have reaped such a benefit following review and it is far more likely that this, and the concomitant reduction in the pro-Labour and pro-Liberal Democrat bias on the same dimension, is to be explained by the operation of the familiar winner's bonus of seats under first past the post than by successful gerrymandering. The Conservatives performed much better and Labour rather worse at the 1999 and 2000 local elections than at the comparable contests in 1995 and 1996. All the other components of our measure of bias have more to do with how votes are cast than how boundaries are drawn.

Table 8.6 Sources of electoral 'bias' at local elections before and after Periodic Electoral Review

	'Conservative' councils		*'Labour' councils*		*'Lib Dem' councils*	
	Before	*After*	*Before*	*After*	*Before*	*After*
Electorate size	15	9	-13	-19	-22	-5
Abstentions	5	-8	43	64	-1	6
Efficiency	-5	20	55	20	37	-7
Third party votes	-2	-2	-21	-10	2	1
Third party wins	17	21	45	43	16	4

Note: A positive value indicates a bias towards that party; a negative value one away from it.

Conclusions

In this chapter we have attempted to assess the degree to which party politics intrudes into the Periodic Electoral Review process and the ability of parties to secure electorally favourable outcomes. For its part the Commission appeared confident that it was now able to spot any blatant attempts to gain partisan advantage from a review. Moreover, the rules imposed such constraints on what could be proposed that in many authorities there was cross-party consensus on broad-brush issues with differences confined to matters of detail. The national parties concentrated their efforts on providing procedural information and advice to their local members, acknowledging both the lack of room for manoeuvre and the logistical impossibility of providing a tailored service for each locality. Indeed the truth is probably that a party could more surely gain an electoral pay-off from a targeted campaign in an individual ward(s) than from attempting to secure its position by shifting a few streets during an electoral review. Nonetheless, we did find plenty of evidence that local political parties became engaged with the review process and that disputes were engendered by it. In extreme cases opposition parties, powerless to overturn the majority on the Council, resorted to airing their grievances in the local press. Officers and members sometimes took rather contradictory views on how much a role partisan politics had played in the process, but most politicians were happy to accept that it was only natural for them to at least explore whether any advantage was available. Yet, time and time again, even they returned to the central issue of being guided by the need to satisfy the Commission.

Party political manoeuvring might never have been far away during deliberations and lobbying on electoral reviews, but we found little evidence that re-districting itself made dramatic differences to the pattern of representation in local authorities. Boundary changes have the potential to add the odd ward to a party's safe seat tally, as in the examples from South Hams and Welwyn Hatfield discussed earlier, but any system which seeks both electoral equality and geographical integrity will militate against radical change. Indeed the examination of the origins of 'bias' in electoral outcomes shows that party fortunes depend much more heavily on factors such as levels of turnout and patterns of party competition over which the Commission can have no influence. It is right no longer to pretend that party politics has no place in an electoral review, but it must also be acknowledged that the ability of parties to get their own way by riding roughshod over either the rules or their opponents seems strictly limited.

Chapter 9

The Evaluation of Process and Outcomes

This chapter provides an analysis of the review process and outcomes from the perspective of those whom the Commission calls its stakeholders. These include the members and officers in local authorities subject to review, the political parties and others who make representations to the LGCE, as well as the sponsoring government department, the Department of the Environment, Transport and the Regions. Our information comes from a number of sources. The questionnaires we sent to officers and members, together with the Commission's own stakeholder surveys to which we had access, provide a common core of data from a wide range of local authorities. These are supplemented by the interviews we conducted with Commissioners and their staff, and with local government officers, councillors, and party activists. Our research also happened to coincide with the quinquennial Financial Management and Policy Review (FMPR) of the Commission carried out on behalf of the government. The FMPR reports provide an important additional perspective on the work of the Commission in terms both of its current organisation and management and of its future structure and role.

Evaluation by the Commission

The Local Government Commission for England is committed to the constant review and evaluation of its own activities. The mechanisms used in this process include an annual report to Commissioners detailing the electoral reviews conducted during the preceding twelve months and the feedback received, and an annual Corporate Plan which puts the Commission's work in wider context and sets out a number of objectives against which it can be judged in the following year. A number of the Commission's objectives relate to staffing policy and the management of resources and do not concern us here. Other material, such as the impact of reviews on electoral equality and council size, has been dealt with in earlier chapters. Of more immediate interest are the surveys of stakeholders and, in particular, the way in which these are used in reviewing and modifying Commission practice. We have examined the results and impact of the surveys conducted in the three years 1996/7, 1997/8 and 1998/9.

The clear trend is one of a growing satisfaction with both the Commission's overall work and of various aspects of the process – see Table 9.1. Questions asking about the conduct of LGCE staff and the clarity of documentation received even more positive responses. This feedback, together with accompanying comments and the observations of those doing reviews, informs Commission attempts to improve its procedures. For example, the Preliminary Period during which local authorities are notified about and may make initial preparations for a PER was introduced following analysis of the first stakeholder survey and later extended in length – see Chapter 3. Similarly, the Commission has been receptive to representations asking for more flexible review timetables during the Christmas and summer holiday periods, and for clearer guidance on matters such as electorate projections and parish reviews. On the other hand, it is constrained by its statutory remit from doing much more than noting calls for less attention to be paid to numerical parity between wards, or for rapid re-reviews further to consider perceived anomalies.

Table 9.1 Satisfaction with the work of the Local Government Commission

	1996/7	*1997/8*	*1998/9*
% overall conduct of Review 'excellent'	5	20	34
% notice given of Review 'sufficient'	57	79	91
% public announcement of Review 'effective'	44	68	77
% 'no problem' understanding Commission's policies	62	62	74
% consultation period 'sufficient' for representations	57	65	86

The Commission also noted that the most troublesome reviews tended to be in places where it had been unable to brief members at an early stage. It is now much more proactive in seeking a cross-party meeting with elected members during the preliminary period/Stage One in order to explain the 'rules' of the review. The Chief Executive believes that this is an important step in managing expectations. If political parties are made aware of what will and will not be accepted at the outset, time is saved and inappropriate submissions avoided later. For example, since such meetings became the norm, fewer local authorities have sought to preserve the *status quo*.

Evaluation by local authorities: Process

Responses to our own survey of reviewed authorities pick up many of the same points, though they are enhanced by asking additionally about PERs from the perspective of local authorities and elected members.

Preparation and Consultation

In some contrast to the early days of Periodic Electoral Reviews, a substantial majority of councillors and officers believed that there was sufficient time to formulate a submission to the Commission at Stage One and to respond to the Draft Recommendations at Stage Three. Indeed, most complaints on this theme came from authorities whose review had taken place before the introduction of the Preliminary Period in 1988. One officer, who wished to remain anonymous, told us that in his local authority, 'Notice of the start of the review was not received from the Commission until the day the public notice was published', and a councillor in Alnwick said that the length of Stage Three 'was a major bone of contention with us and we protested to our Council about this at the time'. Such views were rare. It was more common to find respondents who thought the timing of the PER to be unhelpful. Clashing with local elections could result in the control of the council being changed mid-way through a review as happened in West Lindsey,

> 'The timetable cut through local elections that were significant not only for newly elected members but the whole outlook of the Council. We have been under no overall control since 1974; the 1996 elections changed that.'

In Chester, not only was Stage One timetabled for August, but Stage Three fell during the Christmas holiday period. The council reported 'enormous difficulties' in arranging meetings. There were similar problems in Carlisle where it was,

> 'Impossible for the cycle of City Council, Parish Council response and City Council consideration of Parish response to be completed within Stage One, especially with Christmas/New Year included in the period',

and in Harrow,

> 'Stage One was largely over the Council's Summer Recess period and this, together with the short notice given and the need to create a special panel, made agreeing dates for meetings of the panel very difficult to organise'.

Occasionally, timetable problems were caused by local authority response rather than Commission deadlines. In Bristol, one councillor wrote that his party did not have the full length of the review to work on their submission,

> 'We should have been given figures at the start of the consultation period. As it was, the figures that are fundamental to the proposals were given to us three days – count them – before we had to submit. This was not acceptable.'

A more general concern among stakeholders was that it was impossible to conduct full and proper consultation during Stage One and/or Stage Three. Options were discussed by councillors, but usually only a single, preferred option was put out for consultation among the public. Being invited to do little more than nit pick over particular boundaries, about which they had insufficient information to formulate different proposals, it seemed no wonder that there was not more interest. An officer from Derbyshire Dales argued that,

> 'Stage One was very tight and our proposals were not recommending vast change – had we needed to visit more parishes to discuss the proposals in greater depth, then it would not have been possible to do the job properly. As it was we had to send out documents for comment at short notice with little time for parish councillors and ward members etc. to respond',

and one from Elmbridge spoke for a number of authorities when commenting,

> 'If consultation/participation for the community is to reach beyond the activists, then greater time will be needed. On a sceptical note, I doubt if this would impact on the end solution as it was hard enough to engage the activists.'

An 'opposition' councillor who wished to remain anonymous made a related, but rather different point. He noted that 'the Commission rejected our call for a smaller council because we had not shown public support for it. How were we supposed to resource that?'

Although greater time and more detailed consultation would perhaps have helped to smooth out some of the problem areas that became apparent as various reviews proceeded, the Commission seems rightly keen to avoid the kind of slippage in the timetable that characterised some of the LGBC's reviews – see Chapter 2. Most local authorities are content with the time allowed, and the Commission showed itself sufficiently flexible to react to exceptional circumstances when all the councils in Wiltshire were offered the opportunity to revise their scheme in the light of the government's White Paper on Modernising Local Government – see Chapter 4. A councillor from Exeter probably put his finger on the spot when commenting to us,

> 'You can always do with more time – but I suspect the work would still be crammed into the final deadline period.'

The work of local government officers and councillors

In dealing with something as infrequent and technically complex as an electoral review it is inevitable that councillors place a heavy reliance on the interpretations and advice provided for them by officers. Most were content with the work of officers in their authority. Positive comments about their work included, 'Officers gave every assistance to *all* submissions' (Bexley), 'We were satisfied with their professionalism' (Peterborough), 'Very content. Excellent officer input' (South Shropshire), 'They all operated in a very professional manner to everyone's full satisfaction' (East Hertfordshire), and 'The work carried out by our officers was of the highest calibre and regarded by members as such' (South Somerset). Other respondents mentioned that officers kept them involved and informed about the review, and gave good notice of when and where the Commission was visiting. Overall, councillors suggested that officers performed their role of providing neutral advice and information very well. In High Peak,

> 'The officers were informed, available and extremely helpful in offering information and, where requested, advice on an impartial basis to all concerned';

and in Redbridge,

> 'We were warned and informed and they arbitrated effectively between parties where necessary.'

On the other hand, some councillors felt the officers too powerful, especially where time constraints led to them taking responsibility for formulating the council's scheme. A councillor from Hackney complained that the, 'Officers ignored the views of the political groups and produced their own 'politics-free' scheme', and a colleague from South Gloucestershire wrote that, 'The officers' informal contacts with Commission staff can lead to suspicion that schemes are being designed out of sight of democratic scrutiny.'

Indeed, some councillors who believed that the process was essentially 'political' welcomed the fact that officers had not been involved. A respondent from Bath and North East Somerset commented, 'I was satisfied with their role in the sense that they have very little impact'. The converse of this attitude was the relatively widespread impression among opposition politicians that the officers simply served the party that had political control of the local authority. Responses to our survey included the following, 'they operate under instructions from the controlling Labour party' (Bristol), 'the officers were acting on the Labour majority group instructions' (Stevenage), 'Their work was governed by the wishes of the ruling group' (Medway), 'The officers produced a political submission in line with instructions from the majority group' (Richmond-upon-Thames), 'They were clearly working to a Labour party brief, but were not themselves seeking political advantage' (Harrow). One disgruntled councillor described in some detail the role played by officers in his authority and the effect this had on the review,

> 'The officers in this authority simply followed the instructions of the ruling Tory group. Labour and Liberal Democrats got no support with their submissions. Also, I think we were misled at the outset into recommending only marginal changes because of the strong possibility of reconsideration of wards due to revived unitary status and regional government. Our officers also advised us (incorrectly) that no changes in parish boundaries could be considered. This affected our recommendation, particularly with regard to non inclusion in Macclesfield Town of some adjoining housing estates technically in 'rural' parishes (and wards)' (Macclesfield).

Elsewhere, however, it was believed that a good working relationship between officers and councillors helped to make for a smooth running review. For example, a different respondent from South Gloucestershire commented that,

> 'Joint working between officers and members throughout the whole process, together with regular consultation with Parish Councils, contributed significantly to the review being far less troublesome than we first thought it might be.'

The work of the Commission

The Local Government Commission 'attaches great importance to establishing a good working relationship with local authorities and other interested parties' (Corporate Plan 1998/9, 1998: para 37). One means of seeking this is the structured questionnaire sent to all stakeholders following a review asking for their views on aspects of its process and conduct. Our own survey attempted to elicit a broader range of reaction from these stakeholders by allowing them more open-ended opportunities to voice their opinions.

Once again the more serious complaints seemed to come from those authorities that had been in the first tranche of reviews. For example, the Commission's early stakeholder surveys revealed dissatisfaction about the inexperience of its staff. Comments included, 'Some staff were clearly on a learning curve', 'Some of the staff did not have the knowledge to recognise the different needs of communities within our rural area', and 'Through obvious inexperience some staff underestimated the significance of the public meeting process at the outset'. Councils in Lincolnshire raised this and other issues in response to our own survey. For South Kesteven,

> 'Although the Commission's staff were full of enthusiasm, some did not have sufficient knowledge of local government to give good advice. A definite learning curve. We believe that ultimately this led to at least one very dubious decision implemented against the Council's advice. The solution would be the employment of personnel with general local government experience.'

Others criticised the lack of communication with the Commission. East Lindsey felt the process 'set off badly when we received notification of the start of the review via the local media', and North Kesteven complained there was 'not sufficient guidance about what the Commission expected. They didn't appear to be clear about what they were trying to achieve'. Interviews with officers and Commissioners confirmed that there were difficulties at the start of the PER round, but these were believed to be small compared to the problems starting the earlier structural reviews. However, staff who had been working on the future of local government did find it a significant gear change to move to dealing with the relative minutiae of drawing up ward boundaries. They had acquired in depth knowledge of local government issues, but had no experience of electoral re-districting.

As the reviews proceeded there were a smaller number of complaints of this nature and the majority of authorities responding to us seemed very happy with the work of the Commission. For example, an officer from Bristol wrote that, 'The working relationship was ideal. We cannot fault the Commission in any way'. In Peterborough they '...found the Commission's officers to be helpful and easy to contact', and for Harrow 'formal and informal advice was always available when we needed it and was very helpful'. In some cases, however, satisfaction was tempered by a feeling that the Commission was too desk bound. An officer in Castle Morpeth observed 'it is always difficult when such Commissions are based in London', and a colleague in Exeter commented,

> 'We found the Commission easy to work with and they were extremely professional. We would have liked them to spend more time in the City. They only had one officer spend half a day in Exeter, as a result a great deal of time was spent on the telephone trying to describe physical features that could have been more easily shown'.

Most councillors seemed similarly content with the Commission's work, although their view was sometimes coloured by the degree to which their own pet schemes had been accepted. A member from High Peak had 'no complaints and feel that our representations were carefully considered and more important largely accepted', and one in Peterborough was 'very satisfied – they actually listened to us'. One respondent quoted from a letter sent to the Secretary of State on 31 December 1996,

> 'The City Council's Liberal Democrat Group applaud the Commission for the careful consideration they have given to the evidence and opinions submitted to them from all sources during both Stage One and Stage Three' (Rochester and Medway).

There were also more general plaudits from members for the Commission's professionalism. From St. Albans, 'very satisfied, they were communicative when required. They were also prepared to phone for detailed clarification of a particular point'; from Bristol, 'they were helpful in clarifying the viability of potential schemes'; from Lewisham, 'took our concerns into account. All documentation was very clear and well presented'; and from Thurrock, 'worked extremely well with civil servants *[sic]* establishing a good working relationship which proved very helpful in the long run'.

Criticisms of the Commission covered a range of topics, but were perhaps most serious where they involved accusations by local authorities or members that they had been misled or subject to the inconsistent application of rules. One council reviewed in 1997/8 felt that,

> 'The message given about the acceptable range for councillor/elector ratios was not clear. Firstly, we were told 0% variation; then 4%, but in fact the Commission itself used 10%' (Spelthorne),

and another that,

> 'With hindsight, we were not aware just how far they were prepared to go to obtain electoral equality. We understood that if we did not want change (the electorate, not just Copeland), it wouldn't be thrust upon us – unfortunately this was/is not the case' (Copeland).

Similar complaints of inconsistency were voiced in early 1999 onwards at a time when the Commission seemed not to refer to its guidance document on variations in electoral equality. Instead, authorities were advised informally that a maximum variance of 2-3% only would be acceptable. Southwark commented that 'the goal posts seemed to change – numbers had to be tighter the second time around, which caused more work', and a councillor in Chester felt that, 'the guidance from the Commission changed during the process and this caused difficulty'. There was concern in at least two London boroughs about the advice given by the Commission regarding multi-member wards. An officer in Wandsworth told us that,

> 'The Commission gave members and officers of the Council a misleading impression that only entirely three-member ward schemes would be acceptable. This was not the case, as other London boroughs were the subjects of Draft and Final Recommendations that proposed two- and one-member wards in some instances',

and a councillor in Harrow added,

> 'Our original all three-member ward solution was based on advice from the Commission. Since then, some other London boroughs have successfully argued for a mixture of one-, two- and three-member wards. Had we known this, I think that we would have put in two options, indicating that we preferred the mixed size ward option.'

In some cases the Commission was accused of making mistakes which affected the Recommendations it made. In North East Derbyshire there was surprise that 'the final proposals contained a number of mistakes with the summary not consistent with the details', and in South Gloucestershire one councillor asserted that,

> 'Our only contact with the Commission staff was through correspondence. We were extremely angry that the Commission's Draft Recommendations for one area (which we supported) contained a significant error, because the mapping did not correspond with the text and tables. This led the council (and us) to submit inappropriate representations at Stage Three. We felt that this may have been a contributory factor in the Commission's decision to make alternative proposals in their Final Recommendations. The Commission, when the error was identified, should have written a letter to all respondents explaining the true position, and extending the time for Stage Three submissions.'

Finally, in one authority, an officer complained that the way the Commission went about its business amounted almost to a case of *lèse-majesté*!

> 'The views of an individual resident seemed to be given equal weight to the views of

the City Council which makes the decision as the democratically elected representative body with detailed knowledge and understanding drawn from each ward by the sitting councillors' (Carlisle).

Evaluation by local authorities: Outcomes

Although satisfaction with outcomes was heavily influenced by the degree to which local authorities and/or political parties had got their own way, some councils took a measured view. Ellesmere Port and Neston were 'glad the PER took place as our ward structure was well out of date', and South Somerset acknowledged,

> 'If we had not carried out this exercise we would have had a huge elector /member ratio in some wards, in Yeovil in particular. This has eased the workload of some members and will give the public better access to those members.'

Others were more bullish about their perceived political success. In Stevenage, for example, the council was highly satisfied because 'the LGC agreed with every aspect of our submission and made no changes', and in Ealing they were 'very satisfied as the Final Recommendations coincided with the Council's view except for minor details'. In the majority of cases disagreement with the Commission focused on particular wards or areas. South Northamptonshire noted that,

> 'The vast majority of our proposal was accepted and recommended by the Commission. We disagreed with the Commission on only one ward. We proposed two single member wards, they proposed one ward with two members. This highlighted the inherent contradiction in the review between equality of representation (the mathematics) and clarity of accountability (a preference for single member wards)',

and South Gloucestershire was 'generally satisfied' despite

> 'not all aspects being as individual groups would have liked. There has been no wish expressed by any group to take issue with the final proposals. Everyone seems generally resigned to accepting it – the overriding concern is to see the changes in place for the 1999 local and parish elections.'

Criticisms of the final review outcome centred around three main themes. First, that the review was just a number crunching exercise. Second, that the Commission disregarded arguments showing how communities would be broken up as a result of a disproportionate focus on numbers. Third, that the Commission was vulnerable to being hoodwinked by political parties. Because of the stringent rules regarding electoral equality and the difficulty of reconciling this with the preservation of community ties, the Commission's recommendations were unlikely to be universally popular. Two councils in Wiltshire highlighted this tension. North Wiltshire did 'not dispute the improvements in the councillor/elector ratio' but added that 'the creation of two member wards will be unwelcome', and West Wiltshire was 'deeply unhappy about multi-member wards in rural areas. Members felt that the review was driven by arithmetic not community identity'. In Macclesfield they 'found the whole exercise too mathematical with little leeway for local historical arrangements', and in Carlisle there was disappointment that there was 'no mechanism to give weight to community identity, ties and local history'. Such feelings were multiplied where it was felt that the Commission had ignored strong local representations. A respondent from Copeland protested that,

> 'No notice was taken of submissions from Copeland Borough Council, local councils associations, parish councils and political parties over the issue concerning the combining of two entirely different wards',

and in West Lindsey they were 'not satisfied that the Commission gave weight to local views'. The comments of an officer in Alnwick summed up a view of the Commission which seemed especially prevalent in rural areas. His authority was,

> 'Not very satisfied: local community links and the difficulties found by rural members with very large wards seem to have been given less priority than the statistical homogeneity of the councillor/elector ratio. This works in cities, but not in a district like Alnwick, with a population of 33,000 in an area the size of half of that bounded by the M25!'

The third family of criticisms suggested that party political interests could sway the Commission, especially where these were dressed up in the guise of the protection of 'community ties'. Officers, writing on behalf of the council but probably expressing the views of the ruling group, told us,

> 'The final proposal as amended by the Commission disregarded a number of our recommendations. They have adopted the Liberal Democrat proposal in some areas where political motives were behind the scheme which was surprising. There are also some 'strange' ward boundaries to be adopted' (Waltham Forest), and

> 'The Council wrote to the Secretary of State on 10th September 1999 urging that the Commission's recommendations be rejected due to the flaws that the Council had identified. The Council was concerned that the Commission appeared to give undue weight to letters forming a write-in campaign organised by one political party, and that the Commission's approach to three-member wards was inappropriate given that Government's commitments to elections by thirds now appear to have been shelved' (Wandsworth).

Councillors were even more likely to be upset if the Commission did not use their scheme as a basis for the boundary changes. Some of their comments included,

> 'The Commission seemed to be unable to distinguish between real identity of community and so-called community identity invented to justify party advantage' (Bristol).

> 'Most dissatisfied that they chose the easiest option (presumably to save themselves a lot of work) i.e. swallowed wholesale the recommendations of Stevenage Council i.e. Stevenage Labour Party' (Stevenage).

> 'In general, the Commission appeared to simply accept the borough's submission (i.e. the Tory group). This meant that they were inconsistent in their application of their so-called 'principles'. They effectively contradicted themselves in their report' (Macclesfield).

One respondent went further by accusing the Commission itself of being 'political',

> 'We believe the Commission were politically motivated. The result was crazy, 80 members with some wards having two-members and others three-members is difficult to administer, is far too large and is proving to be unmanageable' (Medway).

We have shown in Chapter 8 that the scope for significant gerrymandering during the review process is limited, and that most reviews result in no more than a marginal change in party political fortunes. Against that background the Commission can probably afford to regard such attacks from disappointed parties as merely an occupational hazard.

Evaluations by local authorities: Improvements

A natural extension to asking PER stakeholders to evaluate the process and outcomes was to invite them to make suggestions about how reviews might be improved. We have divided the comments received into categories covering a range of issues relating to both local authorities and the Commission and to the interaction between them. Much of what we were told reflected the lack of experience among both members and officers in dealing with an electoral review.

Staffing

Many local authorities discovered that a Periodic Electoral review can be a very labour intensive task. The biggest problem they faced was that work on the review was additional to all other staff duties. An officer from Salisbury spelt out the consequence of this,

> 'It is unrealistic to expect members to not want delivery in other areas over the protracted period of the review – thus very long hours had to be worked by staff.'

This was exacerbated by councils often underestimating the time involved in preparing a submission and responding to Recommendations. The feeling of a number of officers is nicely summed up by reactions from two London boroughs. One from Waltham Forest wrote,

> 'It would have been helpful to have been given some idea of the time the submission would take to prepare. This had to be done along with other work which resulted in officers working extra hours',

and a colleague from Ealing added, 'until you have been involved in the process it is difficult to envisage the time commitment'. The easy solution of extra staff was seen as 'unlikely to happen in the 'real world'' (North East Derbyshire), and in any event a PER 'was not the type of project that you could import casual staff to work on' (Exeter). Several councils saw merit in appointing dedicated teams that made use of particular staff expertise rather than 'having the responsibility placed upon one officer' (Northampton). In Lewisham, they came to the conclusion that 'a wide range of experience is needed. Identify people with knowledge of the borough – especially 'natural communities'', and in Kensington and Chelsea,

> 'We would appoint a dedicated team from outside existing electoral services resources. It was very difficult doing the PER and preparing for the European Parliamentary elections.'

Indeed councils that had adopted this team approach seemed to feel that they had coped well enough with the review. A respondent from South Derbyshire wrote that, 'Staffing levels were about right. The PER process requires a multi-disciplinary team'. The authority had a team of six, including the Chief Executive, District Secretary, Policy Officer, Planning Officer, Assistant Director of Planning and Economic Development and the Elections Officer. Elsewhere a warning was sounded against using too many people. Southwark thought it,

> 'Difficult to see how we could have had a much larger team. You can't develop proposals 'by committee' or devolve too far because of the domino-effect of making changes to wards.'

Preliminary planning

When asked how an authority's preliminary planning might be improved, several officers suggested greater concentration on the production of electorate projections. Comments from respondents included, 'Spend more time preparing population and housing projections at ward and parish polling district levels' (Carlisle), 'Have closer liaison with the County Council and establish a County wide policy on method and criteria for calculating population figures to year 2001 before ward statistics were required' (South Kesteven), 'Inform the London Research Centre of planning permissions annually for more accurate predictions' (Ealing), 'Sort out the validity of the electoral data earlier and agree a process of forecasting' (Barnet), and 'Sort out the electorate projections much sooner. This would have allowed more time for the consideration of the different plans' (South Derbyshire). Other areas for improvement included, 'Allow more time for radical changes to be considered' (Vale Royal), 'Draw up several draft proposals for discussion as a pre-review exercise' (Derbyshire Dales), 'Consult other bodies about their views in addition to the political parties' (Northampton), 'Seek journalistic coverage in the local media' (Chesterfield) and 'Look at GIS systems for mapping different models' (Bexley). Another London Borough commented that,

> 'With greater notice and more lead-in time, we would have used our IT resources to

> link the Electoral Roll with the Council's GIS system, which – if it had been available – would have greatly speeded up the production of alternative schemes of ward boundary changes and their resultant electorates' (Harrow).

A final suggestion came from an officer in Exeter who wrote that,

> 'It might have been useful to have applied 'Project Planning' principles to this project. It felt at times that we were losing our way and our timetable was going astray.'

Decision-making process

The ways in which local authorities had organised themselves to make decisions about submissions to the PER varied considerably. With hindsight, several regretted not involving members more fully from the outset. In Alnwick it was resolved to 'try to involve elected members earlier and seek more detailed views', and in Surrey Heath it was thought that 'a small member working party would have been helpful both to the options review and consultations elements'. Similar comments came from Bristol and West Wiltshire, although in Lewisham there was concern that 'it would be difficult to get cross party agreement on this issue' using a working party. Some councils which had experienced such member involvement were not convinced of its utility. For Bexley,

> 'It would have been better not to have set up a formal Council working party and just let the three Groups get on with it',

and South Lakeland took the view that,

> 'If possible, we would delegate the entire review to officers. The councillors had too close a 'vested interest' in the make-up of the new wards.'

In South Kesteven the presence of seven party leaders meant that a consensus was not easy to achieve and the council 'missed the final deadline because a decision of the working party was overturned at a Council meeting'. Several councillors commented that on future occasions they would be more aware of the scope for the party political manipulation of the decision-making process. A respondent in High Peak said that he would,

> 'Ignore the pretence that the controlling Labour group made towards 'dialogue' and spend more time attempting to canvass local opinion about boundaries and their relationship to actual as opposed to supposed community of interest' (High Peak).

Consultation

It is difficult for a local authority to decide which type of consultation is best for a particular project. It is also problematic to discover whether a consultation exercise has been successful. Was there no response to a council's scheme advertised in the local press and on posters in libraries because people were happy with the proposal or because the advertising failed to reach its target and explain what was happening? At least one authority took the former view and argued that they would not change their consultation strategy as, 'The Council received no complaints about the lack of consultation from any person or groups in the Borough'. However, the results from our survey showed that many local authorities accepted that improvements could be made to the public consultation process accompanying electoral reviews. These ranged from the need to 'Hold more Public Meetings and greater consultation with all members of the Council' (Durham), to a belief that 'A wider and more pro-active approach to dissemination and information with some face to face sessions may have proved informative' (Surrey Heath), to a commitment to increase the level of advertising as, 'Most members of the public had no idea the review was on' (Bristol). An officer from South Northamptonshire resolved to

> 'try to be present at Parish/Town Council meetings when it was discussed in order to explain the requirements and conflicting criteria in more detail.'

In some cases better time management was the key with officers suggesting that if they went through a PER again, consultation would take place much earlier than it actually did. One respondent wrote that,

> 'Because of the difficulties with the decision-making process, the Council's draft scheme was not agreed until late in Stage One, resulting in the public consultation period being squeezed and the need to ask the LGCE for an extension of time to get the results of the consultation to them' (Harrow).

Despite such good intentions, authorities also pointed out the difficulties of consulting the electorate on this issue. A respondent from Salisbury explained the situation in his authority,

> 'By consulting on each stage the Parishes/Consultees did not always find it easy to understand where we were at. Also by the District undertaking the review many thought it was our review not the Commission's. The Commission should be more involved.'

Some councils believed that increased advertising would still result in a low level of response because people are generally apathetic, and one officer admitted that,

> 'We should have targeted the consultation more carefully at local community groups. A newspaper advertisement to everyone in the borough was a bit of a waste of time – not many people are interested. We targeted more carefully in Stage Three' (Lewisham).

Councillors also saw the need for greater public consultation, perhaps even at the expense of making it a more difficult process to manage politically. Next time they would,

> 'Consult earlier with Parish Councils and other Community organisations and seek

> advice from national political office' (South Hams);
>
> 'Consult much more widely than we did. The decisions taken were on the basis that we would be revisited again in a fairly short timescale. That turned out not to be the case, and we may well have imbalance in some wards within a fairly short number of years, certainly we will have before the Commission come again' (Halton);
>
> 'Be far more public in asserting our wishes. Whilst some residents did write in, their views were ignored. Perhaps, a public campaign in the local press might at least have made residents more aware about what was going on' (Richmond-upon-Thames);

or

> 'Go out more to public consultation – let us have less from the political groupings' (Peterborough).

Respondents also believed it important that the public should be encouraged to voice support for proposed changes or, indeed, the *status quo* quite as much as they articulated dissatisfaction with them.

Contact with the Commission

Most authorities were content with their contacts with the Commission. Positive comments included, 'The contact was excellent' (Watford), and 'Contact could not be bettered' (Bristol). For the small minority who complained, a key issue seemed to be closer liaison. One council wrote,

> 'It would have been better if we could have met with the Commission to submit our proposal and discuss the reasoning behind our submission' (Waltham Forest);

another believed that,

> 'The Commission should have held a meeting with our Council over one or two problem areas which were in the end not resolved to the Council's satisfaction' (Teignbridge);

and a third said,

> 'The chance to meet and explain our ideas to the Commission would have been helpful' (Shrewsbury and Atcham).

A radical suggestion on these lines came from West Lindsey,

> 'Perhaps, the Commission should second an officer to work with the Council in the Council offices – rather than trying to work from London'.

There were also calls for the Commission to offer enhanced services to authorities being reviewed given that the gap between PERs meant that it was unlikely that anyone in an authority had prior experience of them. These services included, issuing an 'approved process/methodology for forecasting electorates' (Barnet) together with 'guidelines on the process (setting up a working party, some idea of resources needed etc' (Lewisham). Hertsmere mentioned that they had requested a model submission as an example to work to. Although not official Commission policy, a number of Review Managers do now send out their 'favourite' submission as a template for authorities undergoing a PER. An officer in Ealing told us that 'copies of other submissions were helpful'.

A very few councils had more general dissatisfactions. An officer from Wandsworth commented that 'The whole process was rushed, poorly organised and poorly thought through'; a member in Richmond-upon-Thames took the view that the Commission's 'operation appears to have been entirely opaque'; and from North Kesteven we were told,

> 'The contact with the Commission was not effective, it was difficult to obtain responses and guidance. The Commission's lack of knowledge of the local situation hindered progress.'

In other cases the frustration was 'not with the staff but with the criteria' (West Somerset). Alnwick seemed to find it curious that the Commission's staff were 'more interested in sticking to figures and rules, rather than ensuring fair treatment to the rural wards', and the emphasis on electoral equality in the briefing given to council leaders in Wiltshire was deemed 'not satisfactory'. A councillor from St. Albans reported to us how he had spoken,

> 'directly with the Commission regarding probable electoral arrangements and found them polite and friendly in terms of advice/information but 'close-minded' as regards suggestions.'

It is likely that his 'suggestions' included asking the Commission to ignore the rules to which it is bound.

Implementation of Reviews

Once the LGCE has sent its Final Recommendations to the Secretary of State it has no further role to play. However, councils are naturally interested in when elections on the new boundaries will be held. In a number of cases they complained of a delay in the implementation of the new arrangements. In Surrey Heath it was,

> 'the Council's understanding that the implementation of changes would be made in time for the Borough Elections on 6th of May 1999, and it was not made clear that this would not be the case until after publication of Draft Recommendations',

and Derbyshire Dales found it,

> 'disappointing that we have not got an outcome in time for our elections this year and that long term there has been no clear indication of a likely date when the order is going to be made and what arrangements are to be made for holding elections in the future.'

For South Kesteven the delay brought other uncertainties,

> 'It is now the middle of August and we have yet to receive the final Order. The canvass for the Register of Electors looms and to make sense needs to be based on the review. I think someone, somewhere needs to look at the administration of the whole process, especially in view of the Government's strategy concerning local government'.

On a slightly different tack, for at least one council all out elections following a PER seemed like a case of using a sledgehammer to crack a nut,

> 'The Council was not satisfied with the Minister's decision to impose all-out elections in 1999. The boundaries of nine wards were not amended following the review, however, as a result of the decision councillors elected for such wards in 1998 would have their term of office reduced to one year' (St. Albans).

The government has not deviated from its policy of requiring fresh whole council elections regardless of the scale of changes introduced following an electoral review, but in July 1999 it did seek to clarify a timetable for implementation. The Minister for Local Government announced to Parliament that,

> 'we intend to implement the Local Government Commission's recommendations as follows. For district councils that hold whole council elections and where Final Recommendations are received by July 2002, implementation is to be on the normal election date of May 2003. For district councils that elect by thirds, where Final Recommendations have already been received, implementation is to be on the normal election day in May 2000; where Final Recommendations are received between August 1999 and July 2001, implementation is to be on the normal election day in May 2002; and where Final Recommendations are received no later than July 2002 on the normal election day in May 2003. The Commission's recommendations for a county council are to be implemented only after recommendations have been made and implemented for all the district councils in a county area. Subject to this, where Final Recommendations for county councils are received no later than July 2000, they are to be implemented on the normal election day in May 2001; subsequent Final Recommendations are to be implemented on the normal election day in 2005' (LGCE Corporate Plan 2000/1, 2000: 14).

This explicit commitment to publishing Orders implementing all Final Recommendations received by a certain time was new, but contained echoes of similar undertakings given but not always adhered to in the days of the LGBC – see Chapter 2. It also required a complete revision by the Commission of its planned PER timetable.

Changing the Rules

Given that many of the comments made by local authorities and councillors about the review process and outcomes contained at least implicit criticisms of the rules to which the Commission is obliged to work, it was no surprise to find a number of respondents putting forward suggestions for radical changes. For some it was important to investigate ways of entirely removing PERs from the taint of party politics. This would presumably involve the Local Government Commission being proactive in the re-warding of authorities in the same way as the Parliamentary Boundary Commissions produce initial proposals for constituencies which are then the subject of public consultation. A councillor from Runnymede argued that,

> 'Political parties should not be involved in the process. The Borough Council should not be involved either. It should be a totally independent group appointed to deal with this, or preferably carried out along the same lines as public enquiries with interested local groups being allowed to make verbal inputs',

and a colleague from Ealing called for 'an objective body drawing up alternative draft proposals'. A somewhat less far reaching proposal came from a member in Macclesfield who thought that,

> 'Submissions should not be allowed under authority names, which give no indication of support from minority groups. Political and other groups and individuals only should make submissions.'

Even in these circumstances an advantage might rest with the majority party, hence a councillor in Haringey arguing that 'if the PER outcome is meant to be apolitical, then equality of input in terms of resourcing support should be provided for opposition parties'. This was supported by a comment from Chesterfield to the effect that,

> 'we were not given any funds or means to consult widely on our proposals. The party in power had the means to advertise their proposals – we didn't. This area needs examination.'

For some, mainly rural authorities the perceived metropolitan centred nature of the Commission and its decisions needed to be addressed. In the view of a councillor from West Somerset,

> 'As usual, Whitehall and Westminster write the rules from their blinkered metropolitan perspective with no regard to their applicability to rural areas. This is true whichever party is in Government.'

Such sentiments tended to encompass barely disguised pleas for the introduction of rural weighting, the retention of single member wards and the restoration of the powers of principal authorities to determine parish boundaries (which had, in fact, been granted by the 1997 Local Government and Rating Act). As we were told from Salisbury,

> 'There was little thought for rural communities. Two or more member wards normally means one councillor is massively overworked',

and from Tynedale,

> 'The Commission did not appreciate the importance locally of natural and sometimes cultural boundaries. The re-arrangement of parish boundaries should be a local decision.'

Other issues on which local authorities sought a change in policy included setting a shorter and more certain gap between reviews (Kensington and Chelsea); better co-ordination between both district and county PERs (High Peak) and local and parliamentary electoral reviews (Merton); and, unsurprisingly, the amendment of the 1992 Local Government Act to allow boundaries better 'to reflect the identities and interests of local communities'. A councillor from West Lindsey combined many of these concerns in a general condemnation of Periodic Electoral Reviews,

> 'The determination of criteria, the lack of any local members [of the Commission], the recognition of spurious 'representation groups' (one such group was quoted freely by the Commission to legitimise their proposals – no one knows who the group are and suspects it is a cover for a political party) and the lack of any effective appeal gives us little confidence in the PER system. The present system is shoddy, undemocratic and in our case will have to be undertaken again within the next 10 years – what a basis to restore the public's faith in local government!'

Evaluation of the Commission

In addition to the continuing internal audit and evaluation of the Commission's processes, the government carries out a review of all non-departmental public bodies every five years. The terms of reference for the Financial Management and Policy Review (FMPR) of the Local Government Commission for England were,

> 'To undertake a comprehensive review of the LGCE, consisting of first a prior options assessment of the LGCE and its functions and second, having regard to that assessment, a review of all aspects of the Commission's organisation, operation and procedures.'

The Prior Options study, conducted by Professor Robert Hazell of University College London, aimed to answer three main questions:

- Are the functions of the Commission (structural, boundary, parish and electoral reviews) still necessary?
- If so, are they best undertaken by the Commission or some other body?
- Are there additional functions which the Commission could undertake?

The report published on 1 July 1998 concluded that, as far as the electoral review functions of the LGCE were concerned, they were essential and 'must be carried out by an independent commission to preserve the fairness of the electoral system and to maintain 'one vote, one value' (FMPR Prior Options Report, 1998: para 7). The

Commission remained 'the most appropriate and cost-effective body' to undertake this task (para 9). Other key findings included recommendations for electoral reviews to be undertaken on a rolling basis in order that areas with the greatest electoral imbalances could be prioritised, and for a merger between the LGCE and the Parliamentary Boundary Commission for England the better to co-ordinate their various tasks. The Prior Options study resisted calls for a significant shortening of the review timetable and for the relaxation of the Commission's target of a maximum 10% electoral imbalance. It also affirmed that while reviews should continue to be based on initial submissions by local authorities, it would not be appropriate for them to play a greater role given that they 'are generally working under political direction' (para 15.3). Minutes of a Commission meeting reveal that there was some uncertainty regarding the benefits of a merger,

> 'The Commission had approached the FMPR with an open mind on the benefits to be derived from some kind of merger with the PBC. However, it still had not seen a convincing intellectual argument for such a change' (February 1998),

but the 1998/9 Corporate Plan merely said 'we welcome the Government's response to the Prior Options report, and will await with interest its final decision on the case for merging our work with that of the PBC' (Corporate Plan 1998/9, 1998: para 68).

The second stage of the review examined in detail the internal organisation of the Commission. It aimed to assess the performance of the Commission and whether it offered good value for money. A list of twenty-two recommendations was produced, mainly relating to improving the management of the organisation and the review process, and an action plan for their implementation agreed. Examples of recommendations included inviting the Commission to consider how it could achieve a higher national profile for its work, and urging the Department of the Environment, Transport and the Regions to undertake to make Orders giving effect to Final Recommendations within a set period of time following submission to the Secretary of State. The current position regarding the implementation of proposals made at each stage of the FMPR will be reviewed in Chapter 10.

Conclusions

This chapter has examined a number of types of evaluation of the Periodic Electoral Review work of the Local Government Commission for England. These included the Commission's own self-audit and analysis, as well as the views of its stakeholders in both local and central government. The general conclusion on all sides is that the Commission does a difficult and potentially controversial job well, and that it is always willing to respond to suggestions for improvement in the way in which it carries out its tasks. In the years since the current round of PERs began in 1996 it is clear that the Commission has 'learnt the ropes'. This is reflected in a decrease in complaints about process and in a growth in the satisfaction expressed by those subject to review. It is confirmed by the findings of the official Financial Management and Policy Review which gave explicit backing to the Commission's continuing performance of its functions, and largely confined its recommendations to particular aspects of internal organisation and procedure. We were also interested in how those involved in reviews in the local authorities evaluated their own experience of the process. Many were able, like the Commission itself, to reflect on the lessons learned and on what might be done better in the future. Once again, such ideas tended to involve adjustments rather than wholesale changes to the system.

That is not to say that no serious criticisms or dissatisfactions were voiced. The Commission was widely seen as seeking electoral equality between wards and divisions at the expense of respecting community ties. This led to several authorities launching quite vehement attacks on the Commission's approach and even, on occasion, its integrity. For its part the Commission insists that it does not adopt a rigidly mathematical approach to electorates and that it is sensitive to community interests. However, the Act does require it to ensure that 'the ratio of the number of local government electors to the number of councillors to be elected shall be, as nearly as may be, the same in every ward in the district'. Having regard to the 'desirability of fixing ward boundaries which are and will remain easily identifiable' and to 'any local ties which would be broken by the fixing of any particular ward boundary' are clearly subsidiary goals. We consider in Chapter 10 whether these tensions might be resolved by a change in legislation. There is also clearly discontent within local authorities that the party in power can have an advantage over its rivals when it comes to preparing and consulting on submissions to the Commission. Although the Commission prides itself on giving equality of treatment to all representations received and although the Prior Options study recommended no change in the way in which local authorities contribute to the PER process, there were calls for party political influences to be curtailed.

We now move to our final, concluding chapter which considers the evidence gathered about Periodic Electoral Reviews, assesses the degree to which they meet the requirements of a representative and democratic system of local government, and analyses current and potential proposals for altering the functions and role of the LGCE.

Chapter 10

Conclusions

Local electoral re-districting is a detailed and painstaking process designed to secure a lofty democratic ideal. However, although 'one vote, one value' is a cherished goal in theory, it is clear that many people see the equal representation of people as less important than the proper representation of place. This tension between a mathematical as opposed to organic approach is commonplace wherever geographically-defined electoral units are drawn, but it has been heightened in Britain by the existence of often conflicting and contradictory re-districting rules. Rossiter *et al.* (1999) have clearly spelt out how these have impacted on the work of the Parliamentary Boundary Commissions; here we have tried to show how many of the same issues apply equally to the drawing of local ward boundaries.

Aspects of the Periodic Electoral Review process

The Local Government Boundary Commission, set up in 1972, was the first body to be charged with conducting an independent, coherent and comprehensive review of local electoral boundaries, and as such was widely welcomed. In 1992 the Local Government Commission for England inherited from its predecessor not only a number of rules and procedures, but also a reputation for being strictly impartial and non-partisan. The LGCE soon learnt, however, that many of these rules were ambiguous at best and that it needed to set out how it intended to operate and interpret various aspects of the legislation to which it was subject. This process proved to be an on-going one as the Commission responded, first, to feedback from its initial reviews and then became caught up in potential policy changes by the new Labour government elected in May 1997. Procedural issues on which the Commission acted included, the introduction and then extension of a Preliminary Period during which local authorities are notified about a Periodic Electoral Review and have time to prepare for it; the lengthening of some stages within the review timetable; proactively seeking to meet with both members and officers before a review to explain its scope and the statutory criteria; attempting to increase the effectiveness of local publicity and thus have more people and organisations engage with the review. The Commission claims that these have been successful refinements, and certainly the evidence from both its stakeholder surveys and the responses to our own questionnaires show fewer complaints about and greater satisfaction with the process over time. The Commission also attributes the increase in the number of submissions that it is able to put before the Secretary of State without amendment to the greater attention given to the prior briefing of local authorities.

There can be little doubt that developments in government policy brought some uncertainty to the Commission's work during the period of our research. On the one hand, there was widespread discussion about introducing annual elections for London and some urban unitary authorities, and 'half-and-half' elections for the remaining two-tier areas of England; on the other, there was no firm commitment about whether or when such changes would apply. In the circumstances the LGCE could do little more than keep local authorities informed of government thinking, advise them that they may wish to take that into account when devising re-warding schemes, and subtly alter its guidance concerning its attitude to single- and multi-member wards. The provisions of the Local Government Act 2000 do allow for the Secretary of State to alter the electoral cycle of local authorities on his own initiative and for the Commission to recommend county council electoral divisions with more than one member. Neither has yet been invoked.

For many councils the issues of ward structures and electoral cycles were merely another irritant in what they often perceived as a centralising, 'top down' process. Although the Commission has adopted a flexible and consultative approach, it has often clashed with local authorities over the interpretation of the rules. The LGCE sees the legislation as requiring it to seek electoral equality between wards, with some room for discretion at the margins; many at the local level choose to put greater faith in those clauses which speak of 'the interest and identities of local communities' and the preservation of 'local ties'. Where the two interpretations clash, the Commission can be cast into the caricature role of an ogre from London trampling over the wishes of ordinary folk. Indeed, it is precisely to avoid such an image that the Commission places so much importance on transparency and consultation. On occasion, it has moved to meet evidenced objections from local residents and others to its proposals; elsewhere, it has insisted that electoral equality must be paramount.

It is not only the Commission whose decisions vary from place to place. It soon became clear to us that every review was different because the culture and make-up of every local authority was different too. In some, officers were left to get on with designing a scheme for the council to submit, in others, councillors exercised their right to oversee every stage of the process. In some, the political parties co-operated in producing a consensual submission, in others, political rivalry and a desire to achieve partisan advantage led to every political group forwarding its own scheme to the Commission. This variation was also reflected in the degree to which local authorities enabled and encouraged consultation about their proposals, and even in the level of contact and co-operation with the Commission.

Against this background it becomes possible to see the need to ensure that 'the ratio of the number of local government electors to the number of councillors to be elected shall be, as nearly as may be, the same in every ward' as a clear and consistent standard for the Commission to aim at whatever the context and circumstances of the review. Indeed, the Commission uses this as a measurable benchmark in the evaluation of its own performance. Our own analysis in Chapter 7 provided powerful evidence of the effect of PERs on reducing electoral variances, and some confirmation that the LGCE had a better record in doing this than the LGBC before it. However, the continuing pressure on the Commission from within local authorities to pay as much attention as possible to community identity when drawing boundaries can also be seen in the 'slippage' in levels of equality between its Draft and Final Recommendations.

One of the clear advantages claimed for the Commission, as opposed to legislative, approach to electoral re-districting is its political neutrality. Although the LGCE has on rare occasions been accused of bias by disappointed supplicants, its integrity is widely respected. Nonetheless, party politics does intrude into the process whenever submissions are made which attempt to reap a partisan advantage for one side or the other. Sometimes such an advantage is, happily for the party concerned, a proper consequence of the application of the rules; at others, attempts at sharp practice need to be snuffed out by the Commission. The evidence suggests that the constraint of the statutory criteria means that it is easier for a party to get its own way in a couple of wards or over a small area rather than across an authority as a whole. Indeed, we could find no instance of wholesale gerrymandering among our sample of reviewed authorities, and such advantages as did accrue to particular parties were more likely to be the product of patterns of electoral behaviour rather than electoral geography.

The Future of Periodic Electoral Reviews

In the view of most evaluators the LGCE has been doing its job efficiently and well. However, the Financial Management and Policy Review raised a number of issues about the Commission's future. For example, the Prior Options study was certain that electoral reviews ought to continue to be conducted by an independent Commission, but strongly flagged the perceived benefits of a merger between the LGCE and the Parliamentary Boundary Commission for England. It also floated the idea that the role of the LGCE could be expanded to include providing advice about and the oversight of local electoral arrangements and expenditure. Similarly, the second phase of the FMPR, whilst largely concentrating on administrative and management matters, alerted the Commission to the need to secure a higher national profile and to make use of Geographic Information Systems (GIS) in its work.

In the event the government pre-empted much of this by setting up an Electoral Commission (EC) in February 2001. The Political Parties, Elections and Referendums Act 2000 gave the Electoral Commission wide powers relating to the regulation, financing and conduct of elections and referendums, and contained provisions for the transfer to it of the functions of the parliamentary and local government commissions in each part of the United Kingdom. In March 2001 it was announced that these provisions would be activated from 1 April 2002 in the case of the Local Government Commission for England. This organisational change is to be accompanied by the transfer and variation of other powers. Most important of these is the transfer to the Electoral Commission of the Secretary of State's current functions relating to the implementation of the LGCE's Recommendations. In future the EC itself will be empowered to make statutory instruments following electoral reviews. This power will be exercised in part for those reviews due to be implemented on the normal election day in 2003, and for all reviews thereafter. The Electoral Commission's English Boundary Committee, the body that will supersede not only the LGCE but, in time, the PBCE as well, will also be able to determine when to conduct electoral reviews and to undertake reviews covering only a part of a local authority's area. These reforms have often been mooted by those concerned that the current PER cycle can be an inefficient and long-delayed way of dealing with particularly severe electoral imbalances built up across councils as a whole or in individual wards. The Local Government Act 2000 will also have an impact on the PER process. As we noted earlier, the Secretary of State has taken powers to specify a particular scheme of elections to apply to a given local authority and to change the years in which elections are held – both without the need for prior Commission recommendations.

Although these changes are quite radical in one sense, they still leave untouched many of the detailed aspects of the electoral review process. The Electoral Commission will have the discretion to develop its own guidance and practice as it begins to undertake its new responsibilities, and it may wish to address some of the issues which our research has identified as causing concern or provoking controversy:

The primacy of electoral equality

There is an uncomfortable irony in spending so much time (and money) in ensuring that the councillor/elector ratio in each ward of a local authority is as equal as possible at the same time as the numbers actually bothering to participate in local elections continues to fall. We noted very few spontaneous calls from reviewed authorities for votes to be made of equal value, but recorded plenty of complaints about the destruction of boundaries with which electors identified and felt familiar. Given that evidence from Britain and elsewhere suggests that community identity and involvement are positively correlated with an individual's likely propensity to vote (Lijphart, 2000), it could even be argued that fiddling with boundaries is one of the several causes of declining turnout.

There is a case, therefore, for thinking again about the acceptable variation from the mean in terms of each authority's ward electorates. This is not to say that the 10% and 20% markers which have served both the LGBC and LGCE should be abolished, rather that the push towards keeping variations 'to the absolute minimum' (Guidance, 1996: para 23; Guidance, 2000: para 3.12) should be reconsidered. Although a slightly more relaxed approach would make it harder for inexperienced staff to make judgements about the appropriateness of the schemes proposed, and easier for parties to attempt to gerrymander boundaries, it would allow the EC to pay greater attention to the 'identities and interests of local communities'. It somehow seems inappropriate that local authority wards should be expected in practice to meet higher standards of equality than parliamentary constituencies at a time when the reduction in the tax and spending powers of local government has led it to seek an elevated role in giving expression to local needs and interests.

Electoral structures and cycles

In other areas of its PER responsibilities, however, the LGCE has been keen to allow and respect local discretion. Here, we would argue its approach has contributed to stasis in the local electoral system and served to maintain a number of features which electors find complex, confusing and ultimately perhaps, off-putting. By starting 'from the general assumption that the existing number of councillors…already secures effective and convenient local government'(Guidance, 2000: para 3.6), the Commission is at least tacitly encouraging local authorities to adopt a position of minimal change. This also has the effect of 'freezing' what are essentially rural or sparsity weightings, whereby authorities like Alnwick and Tynedale retain councillor/elector ratios of less than 1,000 merely as reflections of what went before. In the light of the provisions of the Local Government Act 2000 concerning the introduction of new styles of political management, and the recent desire by unitary authorities such as Southend-on-Sea and Brighton and Hove to seek radical changes in council size (albeit in opposite directions), the EC may wish to revisit the appropriate councillor/elector ratios for different types of authority. Among London boroughs, for example, these continued to vary by as much as between 1: 1,877 in Kensington and Chelsea and 1:3,611 in Barnet following the recent PERs. Indeed, in the fifth edition of its Guidance, the Commision admits that there is now 'a real case for ... fresh consideration of the council size appropriate for each local authority area.' (Guidance, 2001: para 3.9).

Whilst we can understand how the LGCE felt obliged to respond to developing government policy on annual elections and multi-member wards, it nonetheless missed its chance to systematise the local electoral timetable. We would hope that, over time, the Electoral Commission will be able to simplify and thus make more voter-friendly English local electoral arrangements. A basic rule should surely be that all electors in an authority have the opportunity to go to the polls whenever their council has elections for other than casual vacancies. However, as things stand, the Commission has presided over the survival of systems in which not merely the odd ward, but sometimes a substantial proportion of the electorate is excluded in any given year. We would contend that the situation in Bristol, where there are elections each year only in a proportion of the 35 two-member wards, comes perilously close to breaking the statutory requirement to 'secure effective and convenient local government'. Electors can never be sure who has a vote when; are likely to find it frustrating not to be able to vote if a particular issue raises its head in one their ward's 'off' years; and, if all this is accompanied by a situation in which it is impossible to get rid of the party running the council however they vote, are likely to be less inclined to participate at all. This problem will be exacerbated if the government legislates for biennial 'half-and-half' elections in areas of England which retain single-member county electoral divisions.

The current electoral systems in both London and the metropolitan districts avoid this problem. However, the Electoral Commission is soon likely to discover two other disadvantages of having multi-member wards. First, the larger the area covered, the more likely are local ties to be cut. Second, the larger the electorate in a ward, the less flexibility subsequently available to the Parliamentary Boundary Commission in designing constituencies. In Birmingham, for example, where wards average 18,500 electors, the PBC is faced with a choice of either transferring very large blocks of electors between constituencies in order to try to meet its criteria or leaving well alone. In Cornwall, on the other hand, where there are 133 district wards with an average electorate of fewer than 3,000, the PBC has a much freer hand to fine tune its recommendations.

Electorate projections

The technical issue that causes most concern during PERs is the construction and accuracy of electorate projections. We found evidence not only that local authorities tended to over-estimate the growth in their electorates, but also that they would welcome tighter rules and clearer guidelines about calculating these figures. The

LGCE concurs that most authorities 'over-estimated the potential for electorate growth in their area' (Guidance, 2001: para 3.23). There are a number of options open to the Electoral Commission. It could base its proposed boundaries on current electorates; it could reduce the time span over which projections were to be made – in Australia, for example, it is three and a half years; or it could insist that an agreed occupancy level was applied to different types of property development. The figure commonly used of two electors per property (see Chapter 5) is likely to be an overstatement given present lifestyle patterns. Reliance on such projections means that there can be an almost illusory accuracy to the calculation of the variance in ward electorates. Another argument perhaps for being a little more tolerant of deviations in order to acknowledge community identities.

The role of local authorities

It would be possible, but not very practicable for PERs to be initiated in the same way as parliamentary boundary reviews. In their case, preliminary proposals are drawn up centrally and then put out to local consultation. However, the PBC works with limited and defined building blocks in the shape of wards, whereas local electoral reviews can and do use units as small as individual houses in adjusting boundaries. Because such a process requires fine-grained local knowledge, it is probably inevitable that local authorities (and other interested parties) will retain the opportunity to make the initial proposals. Not that this process is without its critics.

Local authorities often complained that electoral reviews are expensive and time-consuming, and would be the more so if they became more frequent. There was also a perception that they were being required to expend their own resources on what was essentially a 'London-driven' process. To them, the solution was obvious. Several would have liked 'enhanced resources' to be made available to authorities undergoing a PER: one or two even suggested that a member of staff from the LGCE could be seconded to them for the duration. Neither is likely to happen, but the Electoral Commission ought to be aware of the need to address and manage this at least latent discontent.

A potentially more fundamental problem is the advantage the system gives to the party(ies) in power in the local authority. Although we found little evidence of *successful* attempts to manipulate electoral reviews for political gain, schemes devised by those in the majority – whether submitted in the name of the council or the party – often benefited from the work and input of officers. Minority parties, on the other hand, complained that they had few resources and were not accorded equal access to officers. The position is likely to be even worse in those councils where one party enjoys almost a monopoly of seats, but not an equal measure of electoral support. If the integrity of the electoral review process is to be preserved, there is clearly a need to ensure that opposition views are not only treated equally, but have the opportunity to be articulated equally as well. The LGCE does take care to ensure the former, but can do little about the latter. In this context a suggestion made to us by a councillor from Macclesfield is intriguing,

> 'There must be a market for a piece of software to produce recommendations for ward boundaries. In most authorities the electoral register is computerised. One needs to graft on to that, geographic information on contiguous blocks of houses (postcode is also stored!). One could then go through an interactive process (using local experience) to modify first recommendations – and so on – until final version recommended. A generally available tool of this nature would be fairer to those with fewer resources.'

Such an innovation may still lie in the future, but it is clear that the EC is likely to feel an even greater obligation than the LGCE to try to ensure free and fair access to its deliberations by all interested and affected groups and individuals.

Communication and consultation procedures

An important role in achieving this is played by the Commission's consultation processes. However, although clear procedures are in place for communicating and consulting about electoral reviews, we found plenty of evidence that these worked imperfectly or were found to be unsatisfactory. There were calls for more time to be allowed for consultation and for it to be undertaken earlier in the review process. Some councils even admitted that their consultations were effectively little more than window-dressing. The LGCE itself has calculated that it received just 4,800 representations from among an electorate of 18.7 million in the authorities reviewed in the period to July 2000. Moreover, in the words of the Commission's Chairman, these were 'mostly from the self-interested'.

The EC has a remit to promote public awareness of and participation in the democratic process, and it may well be that in time its 'brand image' will help to stimulate interest in all aspects of its work. Certainly the explicit linking of local and parliamentary boundary revisions may lead MPs, national party officials and political activists in general to take a greater interest in the lower tier activity of PERs. Attracting public attention is likely to remain difficult, however. In the meantime it might wish to review the effectiveness of the publicity for the review programme as a whole, and to consider whether press advertisements are little more than a smokescreen for proper, pro-active consultation. The LGCE clearly feels that holding a greater number of formal public meetings would achieve little. Certainly evidence from the parliamentary reviews suggests that such meetings were an elaborate and expensive way of providing the political parties with an opportunity to persuade a new and influential third party (the Assistant Commissioner) of their case. (Rossiter *et al.*, 1999: 401). On the other hand, and in keeping with the EC's commitment to openness (almost to be 'the citizens' friend'), there may be scope for introducing a stage at which the Commission's proposals can be appealed. This, though, may prove difficult given the circularity of the legislation on which PERs are based and case law which has tended to allow Boundary Commissions almost total discretion within it.

The LGEC as a case-study for political science

Our story has shed light, at least by implication, on a number of issues that have been central to the concerns of political scientists. In particular, the PER process is an excellent case study of policy making and implementation in a liberal democracy. The tensions between competing criteria and the centrality of gloriously vague notions such as 'effective and convenient' local government are the very stuff of pluralist policy-making. It throws the onus on to the implementers and allows them considerable discretion in how they interpret both the rules and their role (Hill, 1997; Parsons, 1995). In its early days the LGCE was rather uncertain about what to do, but then showed signs of relaxing and maturing as an organisation by adding its own imprint to the process through the introduction of the preliminary period and the extension of briefings for councillors and officers. Similarly, although the Commission felt constrained to acknowledge emerging government policy on, for example, annual elections, its willingness effectively to anticipate legislation on these varied between different types of authority.

The Commission's stakeholders also approached the review process in very different ways. Although many local authorities may feel that they have become mere administrative tools of central government, we have witnessed enormous variability in how they respond to the demands placed upon them. Some planning for PER with great care, others allowing it to creep up on them; some co-operating with the LGCE, others being obstructive; some wilfully misinterpreting or ignoring the Commission's guidance, others simply ignorant of it; some genuinely engaging in open discussion and consultation, others going through the motions or disguising the pursuit of their own agenda behind a consultative smokescreen. This variance is also reflected in our evidence about the relationship between elected members and officials and the level of mutual trust that exists (Elcock, 1994; Rao, 1994). In some authorities councillors were happy to delegate tasks that were properly their own to officers, in others the elected members interfered in the minutiae of administrative detail about an electoral review. In some councils officers were seen by the opposition groups as being in the pocket of the ruling party, elsewhere they were seen as a valuable and neutral protection against a tyranny of the majority. Sometimes even the assessments provided by different groups about their own and others roles were diametrically opposed! It was by no means clear from our research that these patterns varied systematically according to which party, if any, controlled the council and the size of its majority. Rather the explanation needs to be sought in a study of local political cultures and how they have evolved over time. In some places the flavour of the process may even be determined by whoever happens to be able or willing to be a key actor in the PER.

Local political parties equally, of course, reflect these differences. Even if party systems are similar in a formal sense, as measured for example by the effective number of parties, in practice some tend to operate in a consensual or at least accommodating way whereas in others politics is clearly regarded as a 'zero sum' game (Maor, 1997; Webb, 1999). We found examples of parties co-operating with others, of them going it alone, and of two parties ganging up on a third. Their goals varied from protecting their own fiefdoms (and, by extension, those of their rivals too) to attempting to maximise their position against all-comers. That local parties were able to make these tactical and strategic choices speaks volumes for the lack of oversight of electoral reviews maintained by the central party organisations. Any advice and guidance provided by the centre was of a general rather than specific nature, and we could find little evidence of overall attention being paid to the consequences of a local electoral review for future parliamentary constituency boundaries. In one respect, however, the review process did appear to reflect the current state of the national parties. On balance, Labour groups were more organised and rather cuter than their Conservative counterparts in presenting their case to the Commission, and the Liberal Democrats tended to participate in the process only in respect of those authorities and wards where they had a direct (or potential) electoral interest.

Finally, it is worth reflecting on what the PER process can tell us about the operation of the system of representative government. It seems clear that the attempt to pursue at best ambiguous and at worst contradictory goals has necessitated the legislation on re-districting being open to widely different interpretations. However, the mechanisms to address this potential democratic deficit are themselves flawed. The consultation procedures adopted and developed in good faith by the Commission work unevenly and contain the risk of being subject to manipulation by vested interests. Moreover, many consultees feel that their concerns are dismissed for reasons that they do not consider legitimate. The deficit is increased yet further by the proven ability of the LGCE (and like bodies such as the Parliamentary Boundary Commissions) to have almost any interpretation of the legislation protected by the courts precisely because of the ambiguity of the rules to which it is subject. The transfer of the LGCE's functions to the Electoral Commission, which itself reports directly to parliament, will introduce a clearer line of democratic accountability, but it is ironic that this coincides with the Secretary of State taking powers to specify schemes for local elections in individual authorities. Although the re-drawing of local ward boundaries is but one tiny corner of the British political system, it too contributes to the overall quality of representation available to citizens. It is to be hoped that the Electoral Commission will remain aware of its wider responsibilities for this as it strives to balance good local estate management, the appropriate recognition of communities and the principle of 'one vote, one value'.

Bibliography

Local Government Commission for England

Various publications and papers of the Commission are referred to throughout. The main sources include:

Consultation (1995) *Periodic Electoral Review: a Consultation Paper.* London, LGCE.

Guidance (1996) *Periodic Electoral Reviews: Guidance and Procedural Advice for Local Authorities and Other Interested Parties.* First Edition. London, LGCE.

Guidance (1998) *Periodic Electoral Reviews: Guidance and Procedural Advice for Local Authorities and Other Interested Parties.* Second Edition. London, LGCE.

Guidance (1999) *Periodic Electoral Reviews: Guidance and Procedural Advice for Local Authorities and Other Interested Parties.* Third Edition. London, LGCE.

Guidance (2000) *Periodic Electoral Reviews: Guidance and Procedural Advice for Local Authorities and Other Interested Parties.* Fourth Edition. London, LGCE.

Guidance (2001) *Periodic Electoral Reviews: Guidance and Procedural Advice for Local Authorities and Other Interested Parties.* Fifth Edition. London, LGCE.

Corporate Plan (1997) *Corporate Plan 1997/98.* London, LGCE.

Corporate Plan (1998) *Corporate Plan 1998/99.* London, LGCE.

Corporate Plan (1999) *Corporate Plan 1999/2000.* London, LGCE.

Corporate Plan (2000) *Corporate Plan 2000/2001.* London, LGCE.

FMPR (1998) *Financial Management and Policy Review, Prior Options Study.* London, University College.

FMPR (1999) *Financial Management and Policy Review, Stage Two Report.* London, DETR.

A reference for and the date of the Draft and Final Recommendations for each local authority area is given in the text. Minutes of Commission meetings, reports to meetings of Commissioners and the like are given their internal LGCE reference.

Local Government Boundary Commission for England

LGBC report 6 (1973) *Electoral Reviews.* London, LGBC.

LGBC report 141 (1976) *Initial Electoral Review: Progress Report.* London, LGBC.

LGBC report 285 (1978) *Enfield Judgement.* London, LGBC.

LGBC report 413 (1981) *Report on Initial Reviews of Electoral Arrangements in Districts and London Boroughs.* London, LGBC.

LGBC report 443 (1983) *A survey of the Commission's work so far and their future programme.* London, LGBC.

LGBC report 550 (1988) *People and Places.* London, LGBC.

LGBC report 627 (1992) *The Boundaries of Greater London and the London Boroughs.* London, LGBC.

LGBC report 688 (1992) *Final Report.* London, LGBC.

A reference for and the date of the Review reports for each local authority area is given in the text.

BBC/ITN (1983) *The BBC/ITN Guide to the New Parliamentary Constituencies.* Chichester, Parliamentary Research Services.

Bonfili D. (1998) *Single-Member Districting in Theory and Practice: a case study of Georgia, USA 1991-5*, M. Litt. thesis, University of Oxford.

Boundary Commission for England (1969) *Second Periodical Report.* Cmd 4084. London, HMSO.

Boundary Commission for England (1986) *Evidence to the Home Affairs Committee, session 1986-87.* London, HMSO.

Boundary Commission for England (1991) *The Review of Parliamentary Constituencies.* London, Parliamentary Boundary Commission for England.

Boundary Commission for England (2000) *The Review of Parliamentary Constituencies in England.* London, Parliamentary Boundary Commission for England.

Bush G. (1995) *Local Government and Politics in New Zealand.* Auckland, Auckland University Press.

Butler D. (1954) The Redistribution of Seats, *Public Administration,* 31, 2.

Butler D. (1963) *The Electoral System in Britain since 1918.* Oxford, Oxford University Press.

Butler D. and Cain B. (1992) *Congressional Redistricting.* New York, Macmillan.

Chilton B. (1996) Repairing the Democratic Machine, *Local Government Chronicle*, 12/4/1996.

Chisholm M. (2000) *Structural Reform of British Local Government.* Manchester, Manchester University Press.

Crossman R. (1975) *The Diaries of a Cabinet Minister, Volume One.* London, Hamish Hamilton/Jonathan Cape.

Elcock H. (1994) *Local Government: Policy and Management in Local Authorities.* London, Routledge.

Hill M. (1997) *The Policy Process in the Modern State.* London, Prentice Hall.

Home Affairs Committee (1987) *Redistribution of Seats.* London, HMSO.

House of Commons Library (1992) *The Parliamentary Boundary Commissions and the Boundary Commissions Bill*, Research Note 92/61.

Jackson W. E. (1966) *The Structure of Local Government.* London, Longman.

Johnston R. and Pattie C. (1996) Local Government in Local Governance: the 1994-5 restructuring of local government in England, *International Journal of Urban and Regional Research*, 20, 4.

Johnston R., Rossiter D. and Pattie C. (1999) Integrating and Decomposing the sources of partisan bias, *Electoral Studies*, 18, 3.

Johnston R., Rossiter D., Pattie C. and Russell A. (1993) The Definition of Parliamentary Constituencies in England: searching for principles in the work of the Boundary Commission, paper presented to annual conference of the Elections, Public Opinion and Parties group, Lancaster.

Keith Lucas B. and Richards P. (1978) *A History of Local Government in the Twentieth Century.* London, Allen and Unwin.

Kelly S. (1996) *The Partisan Impact of Local Boundary Revisions*, M.Sc. thesis, University of Plymouth.

Leach S. (1994) The Local Government Review: From Policy Drift to Policy Fiasco, *Regional Studies,* 28,5.

Maor M. (1997) *Political Parties and Party Systems*. London, Routledge.

McAllister I., Mackerras M. and Boldstein G. (1997) *Australian Political Facts*. Melbourne, Macmillan.

Parsons W. (1995) *Public Policy*. Cheltenham, Edward Elgar.

Pearce C. (1980) *Machinery of Change in Local Government 1888-1974*. London, Allen and Unwin.

Rallings C. and Thrasher M. (1994) The Parliamentary Boundary Commissions: rules, interpretations and politics, *Parliamentary Affairs*, 47, 3.

Rallings C. and Thrasher M. (1995) *Media Guide to the New Parliamentary Constituencies*. Plymouth, LGC Elections Centre.

Rallings C. and Thrasher M. (2000) *British Electoral Facts 1832-1999*. Aldershot, Ashgate.

Rallings C., Thrasher M. and Johnston R. (2002) The Slow Death of a Governing Party: the erosion of Conservative local electoral support in England 1979-97, *British Journal of Politics and International Relations*, forthcoming.

Rao N. (1994) *The Making and Unmaking of Local Self Government*. Aldershot, Dartmouth.

Rossiter D., Johnston R. and Pattie C. (1999) *The Boundary Commissions*. Manchester, Manchester University Press.

Sharpe L. J. (ed.) (1967) *Voting in Cities*. London, Macmillan.

Small D. (ed.) (1991) *Drawing the Map: equality and efficacy of the vote in Canadian electoral boundary reform*. Toronto, Dundurn.

Stanyer J. (1967) *County Government in England and Wales*. London, RKP.

Stewart M. (1997) *The Local Government Commission: Oversized Cloak or Emperor's Clothes?* York, York Publishing Services.

Waller R. (1983) The 1983 Boundary Commission: policies and effects, *Electoral Studies*, 2, 2.

Webb P. (1999) *The Modern British Party System*. London, Sage.

Wood B. (1976) *The Process of Local Government Reform 1966-74*. London, Allen and Unwin.

Young K. and Rao N. (1997) *Local Government since 1945* Oxford, Blackwell.

Index